TOWARDS A SECOND REPUBLIC

Irish Politics after the Celtic Tiger

Peadar Kirby and Mary P. Murphy

PlutoPress
www.plutobooks.com

First published 2011 by Pluto Press
345 Archway Road, London N6 5AA

www.plutobooks.com

Distributed in the United States of America exclusively by
Palgrave Macmillan, a division of St Martin's Press LLC,
175 Fifth Avenue, New York, NY 10010

Distributed in the Republic of Ireland and Northern Ireland by
Gill & Macmillan Distribution, Hume Avenue, Park West, Dublin 12, Ireland.
Phone +353 1 500 9500. Fax +353 1 500 9599. E-Mail: sales@gillmacmillan.ie

British Library Cataloguing in Publication Data
A catalogue record for this book is available from the British Library

ISBN   978 0 7453 3056 3   Hardback
ISBN   978 0 7453 3055 6   Paperback

Library of Congress Cataloging in Publication Data applied for

This book is printed on paper suitable for recycling and made from fully managed
and sustained forest sources. Logging, pulping and manufacturing processes are
expected to conform to the environmental standards of the country of origin.

10   9   8   7   6   5   4   3   2   1

Designed and produced for Pluto Press by Chase Publishing Services Ltd
Typeset from disk by Stanford DTP Services, Northampton, England
Simultaneously printed digitally by CPI Antony Rowe, Chippenham, UK and
Edwards Bros in the United States of America

Towards a Second Republic

*Mary dedicates this book to Emer and Dan;
may the Ireland they grow up in cherish all her
children equally.*

*Peadar dedicates this book to Caoimhe and Bríd;
go mb'fhéidir leosan agus a nglúin sochaí níos fearr
a bhaint amach in Éirinn.*

Contents

PART IV: TOWARDS A SECOND IRISH REPUBLIC

List of Tables, Figures and Boxes

Glossary of Irish Political Terms and Political Titles

Ceann Comhairle – 'chief of the council', chairperson of Dáil
  Éireann, named by the largest party and automatically re-elected
Dáil Éireann – 'assembly of Ireland', the elected Irish parliament
Fianna Fáil – 'warriors of destiny'
First Minister and Deputy First Minister – head and joint head of
  the Northern Irish government
Fine Gael – 'the Irish race'
Junior Minister –TD holding minor portfolio, but not a member
  of the cabinet
Northern Assembly – elected parliament of Northern Ireland
Oireachtas, Houses of the – the two houses of parliament (Seanad
  and Dáil Éireann)
Seanad Éireann – the Irish senate or second house, not elected by
  universal franchise
Sinn Féin – 'we ourselves'
Super Junior Minister – a junior minister with more additional
  responsibility and clout, attending cabinet meetings but with no
  voting rights and not holding a full ministerial portfolio
Tánaiste – 'heir presumptive' or 'crown prince'; Ireland's deputy
  prime minister
Taoiseach – 'the leader' or 'the chieftain', a 1930s term for the prime
  minister in line with contemporary Italian and German terms
Teachta Dála – 'representative in the assembly', elected member
  of the Dáil
Uachtarán na hÉireann – 'superior of Ireland', the president of
  Ireland (a non-political role)

Abbreviations

CAP	Common Agricultural Policy
CPA	Combat Poverty Agency
CSO	Central Statistics Office
DOF	Department of Finance
DUP	Democratic Unionist Party
EAPN	European Anti-Poverty Network
EC	European Community
ECOFIN	Council of EU Ministers of Finance
EMU	European Monetary Union
ESRI	Economic and Social Research Institute
EU	European Union
EU 15	The 15 countries that were members of the EU before the enlargement of 1 May 2004
EU 27	The 27 member countries of the EU: Austria, Belgium, Bulgaria, Cyprus, Czech Republic, Denmark, Estonia, Finland, France, Germany, Greece, Hungary, Ireland, Italy, Latvia, Lithuania, Luxemburg, Malta, the Netherlands, Poland, Portugal, Romania, Slovakia, Slovenia, Spain, Sweden and the United Kingdom
Eurozone	The states in which the euro has been adopted as currency, including the Republic of Ireland; Northern Ireland uses pound sterling
FÁS	State Employment and Training Agency
FDI	Foreign Direct Investment
FF	Fianna Fáil
FG	Fine Gael
GDP	Gross Domestic Product
GFA	Good Friday Agreement
GNP	Gross National Product
HNWI	High Net Worth Individual
HSE	Health Service Executive
ICTU	Irish Congress of Trade Unions
IDA	Industrial Development Authority
IFSC	International Financial Services Centre
IMF	International Monetary Fund
IRA	Irish Republican Army

MEP	Member of the European Parliament
MMP	Mixed-Member Proportional
NAMA	National Asset Management Agency
NESC	National Economic and Social Council
NGO	Non-Governmental Organisation
NI	Northern Ireland
NPM	New Public Management
OECD	Organisation for Economic Cooperation and Development
PDs	Progressive Democrats
PR	Proportional Representation
PR-STV	Proportional Representation Single Transferable Vote
SF	Sinn Féin
TD	Teachta Dála
SILC	Survey of Income and Living Conditions
ULA	United Left Alliance

Preface

This book has been written in the white heat of battle, amid the most dramatic events to have convulsed Irish society and the Irish state since independence. On the one side, the collapse of the economy and the drama of a bankrupt banking system grew worse as every publication of new data revealed that no end was in sight in the downward spiral. On the other side, a traditionally quiescent civil society seemed by and large to accept in silent anger the ever greater burdens of tax increases and cutbacks in public spending that were being imposed to save the international bondholders who had lent to and invested in Irish banks – until, that is, citizens got a chance to express that anger in the privacy of the ballot box on Friday, 25 February 2011. What was expressed was a calculated determination to punish the party that they held responsible for the crisis, the party that had so dominated Irish politics and public life since 1932 that it would be accurate to describe the period 1932–2011 as the 'hegemony of the Fianna Fáil state'. As the dust cleared over the weekend of 25 to 28 February and the final results trickled in, it was clear that the landscape not just of Irish politics but of Irish society was changed in ways that opened new possibilities. This book is an attempt to map out just what has changed and the new terrain this now opens. It can therefore be seen as a communiqué from the field of action, an effort to peer out and delineate the struggles that could give new shape to Irish society. What that shape is likely to be is the main concern of the book.

We are both professional academics, but each of us has set ourselves the task of bridging the gap between academic output and the debates that shape the world of politics and public affairs. The book therefore draws on the theories and evidence that are the stuff of our professional life; but we seek to apply them in an accessible way to illuminate where Irish society now finds itself. While we value the rich contribution of political commentators and journalists, we are convinced that scholarship – if applied with sensitivity and insight – has an essential contribution to make, as it can offer more enduring and solid frameworks to understand and guide the shaping of social change. So we fervently hope that this is received not just as a book for the scholar and student of Irish politics and society, but as a book for the politician, the activist, the citizen whose main concern is to build a better future, an equitable and sustainable society that we can be proud to hand on to our children. We each dedicate this book to our offspring, not with a pride at the society our generation has helped create and is passing on to them, but with a sense of anger at the myopia, the failure of ambition and will, and the lack of social values and solidarity at all levels of our society but most especially among our political, economic and intellectual elites. And it is this anger that also gives us a determination to help achieve change. It will be immediately clear to all readers that we don't write this book from some detached, neutral standpoint, since we believe that such a standpoint, even where sincerely adopted, often hides biases and assumptions insufficiently examined and revealed. And these usually support the status quo. We are clearly committed to changing the status quo since we believe that this had led us into a crisis that is blighting the lives of large sections of Irish society, most especially younger people, robbing them of a perspective of hope and positive expectation for the future. We don't expect that all readers will share the values and convictions that shape our analyses and conclusions – indeed, we would be most disappointed were that to be the case – but we do hope that readers will find it a helpful aide to throwing light on the struggles that lie ahead for all inhabitants of Ireland for the foreseeable future, even if their own commitments are very different to ours.

As always, many debts accumulate in the writing, particularly where this is done under the twin pressures of fast changing events and a looming deadline. We would both like to thank Roger van Zwanenberg, the chair and commissioning editor of Pluto Press, who first invited us to write a book and who has offered warm and friendly support throughout the writing. Thanks also to the Pluto Press team who edited, proofed and prepared the book for publication and to Pat Cooper for initially proof reading the text and checking the references. Peadar would like to thank the dedicated staff of the Institute for the Study of Knowledge in Society (ISKS) at the University of Limerick – Niamh O'Sullivan, Emma Leahy, Anthony Cawley and Sandra Lorenz-O'Sullivan – without whose daily support he could not have carved out of his far too busy schedule the necessary periods to dedicate to research and writing. He would also like to thank other colleagues in the University of Limerick, both in his own Department of Politics and Public Administration, and in many other units of the university, whose commitment to making a positive contribution to society often in quiet ways, is a regular inspiration. He feels a particular debt of gratitude to his co-author, Mary Murphy, whose detailed knowledge of the social forces that shape Irish society and whose deep dedication to being an activist public intellectual gives this book a quality and a groundedness that it would otherwise have lacked. Finally, to Toni, Bríd and Caoimhe, Peadar simply says: 'Each of you is the wonderful daily support of my life and without you nothing of what I am or do would have the same inspiration, enjoyment or commitment.'

Mary would like to thank many people. Firstly to her colleagues in the Department of Sociology in the National University of Ireland Maynooth, for their support and encouragement and to many students for their questions and ideas. There are many who contributed to the ideas in this book, and some were sown in the midst of working with others to try and create political and social change. Special thanks from Mary to friends in activist spaces like Is Féidir Linn and Claiming Our Future, she hopes this work contributes to what we are all trying to achieve and that the book does justice to our work. To Peadar, a very special thank you from Mary for your belief in her and your encouragement not just in this publication but for the last decade of work together and for pushing her to standards she would not otherwise even aspire to. Mary wants to especially thank her wonderful friends and family who patiently support her not only through the birthing pains of this book, but also throughout her life and all its ups and downs. Lastly from Mary to Emer and Dan: 'Thanks so much. I know I am so lucky to share my life with such wonderful children. You have no idea how much I want the future to be bright and happy for you both.'

Peadar Kirby
Mary Murphy
Dublin and Cloughjordan
April 2011

1
Introduction:
Ireland and the Future of Capitalism

The financial crisis that struck western economies with such force in mid 2008 jolted many certainties. Citizens and consumers who had seen themselves as being in the mainstream of society, making what they saw as responsible decisions about how much to spend and on what, and how best to save for the future, were suddenly faced with unforeseen difficulties as banks teetered on the brink of collapse, economies contracted dramatically and unemployment became a real threat. Comparisons with the Great Depression abounded and, after a decade or more of expansion and plenty in many societies, risk and uncertainty came to dominate future horizons. It is paradoxical that it was the exuberances and inequalities of capitalism that brought about this crisis, undermining from within a system that had withstood well what in the post-Second World War period had seemed like a formidable challenge from without in the form of communism. Yet, more effectively than any left-wing analysis, the crisis revealed to many the fact that the capitalist market system, when left to its own devices, served to enrich the few at the expense of the many, to undermine the efficiency and survival of quality public services, to strip away the defences that made life bearable for the most vulnerable in society and to reduce the most precious things in life to commodities to be bought and sold. In a very real way, the crisis raised questions about capitalism itself.

This book is about a small country that has, more than most in the world, embraced with zeal the possibilities offered by the free market. By doing so Ireland managed, through some options made by policy makers and with not a little luck, to create conditions that led to a 15-year economic boom, from 1993 to 2007, which saw employment expand dramatically, and average living standards rise to some of the highest levels in the European Union. Yet, this Celtic Tiger, as it came to be known both at home and abroad, collapsed ignominiously in 2008 as the country entered into a crisis that, in the words of the International Monetary Fund (IMF) 'matches episodes of the most severe economic distress in post-Second World

1

War history' (IMF 2009: 28). In late March 2011, the governor of the Central Bank of Ireland, Professor Patrick Honohan, described it as 'one of the costliest banking crises in history' (quoted in Carswell 2011). As the full scale of sorting out its bankrupt banking system became obvious, the country's deficit as a percentage of its GDP rose to 32 per cent in 2010, a full 10-times the deficit permitted by the European Union and a record for any country outside wartime. Ireland had experienced a series of boom–bust cycles since independence in 1922, but this crisis was different since it was clearly seen as being generated by banking and political elites whose reckless actions in fuelling an unsustainable property boom crashed the economy; however, the enormous costs came to be borne by ordinary taxpayers, by low-income public servants, by the poor, the old and the sick as a wave of austerity budgets raised taxes on moderate and average incomes, and massively cut state spending on welfare, health, education and infrastructure. Again, the question loomed large, what was the future for a model of capitalism that took the citizens of one small country on a rollercoaster ride to the heights of prosperity only to be plunged to the depths of a crisis beyond anyone's wildest imaginings.

In examining the Irish case, therefore, this book places it in the wider context of capitalism and its future. This introductory chapter clears the ground for the analysis of the Irish case to follow. It undertakes two tasks. The first one is to examine the contours of the present global financial and economic crisis to identify the extent to which it is indeed a crisis of capitalism and what issues this throws up for its future. The second task is to introduce readers to the Irish case through briefly outlining the history of boom and bust since the late eighteenth century until the Celtic Tiger boom that seemed finally to mark the emergence of Ireland from its history of entrenched failures. It is this structural feature of boom–bust cycles in the Irish case that requires the present collapse be treated as the latest manifestation of deeper realities. This is also the context that makes the collapse of 2008 all the more poignant for not only did it mock the expectations generated by the boom but, even more importantly, it raised for many Irish people persistent and troubling questions about the malaise that lay at the heart of the Irish project of independence. It is for this reason that this book is entitled *Towards a Second Republic*, as it signals that addressing this malaise requires a refounding of the institutions and culture of the Irish state, and a new development project for the country.

Though the book is centrally about the collapse of the model of development that structured economy and society in the Republic of Ireland, the analysis throughout includes treatment of developments in Northern Ireland, and consideration of the prospects for economic and political reunification of the island in the context of a second republic.

APPROACH AND CONTENTS OF THIS BOOK

The main task this book sets itself is to analyse how Irish political institutions, patterns of interest formation in political parties and civil society, and ideologies have interacted in a distinctive way to produce the Irish variety of capitalism – a variety that has proved to be economically, socially and environmentally unsustainable, as illustrated by the sudden and severe recession into which the country was plunged in 2008 and which has grown ever deeper up to the time of writing in early 2011. A number of themes frame the discussion: how social and economic change and distributional outcomes are determined by the interaction of institutions, interests and ideologies; how these outcomes are highly unequal (in class, gender, distributional and regional terms); how globalisation restricts national states' room for political and policy manoeuvre; and how civil society and the state are interdependent. We make the case that an open participatory public sphere is essential for a healthy society, and that no model of development can be economically, socially, politically or environmentally sustainable if it does not attend seriously and effectively to issues of fairness and equality.

In doing this, the book exposes the Celtic Tiger economic model as fundamentally a political construction and argues for detailed reforms of Irish political and administrative institutions, at local and national levels. The reforms proposed are framed within the call for a 'second republic', namely a more sustainable and equitable successor to the state founded in December 1922. The inclusion of analysis of the Northern Ireland statelet allows consideration of the possibility that the second republic will contain the whole of the island of Ireland. Where relevant, therefore, comparative data from north and south are used, highlighting the commonalities between the two Irish states, but also the differences that have grown between them over the 90 years of separate development.

The book identifies as accurately as possible what forces have shaped and sustained Ireland's variety of capitalism, how this has been done, and how it might be changed. In doing this, it situates Ireland in a wider global context, examining the role of the European Union in helping to create the conditions for the Irish boom and the impact that EU membership has had on Irish political culture, policy making and civil society. Discussion of the EU will also emphasise how the European project itself has been pulled ever more in a neoliberal direction. It examines the stress the present crisis has placed on the Union and the options available to weather these strains. A subsequent chapter compares Ireland to a range of other countries, including Iceland, Spain, Finland and New Zealand, examining in particular the similarities and differences between their political economy models and that of Ireland. The aim is to isolate those dimensions of the political economy models examined that either heightened the vulnerability of their economies to crisis or else helped protect them from the impact of crises generated elsewhere. This will allow a wider discussion of the impact of globalisation on varieties of capitalism.

The book is divided into four parts as follows:

- Part I is on the Irish state and contains two chapters. Chapter 2 is on Irish politics; it describes the historical evolution and distinctive features of the political systems and cultures of the two Irish states. Chapter 3 is on the Irish bureaucracy, sometimes called the 'permanent government' in Ireland. It analyses the power that inheres in the civil service because of the weakness of political party control over it, isolating the historical and cultural specificity of Irish bureaucratic power.
- Part II is on the Celtic Tiger model and contains three chapters. Chapter 4 analyses the nature of the Irish boom, identifying the features which constituted it and which led to its collapse, particularly the links between the political and the banking systems, reflecting the ideology which informed the model. Chapters 5 and 6 identify the distributional impacts of the boom. The first identifies the many losers, illustrating the gendered and ethnic nature of the boom's impact, while the second identifies the winners, reflecting the class and political nature of the boom and what drove it.
- Part III examines the international context and contains two chapters. Chapter 7 discusses the European Union, analysing its contribution to creating the conditions that helped generate the boom, but also identifying how some of these created vulnerabilities that led to the collapse. The chapter goes on to examine how the EU could contribute to a more sustainable

model and what reforms would be necessary for this to happen. Chapter 8 compares Ireland's variety of capitalism with that of a number of other states to which it has recently been compared, both states like Iceland and Spain that face crises with similar dimensions to those of Ireland, and also Finland, which emerged successfully from a similar crisis in the 1990s, and New Zealand, which undertook a thorough neoliberalisation as far back as the 1980s.

- Part IV looks to the future, mapping out the reforms necessary for a second Irish Republic. Chapter 9, 'Facing the Challenges', takes as its subject the content of such reforms, while Chapter 10, 'Achieving the Second Republic', examines how they might be implemented in practice within the conditions of contemporary Irish politics. The chapter ends with a discussion of where Ireland stands in debates on the future of capitalism.

A FAILURE OF CAPITALISM?

In writing about the present crisis, Andrew Gamble highlights the importance of ideas. He writes that 'it matters which explanation of the crisis becomes dominant, because that will shape the political response. Interpretations of the crisis become part of the politics of the crisis.' While the crisis will ultimately be resolved through politics 'one of the main aspects is the battle over how the crisis is to be understood, because that determines what can be done, and what should be done, and who has the legitimacy to do it' (Gamble 2009: 141, 143). This therefore invites attention to the debates about the cause of the crisis and what these tell us about how it can be understood. This is the purpose of this section.

US sociologist of market regulation, Monica Prasad (2009) identifies three emerging theories of the financial crisis each of which focuses on different levels, from the global to the specific level of the housing bubble. At the global level, she argues that growth in developing countries like China, India and Brazil led to a dramatic increase in savings worldwide which led to a larger number of investors seeking investment opportunities. The second level she identifies refers to the US financial system which, with deregulation, allowed an explosion of new financial instruments to attract these investments. These instruments essentially repackaged risk, selling it on in ways that tended to hide it from investors. The fact that the rating agencies themselves failed to understand the risks involved exacerbated the dangers inherent in this situation. The final level for Prasad was the home mortgage bubble, itself caused by deregulation in the financial market, which led to more people buying houses resulting in deeper indebtedness. When property prices began to decline homeowners could no longer borrow more against the value of their property to pay off debts. The collapse in the property market had a knock-on effect on the values of those securities that had been built on top of home mortgages, resulting in some financial firms going bankrupt or being propped up by taxpayers, and making those that survived much more risk-averse (Prasad 2009). This is a representative analysis of the financial crisis, particularly as it manifested itself in the United States, but Prasad argues that it does not reveal a deep flaw in capitalism but instead points to the urgent need for global policies of demand management. It is, in other words, a crisis not of capitalism itself but of a particular variety of capitalism, namely extreme free-market or, as it is often called, neoliberal capitalism.

This is a widely held view, including by many world leaders such as Barack Obama, Angela Merkel and Nicolas Sarkozy. But does it get to the heart of understanding what has caused this crisis? A more comprehensive probing, by the founding chairman of the United Kingdom's Financial Services Authority (FSA), Howard Davies, former director of the London School of Economics (LSE), ranges more widely and delves deeper. Davies sets out 38 distinct possible causes of the financial crisis, grouped under seven different headings, from what he calls 'the bigger picture' of the wider global macroeconomic system, to 'wild cards' such as greed and 'the watchdog that didn't bark', namely the media (Davies 2010). As would be expected, much of his analysis focuses on the failures of regulation, on accountants, auditors and rating agencies, and on financial firms and markets. All of this is consistent with Prasad's analysis except that it focuses on features that she neglects. One of these is the reality of inequality which is a feature of today's capitalism, namely the obscene growth in the incomes and assets of those who run the system (leading figures in global corporations and banks) while those on average incomes resort to borrowing to fund a desirable lifestyle as portrayed in the media. As he puts it in the title of one chapter 'the rich get richer – the poor borrow'. Equally important is Davies's comment which reveals causes beyond regulatory weakness when he says the political environment was 'unfavourable to measures which tightened financial conditions' (Davies 2010: 216) and that the tools regulators had at their disposal were too weak. Focusing on tightening regulation alone therefore is to miss the deeper causes of the crisis in the inequalities of today's global order and in the ideology of those who run it. While this does not amount to a rejection of capitalism, it does focus attention on key features that characterise it: the first of these is its inherent inequality and the second we can label its political economy, namely the relationship between state and market under capitalism. As will be outlined below, both of these issues are central to the approach taken in this book.

The analysis of Davies therefore uncovers deeper features of capitalism that are implicated in the present crisis, showing that this is not just a crisis of the financial system but also a crisis of politics. For at the heart of this crisis is a form of financial capitalism that came to be dominant over recent decades through which finance became uncoupled from the productive economy so that some 90 per cent of global financial transactions had little to do with generating goods and services, and therefore employment, but were for the purposes of speculation to make money out of money (Ferguson 2008; Castells 2001). The origins of this form of financial capitalism lie in the new technological possibilities opened by the invention of the microchip coupled with the liberalisation of the global financial system since the 1980s and the resultant weakening of public regulation. The deregulation of finance spawned a vast array of new financial instruments known as derivatives, such as futures, options and swaps, and an array of new actors trading in these instruments, such as hedge funds and new forms of investment banks. For example, de Goede has detailed how the US energy corporation, Enron, which collapsed in December 2001, had become an underwriter and trader of complex financial products, 'including weather derivatives (allowing companies to hedge against, or simply speculate on, changes in the weather), credit default swaps (allowing financial institutions to resell the risk of a borrower default) and advertising risk management (allowing companies to hedge against fluctuating prices of advertising space)'. Indeed, he quotes one Enron manager describing the goal of the company as 'the commoditisation of everything' (de Goede 2004: 198). Not being a bank, it was exempt from the regulations applying to financial institutions. Moreover, the growth of such complex financial instruments has made it much more difficult for public authorities to regulate because of their complexity and lack of transparency. As a result, since the mid 1990s the Basel Committee on Banking Supervision, a leading international supervisory body, has relied on banks' own internal risk assessment models (ibid.: 199). All of this was done in the name of spreading risk but in doing this it also intensified it. As the chairman of the US Federal Reserve from 1987 to 2006, Alan Greenspan, admitted to the US Congress, the crisis of autumn 2008 had 'found a flaw' in this thinking: 'I made a mistake in presuming that the self-interest of organisations, specifically banks and others, was such that they were best capable of protecting their own shareholders,' he said (*Financial Times* 2008: 6). Thus, the very structural features of the globalised financial system, arguably the core driver of today's globalisation, intensify risk and transmit it across the globe. This is illustrated by the impact of the US sub-prime crisis on the financial system around the world, particularly in those countries where public authorities had handed power to the markets. As will be shown later in this book, Ireland was one of those countries which, in the words of Nobel economics prize winner, Paul Krugman, had 'jumped with both feet into the brave new world of unsupervised global markets' (Krugman 2009). At the heart then of this new form of capitalism was not just a particular relationship between finance and the productive economy but, even more centrally, a particular form of political governance as states systematically ceded power to markets.

It is common to call this form of capitalism neoliberal, focusing on the restructuring of governance institutions such as regulatory agencies so that they embody the logic of the market and see as their objective the creation and policing of conditions for the competitive operation of private markets. Yet, as just outlined, this fails to give sufficient attention to the central role that financial institutions have taken on in this new variety of capitalism, a role that is of key importance in the current crisis. In this reading therefore, what is in crisis is this model of neoliberal financial capitalism characterised by a generally market-friendly macroeconomic framework, including weak redistributive mechanisms and a practice of excessive payments for senior figures in banks and enterprises, so that a culture of inequality came to be part of the prevailing situation. This discussion focuses attention therefore on what has been called 'varieties of capitalism' rather than on capitalism per se. In their influential work on varieties of capitalism, Hall and Soskice distinguish between liberal market economies (LMEs) and coordinated market economies (CMEs) depending on the extent to which the state defers to the interests of the private sector, with LMEs preferring to create the incentives for the private sector to make its decisions rather than seeking to coordinate the private sector and therefore shape its decisions as do the CMEs. Hall and

Soskice also note a link between their varieties of capitalism and Esping-Andersen's varieties of welfare capitalism, namely liberal, conservative and social democratic welfare states (Esping-Andersen 1990) when they write that 'virtually all liberal market economies are accompanied by "liberal" welfare states, whose emphasis on means-testing and low levels of benefits reinforce the fluid labour markets that firms use to manage their relations with labour' (Hall and Soskice 2001: 50–1).

When examined with a view to situating Ireland in these different varieties of capitalism, their limitations are highlighted. For example, efforts to situate Ireland as an LME or a CME are difficult due to the very large role played by foreign firms in the Irish economy and due to the existence of the concertative mechanisms, known as social partnership in Ireland, that characterise the CMEs (Kirby 2008). Ireland, therefore, seems to be some sort of hybrid between an LME and a CME, which tells us more about the inadequacy of the distinction between LMEs and CMEs than it does about the nature of Irish capitalism. Similarly, much discussion has taken place as to where Ireland stands in the typology developed by Esping-Andersen (1990). Cousins finds Esping-Andersen's typology problematic for a case like Ireland as it pays no attention to post-colonial peripheral countries that have been highly dependent in the global political economy (Cousins 2005: 10). Instead, it is the emerging literature on varieties of residential capitalism that seems to offer more promise to understanding the variety of capitalism that led Ireland into its current crisis. This criticises Hall and Soskice for focusing too much attention on the strategic interactions between the state and firms, and on how firms access finance, at the expense, for example, of how housing markets operate and are financed. Schwartz and Seabrooke argue that residential property and its associated mortgage debt constitute one of the biggest financial assets in most economies and have important implications for economic growth, wealth distribution, voting behaviour and the structure of taxation systems. They furthermore argue that housing finance has come to be linked to global financial integration, thereby drawing attention to the greater integration across national economies, something missed in the varieties of capitalism literature. For these reasons, they postulate 'varieties of residential capitalism' (Schwartz and Seabrooke 2008). This is very pertinent to the Irish case since it was the growth of the housing sector, fuelled by the fact that Irish banks could easily access capital on international markets due to deregulation of financial systems and membership of the euro, that led to the collapse of the Irish boom.

However, discussion of these different varieties of capitalism takes us only so far as they fail to focus sufficiently on the central feature that distinguishes the different varieties identified, namely commodification – the extent to which essential services and goods (such as housing, health, education and welfare) are treated as commodities to be bought on the private market or are seen as entitlements to be provided by the state outside the confines of the market. Traditionally these issues have tended to be seen as an option between efficiency and equity. For those, usually on the political right, for whom the efficient operation of the economy was paramount, with a view to achieving high levels of economic growth, state interference with markets was seen as leading to inefficiencies and therefore not desirable. On the other hand, for those whose primary concern was greater social equity through guaranteeing basic goods and services to all as an entitlement of citizenship rather than as a result of what they could afford, the state was expected to interfere with markets so as to ensure more equitable outcomes. The basic difference therefore related to the extent of decommodification to be achieved by public authorities. During the era of neoliberal capitalism, economic efficiency came widely to be seen as a much more important value than social equity; indeed, the latter was virtually abandoned as an objective of public policy. However, in recent years alarm bells have come to be sounded about the cost to society of neglecting what is called equality of condition, namely the gap between rich and poor. In their comprehensive work, Wilkinson and Pickett (2009) correlate a range of public ills (such as poor health and education, and high crime) with levels of inequality, thus alerting policy makers and the general public to the importance of balancing the emphasis on economic efficiency with a renewed commitment to social equality.

Over the last decade, a new concern has been forced on to the public agenda which was long neglected by social scientists and politicians, namely the environment. For as scientists present overwhelming evidence that emissions of greenhouse gases are warming the atmosphere to a degree that is already resulting in catastrophic climate change, and as we face the imminent exhaustion of oil reserves which provide the cheap energy to supply us with the goods and services on which our economy and lifestyle depend, humankind faces fundamental decisions of a kind never faced before. As Jackson writes:

A world in which things simply go on as usual is already inconceivable. But what about a world in which nine billion people all aspire to the level of affluence achieved in the OECD nations? Such an economy would need to be 15 times the size of this one by 2050 and 40 times bigger by the end of the century. What does such an economy look like? What does it run on? (Jackson 2009a: 6)

Facing these challenges takes us beyond the varieties of capitalism currently on offer: 'All of them are to a greater or lesser degree bound up in the pursuit of economic growth. Differences in social and economic organisation are differences in degree rather than fundamental differences in kind' (ibid.: 97). And the challenge now facing all governments is 'to provide the conditions for its citizens to flourish – within ecological limits' (ibid.: 98). This will require establishing and imposing meaningful resource and environmental limits on economic activity and finding forms of prosperity that do not depend on economic growth, since, for Jackson, it is the imperatives of economic growth that lie at the heart of the present crisis. As he puts it:

The growth imperative has shaped the architecture of the modern economy. It motivated the freedoms granted to the financial sector. It stood at least partly responsible for the loosening of regulations and the proliferation of unstable financial derivatives. Continued expansion of credit was deliberately courted as an essential mechanism to stimulate consumption growth. (Ibid.: 6)

This model has always been environmentally unsustainable; its social unsustainability has come to be questioned in the light of the gross inequalities it has fostered. Now, it shows itself to be economically unsustainable also. Therefore the really big question facing humankind is whether it is possible to move to a new kind of capitalism in which the market is so strictly controlled and curtailed that it can deliver forms of prosperity that are sustainable – environmentally, socially and economically. Do we need a new variety of capitalism or a move beyond capitalism altogether?

It is paradoxical, and indeed very disturbing, that, at a time when we most need some fundamental rethinking of our socio-economic system, we find ourselves locked tightly into forms of thinking that so constrain our social imagination as to narrow the range of possibilities being considered. Reflecting on the 30th anniversary of the 'winter of discontent' in Britain in 1978–79 that created the conditions for ushering in Thatcherism and the wave of deregulation that is at the heart of the present crisis, Colin Hay writes that the crisis of 1978–79 and that of 2008–09 look very different for one simple reason, 'the absence of an alternative economic paradigm capable of constituting the present crisis *as* a crisis' (Hay 2009: 551; emphasis in original). As a result, solutions are being sought within the terms of the existing paradigm, namely a desperate attempt to seek to reflate the economy, instead of in terms of a new paradigm. He concludes:

> What this perhaps reminds us is that new economic paradigms are difficult to summon up, especially when you need them most. Arguably, Britain didn't really need a new economic paradigm in 1978–79 when it was last offered one. Today, when its parlous economic condition cries out for one, none is on offer. (Ibid.: 552)

Where those seeking remedies for our present plight are looking is to the work of John Maynard Keynes, whose ideas played such a key role in the paradigm of a form of managed capitalism that emerged out of the Great Depression of the 1930s (while we must never forget that it took a world war to create the conditions for the widespread acceptance of these ideas). The ideas of Keynes are used to justify the deficit-financed stimulus spending packages that have been the response of most governments, though these themselves have come under sustained attack from mainstream economists who still believe that the role of governments should be to balance budgets and leave recovery to the private sector (Keynes 2007).

The difference between these two approaches gets us to the heart of the deeper issues required in analysing capitalism, which have tended to be overlooked in the arguments about the more technical issues of deficits, inflation and growth. For, according to Keynes's biographer and economic historian Robert Skidelsky, the theory of demand stimulus he developed rested on a more fundamental distinction between risk and uncertainty; whereas risk is calculable and therefore can be planned for to an extent, uncertainty is by definition incalculable and so acts as a deterrent to private entrepreneurs undertaking the kinds of investment required to create the conditions for economic recovery. Instead, Keynes argued, they will tend to hoard their capital until greater predictability returns. For this reason, Keynes emphasised the requirement that governments undertake the task of economic stimulus. Skidelsky goes further, however, arguing that this distinction rested on a more fundamental divergence between Keynes and the mainstream of the economics profession. Keynes was a heretic never able to integrate his insights into the core of the discipline for the simple reason that he believed economics to be a means to an end rather than an end in itself (Skidelsky 2009). It was for this reason that in 1939 he described his approach as 'liberal socialism': liberal because it sought to protect individual freedoms, and socialism because he sought, as he put it himself, 'a system where we can act as an organized community for common purposes and to promote social and economic justice' (quoted in Block 2010: 112). This reminds us of the core insights of Karl Polanyi writing around the same time and focusing on the same set of issues, namely the relationship of the market economy to society.

Polanyi's (2001) core insight was that the British industrial revolution created a new form of economy, namely an economy that purports to operate according to its own laws of supply and demand. For Polanyi, in all societies previous to nineteenth-century Britain, economic production took place not for the purpose of gain but for the purpose of use and was organised for the satisfaction of social needs. An essential feature of the creation of a market economy was the treatment of labour, land and money as if they were commodities that could be allocated a price and traded between suppliers and buyers. For this reason, he described such an economy as an automaton governed by its own 'economic law'. But the creation of a market economy made necessary 'a more extreme development, namely a whole society embedded in the mechanism of its own economy, a *market society*' (Polanyi 1977: 9; emphasis in original). For treating human labour, nature or money as commodities 'means no less than the running of society as an adjunct to the market'. This resulted in a form of relationship between economy and society that was entirely new: 'Instead of economy being embedded in social relations, social relations are embedded in the economic system' (Polanyi 2001: 60). The harmonious self-regulation that characterised the market system 'required that the individual respect economic law even if it happened to destroy him' (ibid.: 84–9). For 'the commodity fiction disregarded the fact that leaving the fate of soil and people to the market would be tantamount to annihilating them' (ibid.: 137). To counter this 'sociological enormity' as he called it (Dalton 1968: 68), a spontaneous countermovement emerged to check the action of the market. This took the form of more restrictive or regulative legislation in relation to such areas as public health, factory conditions, municipal trading, social insurance, shipping subsidies, public utilities and trade associations, re-embedding the market in society so that it served social ends and not purely economic ones. Therefore, as Block writes referring to the term 'socialism':

> Both Keynes and Polanyi recognized that the term initially had little to do with ending private property or markets; it was simply the idea that the human economy should be subordinated to human society. Human beings are social animals and 'socialism' is the belief that the social should be predominant. (Block 2010: 112)

As Jackson puts it in his consideration of the requirements of an economics for sustainability, 'it will have to be ecologically and socially literate, ending the folly of separating economy from society and environment' (Jackson 2009a: 10). Subordinating the economy to society is therefore the urgent task on which the survival of the planet as a place easily inhabitable by humans now depends. If we keep calling it capitalism, it will be a capitalism in which the role of the market will be so fundamentally transformed, both in how it itself operates and in how it relates to the wider society, that it will be unlike any form of capitalism we have known so far. Far more accurate would be to call it a form of liberal or ecological socialism.

This discussion has introduced the principles and themes that guide this book's examination of the contemporary crisis of Irish capitalism and what needs to be done to address it. Its approach is not predominantly political or sociological or economic, but it combines all three, based on the premise that social outcomes are profoundly shaped by how the state and the market interrelate, and that this interrelationship is itself deeply influenced by social actors – not just political and economic elites, but also the actions of organised sectors of civil society. Central to this book's analysis also is a recognition of the major importance of international factors in shaping the context in which states operate today; this is even more true in the Irish case since it is so heavily dependent on high levels of foreign investment as the engine of growth in its economy. The book therefore focuses on dominant political economy models that structure society in particular ways at particular times, but that also change when critical junctures are reached, such as at the present moment. While configured by national political and social struggles, these models are also heavily influenced by international forces, as the book will emphasise. Critical junctures, arising as the dominant model enters into crisis, do not in any way determine what new model, if any, might emerge – this can only happen through political and social action. Guiding this action, and the proposals that inform it, are basic principles. As has been argued above, two fundamental principles are regarded as of vital importance for the approach taken here, namely social equality and environmental sustainability.

IRELAND'S BOOM–BUST CYCLES

As the latest global financial crisis has confirmed so dramatically, boom–bust cycles continue to be a central characteristic of capitalism. To state that Ireland's economic history has been marked by such cycles, therefore, is not surprising and Ireland is in no way unique in this respect. However, what can be very revealing is to examine in more detail the nature of these cycles in the Irish case and, in particular, to analyse the present Irish crisis in this historical context, thereby helping to identify some deeper and abiding features of the Irish development experience. Much of the academic and popular media comment on the Celtic Tiger boom period of Irish development was led by economists and largely lauded the model's capacity to generate growth. Yet the very vulnerability of the Irish development model, as exposed by the recent crisis, illustrates starkly that the Celtic Tiger largely failed to resolve the country's long-standing development problems. This, then, offers a starting point for analysing the Irish model of capitalism.

When Ireland achieved independence from the United Kingdom in 1922, its economy bore more resemblance to that of a typical underdeveloped country than it did to the more industrialised economies of its nearest neighbours. Overwhelmingly agricultural in what it produced and in its labour force, over 50 per cent of the country's exports consisted of live cattle for the UK market. Except for a small food and drinks agricultural sector, the country was virtually without industry. A region of the UK economy following the Act of Union between the Irish and British kingdoms in 1801, the incipient industrialisation that characterised the Irish economy under its colonial parliament at the end of the 18th century was stifled and, especially following the Great Famine (1845–48), the Irish economy became overwhelmingly dependent on agricultural production. While there have been debates about the extent to which the Great Famine marked a watershed in Ireland's modern history, there is little doubt that it contributed towards profoundly reshaping the country's economy and society, establishing a pattern of emigration that saw the population decline from a high of over 8 million on the eve of the famine, to 6.6 million in 1851 and to 4.2 million by 1926. Within agricultural production, there was a move from tillage to pasture, encouraged by international prices and resulting in intensified land clearances to make way for cattle. While there were periods of growth and recession in Ireland's economy in the nineteenth century, the Great Famine cast a profound shadow that lasted well into the twentieth century characterised by depopulation, a social conservatism and, as Foster puts it in referring to Irish emigrants, 'a race-memory of horror' (1989: 203). The only exception was the north-east of the island which became an industrial growth pole within the British economy, but which, of course, chose to remain with the United Kingdom when the rest of the island became independent as the Irish Free State (Ó Gráda 1994).

The subsequent trajectory of the south's economy can be divided into four main periods of boom and bust. The Free State gained its independence amid an economic boom that had been generated by the First World War; however, it soon entered into a period of economic decline which the fiscally conservative policy of the ruling Cumann na nGaedheal party between 1922 and 1932 did little to counteract. As real agricultural prices fell over the 1920s and output was sluggish, poverty and emigration continued while farmers' living standards dropped by 15 per cent between 1929 and 1933 (Ó Gráda 1994: 413). Membership of the militant Irish Transport and General Workers' Union (ITGWU), founded in 1908, declined from 100,000 in 1922 to 16,000 in 1930. An average of 33,000 emigrated each year over the 10-year period following the foundation of the state, almost double the previous decade (Kennedy, Giblin and McHugh 1988: 38). The one developmental initiative taken was the building of Ardnacrusha hydroelectric generating station which, eight years after it opened in 1929, was supplying 87 per cent of the country's needs. The recession of the 1920s was largely caused by international factors, but was exacerbated by timid and conservative state policy.

The arrival in power of the Fianna Fáil party, representing those who had been defeated in the brief civil war of 1922–23, and also small farmers and sections of the working class, opened a period of developmental nationalism during which the state was used to develop industry and to try to broaden the basis of agriculture. The party initiated a radical policy of state-led industrialisation behind high tariff barriers and extensive social investment, especially in housing and health care. The main thrust of policy was to encourage Ireland's nascent industrial class to manufacture at home what previously had been imported, a typical policy of import-substitution industrialisation (ISI) behind high tariff barriers, the average level of which rose from 9 per cent in 1931 to 45 per cent in 1936, with tariffs on some goods ranging between 50 and 75 per cent. Manufacturing output rose by 7.2 per cent between 1932 and 1936, while the number of Irish-owned industrial concerns quoted on the Dublin stock exchange trebled between 1933 and 1939. Industrial employment rose from 110,600 in 1931 to 166,100 in 1938, and emigration declined to an average of 14,000 a year over the decade 1930 to 1940, one third the rate of the previous period. However, unemployment remained high, peaking at 145,000 in 1936, before improving economic conditions in the United Kingdom saw Irish emigration there begin to increase again. The years of the Second World War, in which Ireland remained neutral, proved disastrous, as the industrial economy shrank and many workers emigrated to find work in the UK war economy. Furthermore, the economic isolation of those years left the state cut off from the European recovery that followed, and economic stagnation was exacerbated by the lack of clear policy direction amid growing balance-of-payments problems and sluggish industrial productivity behind high tariff barriers. Unemployment increased and emigration returned to levels not seen since the 1850s, with over 50,000 people emigrating a year in the mid 1950s. The workforce fell from 1,228,000 in 1946 to 1,053,000 in 1961 (CSO 2000: 108). As Kennedy, Giblin and McHugh describe it, 'Ireland's overall growth performance in the 1950s was one of the worst in Europe, emigration reached record levels for this century, and confidence about the viability of the economy reached an all-time low' (Kennedy, Giblin and McHugh 1988: 55). Having counteracted the impact of the Great Depression in the 1930s through a vigorous project of state-led industrialisation, the deep depression of the 1950s was caused by a paralysis in state policy, exacerbated by political instability, that failed to adapt policy to the new opportunities opened up by the European recovery.

Just as in the 1930s, responding to the crisis of the 1950s led to an about-turn in policy as the state adopted an outward-looking liberalisation of trade and actively encouraged foreign investors to establish manufacturing plants in Ireland. This opened a new boom phase in Ireland's development from 1960 onwards, with a swift growth in foreign enterprises establishing themselves in Ireland for the export market, reflecting the new buoyancy in the global economy. Protection was swiftly dismantled, first unilaterally and then in the context of a free-trade agreement with the United Kingdom in 1966, opening the way for membership of the then European Economic Community (EEC) in 1973. The success of policy in attracting foreign investment led to an increasing dependence on the foreign-owned manufacturing sector and a neglect of domestically owned industries, which faced much stiffer competition. By 1973, overseas firms accounted for almost one-third of all manufacturing employment (68,500 out of 219,000) and by 1983 there were almost 1,000 foreign firms in Ireland, half of them from the United States, one-eighth from Britain and about one-tenth from Germany (Ó Gráda 1997: 115). By contrast, however, there was no employment growth in the domestically owned manufacturing sector from the mid 1960s to the end of the 1970s. Overall, the decade 1961–71 saw the agricultural labour force decline from 360,000 to 272,000, while in industry the labour force grew from 252,000 to 320,000 and in services from 405,000 to 457,000. GDP grew over the decade at an annual average rate of 4 per cent, the highest of all the decades from 1926 to 1986 (Kennedy, Giblin and McHugh 1988: 144). This boom ended in a problem of high levels of international indebtedness, initially caused by an increase in borrowing to counteract the effects of the oil price rise in 1973, but deepened by the policies of the new Fianna Fáil government in 1977, which, following expansionary Keynesian policies, ended up boosting imports and further undermining the domestic manufacturing sector. Political instability in the early 1980s made a coherent policy response difficult; by 1985 the public debt had risen to 35 per cent of total tax revenue, resulting in deflationary policies which depressed the economy further. Overall, between 1973 and 1986 the national debt/GNP ratio rose by nearly 90 percentage points, much more than in the whole of the previous history of the state. Unemployment reached some 18 per cent of the labour force and emigration returned to levels not seen since the 1950s. This third slump, while initially caused by the oil price rises, was severely worsened by domestic policy options and political instability.

The fourth boom period opened with the decisive action of the incoming Fianna Fáil government in 1987, which stabilised the public finances through severe austerity measures. With its financial house in order, the consistent policy since the 1960s of attracting foreign firms, coupled with investment in technical education and training since the 1970s, made Ireland a very attractive location for multinational companies from outside Europe, particularly from the United States, which wanted to establish a base within the then European Community to avail itself of the EC's large market. Investment in upgrading infrastructure (especially in communications) and human resources was helped by EC regional and structural funds which greatly increased in quantity from the late 1980s. These measures laid the foundations for the Celtic Tiger boom which lasted from 1994 to 2007, increasing living standards and employment in Ireland. However, the seeds of its collapse were already visible from the early 2000s, when the Irish economy came to depend more and more for its growth, not on exports, but on domestic consumption, particularly the purchase of property fuelled by reckless bank lending. Export growth declined from an annual average of 17.6 per cent between 1995 and 2000 to an average of 4.9 per cent annually between 2001 and 2006. Between 2002 and 2006, the number of people employed in construction increased by so much that by the end of the period this group constituted 13.2 per cent of all those at work. The details of the boom–bust phase of the Celtic Tiger are analysed in more detail in Chapter 4. It is sufficient here to point to the central role played by lax regulatory and development policy in creating the conditions for the collapse of 2008, even if it was the international financial crisis that triggered that collapse.

With the establishment of the statelet of Northern Ireland in 1920, the most industrially developed part of the island chose to remain a part of the United Kingdom. Home to substantial shipbuilding and linen industries as well as engineering and textile machinery-manufacturing, the subsequent 90 years were to see the two states move in almost opposite economic directions. Of course, despite having its own parliament until 1972 and its own administration, Northern Ireland had limited powers over its economic destiny and was subject to the broad policy directions set in London. As in the south, it initially experienced the recession of the 1920s, but, unlike the south, which countered the Great Depression with its own industrialisation drive in the 1930s, the recession in the North grew deeper until the stimulus of the Second World War greatly boosted the Northern economy. This boost lasted until the early 1960s in the case of shipbuilding, though the linen industry had received only a modest lift in the 1950s before declining to virtual extinction in the face of competition from new fibres. Attempts to diversify the economy in the 1960s, particularly through attracting foreign investment, had very limited success in the context of the emerging Troubles from the late 1960s; indeed, the IRA explicitly targeted some executives of multinationals that had established a presence in the North. Increasingly, therefore, while the Republic was experiencing development through export-oriented manufacturing largely by multinational firms, the North's industrial economy was declining and employment came to depend more and more on the public sector. By the end of the 2000s, this provided almost one-third of all employment and the annual subvention given by the British government was £5 to £6 billion annually, amounting to nearly a quarter of the North's GDP (Adshead and Tonge 2009: 180). Boom–bust cycles in the North, therefore, are explained much more by the decline of traditional industries and the failure to achieve a new industrial development paradigm, a failure explained both by the limited powers of the Northern Ireland administration and also by the three decades of civil unrest from the late 1960s to the late 1990s.

This brief historical survey points to the ways in which processes of policy deliberation and decision making at domestic level failed again and again to respond adequately or in time to the challenges of the international situation. Though each of the severe economic slumps experienced by the southern Irish state has been distinctive in its causes and nature, what characterises them all is severe failures in policy making. This points therefore to the need to devote central attention not primarily to the content of these policy failures, but rather to the institutional and political context that alone can explain the persistence of these weaknesses over the relatively long period just surveyed. However, limiting the analysis to institutional weaknesses alone fails to explain how and why these institutional features emerged within Irish society and, despite huge socio-economic change, how they have survived; clearly culture and values are also important explanatory factors. Only an analysis of this nature can capture the many variables that combine to create the distinctive variety of Irish capitalism that has emerged.

Part I

The Irish State

A key outcome of the current economic crisis has been a focus on the degree to which the political institutions described above are to any degree fit for purpose. This part examines the politics and institutions of the Irish state, how they have evolved since independence, the role of organised interest groups in their evolution and the changing nature of the class coalitions that have exercised major influence over the state in a way that illuminates the economic policy choices it has made since independence. Chapter 2 examines interests (political parties, civil society, gender). It reviews the ideological context of Irish policy making and the generation of ideas in Irish political culture. Finally, it briefly reviews recent political changes in Northern Ireland. Chapter 3 focuses on the bureaucratic institutions of the Irish state and their capacity to implement policy, but also on how the overlap between unaccountable bureaucratic power and political power that is in theory accountable to citizens helps explain the cosy consensus and the Irish style of crony capitalism discussed in Chapters 4 and 6.

2
Irish Politics

Only history will tell whether the scale of defeat for Fianna Fáil in the 2011 general election was a transformative moment in Irish politics. This chapter describes the historical evolution and key features of the Irish political system and of Irish political culture. It draws attention to its distinctiveness and to how these institutions and culture led to the particular approach to development outlined in subsequent chapters. It argues that, even though the dominance of Fianna Fáil in Ireland's 'two-and-a-half-party system' of Fianna Fáil, Fine Gael and the Labour Party may be seen from outside the country as bearing similarities to the dominance of social democratic parties in Nordic systems, in fact Irish politics must be understood as profoundly populist and localist in nature and culture.

The chapter begins by situating Ireland as a small peripheral island state and then briefly outlines the state's key political institutions. The second section discusses two core institutional features, the highly centralised nature of political power and the single transferable vote system of proportional representation (PR-STV); the third discusses how these institutions reinforce a strongly personalist and non-ideological political culture and system, and reflects on how this political culture influences voters. The fourth section turns its attention to interests, and examines the nature of Irish political parties, while the fifth reflects on the dominance of Fianna Fáil in the history of the Irish state and the degree to which the interests of the party have come to be synonymous with the state. The sixth section pays specific attention to the patriarchal nature of that culture and to inequality in political participation and representation; the seventh briefly discusses the particular nature of Irish civil society; and the eighth examines the nature of Irish ideology and ideational debate. The final section looks at the evolution of the political system and of politics in Northern Ireland.

POLITICAL INSTITUTIONS

Though it is a small state, the Republic of Ireland is not a micro-state, and size has rarely been employed as an analytical category through which to analyse it. Though less well theorised, the impact on political culture of being an 'island' state should not be ignored. However, it is not size or geography but the party, political and electoral systems that appear to have a profound impact on Irish political culture, dominated as it is by localism and personalism. Ireland is regularly compared to small European states such as Austria, Denmark, Finland, Sweden and the Netherlands (Mjøset 1992; P. Cox 2010). Yet in reality, the Irish political and party system is quite distinctive in European terms. Ireland is characterised by Lijphart (1999: 67, 114–17, 189) as a unitary and centralised, two-and-a-half-party, semi-presidential system with a bicameral parliament, an elected president, a prime minister who has a medium level of influence, and as being 'weakish' in relation to judicial review and constitutional rigidity.

Key institutions outlined in the 1937 constitution are a seven-year presidential term with the president elected by universal suffrage and a two-chamber national parliament with the main legislative chamber, the Dáil, having 166 members directly elected from 43 multi-seat constituencies through a proportional representation, single transferable vote electoral system. The more limited second chamber, the Seanad, is comprised of 60 members, 11 of whom are nominated by the taoiseach (prime minister), six elected by university graduates and the remainder by elected politicians, both at national and at local-authority levels of power. The president has relatively weak powers and appoints the taoiseach (normally the leader of the largest party or coalition grouping in the Dáil). Elections are constitutionally prescribed to happen nationally and locally at least every five years.

A CENTRALISED STATE WITH A LOCALISED ELECTORAL SYSTEM

Mair (2010) notes a number of paradoxes in Irish politics. Irish political institutions are widely considered to suffer from two key problems (Coakley and Gallagher 2010; Adshead and Tonge 2009): a centralised state with a parliament notorious for its ineffectiveness either in making public policy or in overseeing the executive; and an electoral system that is perceived to promote localism and clientelism over policy making, values and political leadership.

Centralised state

Despite the separation of powers between the presidency, the executive and the two-house legislature, Hardiman (2009) describes

Ireland as the most centralised political system in western Europe. Appointment to the executive, the Irish cabinet, is exclusively from the parliament and almost exclusively from the lower house, the Dáil. This compares to the complete separation of executive and legislature found in France or Norway and the more mixed models which provide for the possibility of external appointment to cabinet in most European democracies. Ireland is alone among small unitary states with a population of less than 10 million in having a bicameral parliament, with an upper house, the Seanad. While originally intended to be a voice for diversity and pluralism, the Seanad is generally considered to play little useful role, often being used by political parties as a grooming or retirement home for aspiring or retiring politicians. As a result of these features, the executive has very tight control over the parliamentary agenda, dominates parliamentary procedures and totally controls the plenary agenda and timetable in legislative committees. The party whip system is tightly exercised, with little tradition of free voting.

The allocation of power between the executive and the legislature is a crucial one and is further discussed in Chapter 9. The present degree of concentration of power in the Irish executive was not necessarily intended by the 1937 constitution. The practical lack of separation of power between the executive and the legislature is more an outcome of political culture and parliamentary practice, as debate can be severely guillotined and legislation passed with little parliamentary scrutiny, while strong party whip systems restrict full political debate (MacCarthaigh and Manning 2010). O'Halpin (1998) describes a parliament that is without bark or bite, has little control over all-important budgetary matters and is unable to hold government to account. The Irish committee system, seen as essential for effective parliamentary work, is considered too weak, ineffective, underdeveloped and under-resourced, and as being controlled by cabinet-appointed chairs and a strong party whip system (Martin 2010). The 2011 Programme for Government reflects the growing political consensus for a range of measures to strengthen the parliament and decentralise power; there is also some less significant focus on devolving power to local government.

Electoral system

One might think that the PR-STV electoral system, which allows a very low threshold to win power in multi-seat constituencies and enables small parties and independents to win seats, would have worked against a concentration of power. Though Ireland is not unusual in having proportional representation, its system, the multi-seat constituency single transferable vote (STV), is unusual. Voters can transfer their single vote in order of preference to as many candidates as they wish in multi-seat constituencies. Thus, if their first preference candidate is not elected (or does not require their vote because she or he has already passed the quota to be elected), the vote is not wasted but is passed on until it elects someone (Sinnott 1999). The result is to pit party candidates against one another for votes in their local area. The policies and perspective they have in common with other candidates of their party are played down in favour of their personal effectiveness in representing constituents' interests. There is mixed opinion about this type of electoral system. Farrell, summarising arguments against, argues it leads TDs to devote 'far too much time to nursing their constituencies to the neglect of their parliamentary duties. It attracts the wrong kind of people to politics, giving rise to a politics of short-termism in which government is never held to account' (Farrell in Mulholland 2010: 44) and leads to a situation in which 'personalism is at the heart of politics' (Collins and O'Shea 2003: 105) and excessive constituency workloads, local rivalries and a high turnover of deputies frequently discourage high-quality candidates. However, Gallagher (1987) observes how Irish voters appear to like this electoral system and to enjoy the intensely personal relationship they have with their elected representatives. The voter interacts with this highly personalised and localised electoral system in a logical manner, often voting for personalities and local issues, but also for party cleavages and national policy issues. The debate about electoral reform is reviewed in Chapter 9. Adshead and Tonge (2009) relate how the 2002 Irish National Election Study showed a fairly even split between the 40 per cent of voters who choose candidates and the 40 per cent who vote for parties, while the remaining one-fifth of voters try to marry the two choices. The 2011 election saw significantly more focus on national policy issues. This system also means considerable opportunity for independent candidates representing local issues: in the 2002 election 14 out of 166 seats (almost 10 per cent) went to non-party-affiliated local candidates, often focused on single-issue health or local infrastructure campaigns. In the 2011 general election, despite the focus on national policy over half the candidates were independents, with 14 being elected (though some stood clearly on national rather than local policy issues).

POLITICAL CULTURE

Institutions and culture are mutually determining. However, the present Irish state is relatively new and some of the characteristics of Irish political culture predate it. They include Ireland's peripheral island location, its conservative, landowning but peasant rural culture and underdeveloped industrial class (Adshead and Tonge 2009: 142), and the powerful, authoritarian and dominant Catholic Church and its promotion of both deference and victimhood as Irish characteristics. Ireland's colonial history placed the pre- and post-colonial nationalist Catholic Irish identity at the centre of national culture. Garvin (1987) argues that this fostered a culture based on loyalty to peasant kinship ties rather than on class solidarity, with values of authoritarianism, conformism and anti-intellectualism predominating – values which Chubb (1982) argues are distinctive features of Irish political culture. Garvin (1991: 42) suggests that Irish political culture is marked by a 'pervasive populism' in which the local publics and political leaders are unusually vulnerable to each other's influences. Power is strongly centralised, but secular political institutions are relatively weak. A combination of an underdeveloped working class and a nationalist stress on the unity of community enabled this populist culture to flourish. The Fianna Fáil party in particular grew from this culture and learnt to foster it for its own political ends.

Once in place, however, the institutions of the Irish Republic also influence Irish political culture and how business and civil society actors interact with this culture. While it would be wrong to blame the electoral system for all the ills of Irish political culture, it does contribute significantly to a policy system 'dominated by the culture of short-term pragmatic politics' (M.P. Murphy 2006: 152). Politicians tend to have little interest in long-term policy planning, and policy tends to be developed 'in an ad hoc and fragmented fashion' (ibid.: 125) in a 'consensus-driven, blame-avoidance, no-losers political culture' (ibid.: 242).* The focus on Catholic subsidiarity meant a vocationalist and corporatist orientation of

---

* The strategic ambiguity of Minister for Finance Charlie McCreevy's increase in the universal child benefit in the 2001 budget offers a good example of this. Faced with various competing demands for state policy on child income support from working mothers, at-home mothers and child poverty campaigners, the political response was a costly increase in universal child benefit which addressed neither the targeted childcare needs of mothers with young children nor the needs of poor families.

the Irish state; this reinforced a consensus-oriented civil society, while highly centralised institutions also failed to foster an accountable or transparent culture. Hay (2004: 205) differentiated states according to institutional characteristics that give rise to 'veto points', where actors or groups have political power to veto decisions. Ireland has a relatively large number of veto points which constrain policy (a relatively rigid constitution, coalition government, bicameralism and social partnership can all be seen as veto points). The state became increasingly captured by vested interests with strong veto power to stop reforms in their tracks; this leads to a frozen landscape of policy reform often characterised by paralysis and failure to respond effectively (Wright 2010; Nyberg 2011). This combination of a highly centralised and unaccountable concentration of power allied to strong vested interests can lead to a political culture of elite 'group-think' (Nyberg 2011). An elite political class surrounds itself with other like-minded elites who reinforce what is politically expedient, while dissenting voices are marginalised and ridiculed, with the result that 'the practice of government itself was subordinated to the imperative of politics' (Leahy, in Mulholland 2010: 31). Examples of how vested interests and political short-termism drove policy are illustrated throughout the book, with examples of decentralisation and FÁS in Chapter 3 and of tax policy and tourism in Chapter 6.

POLITICAL PARTIES

What types of political party thrive in and promote such a political culture? The origins of the party system lie in the emergence of a single Irish nationalist party within the British political system in the nineteenth century. The Irish Parliamentary Party collapsed in the 1918 election. Sinn Féin, as the political expression of the widespread demand for Irish political independence, enjoyed almost 100 per cent electoral support among the nationalist population across the class spectrum and provided political leadership during the War of Independence (1919–21). Following independence and treaty negotiations in 1921, a civil war was fought over the terms of the treaty, which proposed ending British rule in 26 counties but maintaining it in six counties of Ulster which had been constituted as the province of Northern Ireland in 1920. Sinn Féin split into two parties. The more moderate pro-treaty nationalist leaders formed the Cumann na nGaedheal party in 1923, which ran the state up to 1932. Fianna Fáil (FF), an anti-treaty nationalist party, was formed out of the group defeated in the civil war but then accepted constitutional politics and went on to dominate political life in the Irish state until 2011, after first gaining power in 1932. A smaller and more militant group retained the name Sinn Féin and did not recognise the constitutionality of the 26-county Irish state. Cumann na nGaedheal renamed itself Fine Gael (FG) in 1933 and has formed the principal opposition party since then. Thus the national question rather than class remained the main cleavage in Irish politics after partition and independence. While FG sits with centre right parties in Europe, it has formed coalition governments with the left-leaning Labour Party in Ireland. The Labour Party was formed in 1912 during a time of extensive labour militancy. While being Ireland's oldest party, it chose not to contest the key 1918 election, largely as part of a strategy of maximising support for Irish independence in that election. The struggle for independence meant that nationalist issues took precedence over class issues and, until 2011, the Labour Party consistently remained the 'half' of the two-and-a-half-party Irish system.

Smaller ideologically driven parties are less likely to thrive in a populist political culture, and many have come and gone in the Irish political system. On the left, various political parties and political movements contested electoral power. Originating from a split from the now marginal Workers Party, Democratic Left was a small left-wing party that merged into Labour in 2000, as had the Socialist Democratic Party in the previous decade. The contemporary Socialist Party which has maintained sporadic Dáil representation over the last decade, formed as a Trotskyist 'Militant' split from the Labour Party in the early 1980s. In 2004, a broad front of small left parties gathered around the Socialist Workers' Movement contested power as People before Profit and also since 2011 as part of a front known as the United Left Alliance. In that election, the Socialist Party and People before Profit each won two seats under the ULA banner. On the other end of the political spectrum, the Progressive Democrats formed in 1985 out of a split from FF on issues of honesty and probity in public life and economic and social liberal values. This remained a very small (with around 5 per cent of the national vote) but influential party playing a key ideological role in coalition with FF until a severe electoral setback in 2007 finished it off in 2009. A small Green Party (with six members of the Dáil from 2007–11) entered coalition with Fianna Fáil and suffered a significant collapse in votes, losing all its seats, in the February 2011 election. As Table 2.1 shows, until the 2011 election Ireland had a classic two-and-a-half-party system, with the two main parties, Fianna Fáil and Fine Gael, and one smaller Labour Party. All three parties have had to survive in a populist culture. Mair (1992: 409) describes how Irish party politics grew out of a culture which had emphasised 'solidarity, cohesion, and homogeneity'. He argues that this culture was consciously sustained by Fianna Fáil, which saw itself as a party that represented the interests of the Irish people as a whole and decried any attempt to turn sections of this people against others. Fine Gael, while representing a distinct class of larger farmers, urban professionals and entrepreneurs, had to adapt to this culture. Labour acquiesced in this same vision of politics, rarely mobilising, and it never sustained an effective alternative politics or class alignment. This cultural overlap explains the ease with which Fine Gael and the Labour Party, despite clear ideological differences, worked relatively effectively in coalition.

Table 2.1   Republic of Ireland governments, 1932–2011

Year	Main party	Coalition partner
1932–47	FF	
1947–51	FG	Lab
1951–54	FF	
1954–57	FG	Lab
1957–73	FF	
1973–77	FG	Lab
1977–81	FF	
1981	FG	Lab
1981–early 1982	FF	
1982–87	FG	Lab
1987–89	FF	
1989–92	FF	PD
1992–94	FF	Lab
1994–97	FG	Lab/Democratic Left
1997–2007	FF	PD
2007–11	FF	PD/Greens
2011–	FG	Lab

Source: Adshead and Tonge (2009), updated by authors

Opinions polls in 2009 and 2010 showed that for the first time in 60 years over 50 per cent of voters intended voting for a party other than Fianna Fáil or Fine Gael; in the actual election these two parties had a combined vote of 55 per cent. The seismic drop in support for FF from 41.6 per cent in 2007 to 17.4 per cent in 2011 showed that, for the first time since 1932, Ireland's political landscape was not dominated by FF. A coalition of FG and Labour now constitutes a considerable majority of 113 in the 166-seat Dáil. A much smaller FF with 20 seats provides the main opposition, alongside a sizeable Sinn Féin with 14 seats and a small but vocal United Left Alliance with 5 seats; 14 independents complete the 31st Dáil. However, as O'Toole (2011:1) has observed, 'everything and nothing has changed', and it is not yet clear how Irish politics will shape itself over the next decade. Exit polls at the 2011 election showed 50 per cent of voters did not change their voting pattern, while 36 per cent of remaining voters voted out of negative frustration, suggesting they voted against rather than for a party. While dramatic changes did occur, it is less clear whether a more traditional class-based cleavage is about to emerge in Irish politics. Post-election opinion polls confirmed strong support of 39 per cent for centre-right Fine Gael. Future prospects for political realignment are discussed in Chapter 10.

FIANNA FÁIL DOMINANCE

To understand modern Ireland, one has to understand Fianna Fáil. The traditional dominance of FF illustrated in Table 2.1 at first appears similar to the dominance of the Social Democrats in some European party systems, particularly the Nordic ones. However, it differs greatly in ideological terms. For even though clear class bases can be identified for Irish political parties, political culture and discourse, with their historical origins in a cross-class national movement for independence, have been largely non-ideological. One-party dominant system (OPDS) literature (Suttner 2006) sees FF as being similar to the Congress party in India, the PRI in Mexico, the Christian Democrats in Italy and the LDP in Japan, all of which have in common centrist policies and patron–client relations. There can be a tendency for dominant parties to conflate party and state and to reward party supporters by appointing them to public positions. As O'Toole (2011:1) argues, Fianna Fáil is more than a political party; it is a key institution of the Irish state. Through its brokerage style of politics, people learnt to deal with the Irish state, not directly as citizens of a republic, but through Fianna Fáil middlemen (a feature of OPDS systems). FF's populist success forced opposition parties to try to emulate them, but with little long-term success. All the main political parties employ relatively populist language and tactics and appeal to national and community interests over class ones. At times, FF has portrayed itself as the party of the rural and urban working class and therefore as Ireland's natural labour party, but this is always subservient to its vision of itself as a national movement. This 'movement' image is still invoked as the party tries to resurrect itself following its devastating electoral defeat in 2011. FG has been more clearly a middle-class party, representing large farmers and the urban bourgeoisie and professionals, but it too has tended to present itself as a national party. In this political culture, with many workers and trade union members voting for FF, Labour has tended to emphasise how it is different from FF rather than presenting a strong, class-based alternative. Thus 'community' or 'le céile' (the Gaelic for 'together') becomes the language used by all the larger parties to express identity values to the Irish electorate (O'Carroll 2002).

Mair finds 'many echoes' of FF's focus on national unity 'in some of the more extreme populist rhetoric employed in the developing economies of Latin America' (ibid.: 406). But FF's success does more than echo the rhetoric of Latin American populist parties. For, like them, its success lies in having espoused a project of national development through state-led industrialisation and through the extension of welfare measures (Dunphy 1995). However, by doing this it reinforced a strong dependence of wide sectors of Irish civil society on the party (industrialists, property developers, agro-business interests, as well as small farmers, rural labourers and public sector workers). In this way, FF rule corresponds well to Jorge Castañeda's definition of populism as 'a compromise between limited political will to impose reform from above, and limited capacity to fight for reform from below' (Castañeda 1994: 46). During its long dominance of the Irish state, the party consistently conflated the Irish national interest with that of the party, engaging in political business cycles in which key budgetary decisions closely followed electoral cycles. Smith describes the party as being acutely aware of constituency seat issues when making ministerial appointments and spending decisions, and fostering an approach to politics that is 'fertile for corruption' (Smith 2010: 201). Smith points to the emergence since the late 1950s of senior leaders in Fianna Fáil who achieved status and power within the party based on their capacity to raise party funds for winning elections (ibid.: 199). The fundraising activities of these figures were examined by numerous tribunals of inquiry, which exposed elite golden circles of Fianna Fáil politicians and businessmen, a culture of what George Colley, a dissenting Fianna Fáil TD, had described as 'low standards in high places'; Chapter 6 further discusses corruption. This party system and the Fianna Fáil political culture underpinning it lasted from the 1950s to 2011 and Fianna Fáil held power for 80 per cent of that time, making it one of the most stable dominant party systems in the western world. But, it also embedded into Irish politics a power elite, a lack of moral leadership and an absence of political vision. Mair (2010) reflects on 'a lack of real innovation in politics and a lack of room for new ideas and political styles, the result being a moribund political culture'. Further, as discussed in Chapter 3, the use of public monies and public policy for electoral purposes alarmingly accelerated in the last decade (J. O'Brien 2009) and considerably shifted the balance of power between the political system and the senior civil service (Pye 2011). There is some optimism that the lessons we have learnt and the scale of Fianna Fáil's 2011 electoral defeat may mark a seismic break in Irish politics and this political culture. This is further discussed in Chapter 10.

GENDER: *PLUS ÇA CHANGE*

There is considerable support for the view that the macho, testosterone-fuelled world of banking, business and politics contributed to the scale and nature of the crisis (Smith 2009; McCarthy 2010). In this context Ireland's patriarchal political system merits special focus. The absence of women in Irish political and broader public life has to be understood in the context of Irish political culture and the local process through which candidates are selected for political office. Local status in community, family or sports networks or local government is still the entry route for 80 per cent of national Irish politicians and the higher and lower professional classes supply 70 per cent of Irish national politicians. Thus in Irish politics, dominated by male entry routes, excessive constituency workloads and a macho culture, women remain consistently under-represented. The negative pattern of gender representation continued in the 2011 general election, in which only 15.2 per cent of candidates (86 out of 566) were female, and only 23 out of 166 elected TDs are women, constituting 15 per cent of the total. This continues a long-standing pattern of gender inequality in Irish politics, resulting in Ireland being ranked by the UN as 78th in the world for female representation in parliament. This is a deeply embedded pattern of gender inequality. Despite Irish women winning the vote in 1921 and the government elected by the 1st Dáil including a woman minister (Countess Markievicz), the patriarchal nature of the Irish state soon became evident. The role of women in Irish public life evolved from an early public mobilisation at the time of independence to a private, domestic, marginalised and subservient role, captured in the conservative view of women in the 1937 constitution. This was punctured by the emergence of women's groups from the 1960s in various and changing guises. Although women have served as presidents of Ireland for the past two decades (Mary Robinson 1990–97; Mary McAleese 1997–2011), this role is relatively symbolic; the symbolism of a woman president has not translated into more structural shifts in gendered patterns of political representation. In almost 100 years, Ireland has had only eleven female cabinet ministers, only two female tánaistí (deputy prime ministers), and has never had a female minister of finance or taoiseach.

Opinion poll evidence shows public support for more women candidates and that voters are as likely to vote for women as for men (Bacik 2009). As in other countries, the five Cs of childcare, cash, confidence, culture and, most of all, candidate selection are agreed to be the main barriers to women's political success (Bacik 2009). The 2011 Fine Gael and Labour government is to request a constitutional convention to examine 'amending the [constitutional] clause on women in the home and encouraging greater participation of women in public life' (Programme for Government 2011: 18), and to make recommendations as to how the number of women in politics can be increased (ibid.: 21). Separately, there is a commitment that public funding for political parties will be tied to the level of women candidates those parties achieve (Programme for Government 2011: 21). Despite such commitments, patriarchy continues, and only two women were appointed to 15 cabinet seats by the incoming 2011 government. This confirms a patriarchal culture in which men are beneficiaries of 'a patriarchal dividend' of prestige, status, power and male networks. Valuing equality needs to be at the heart of a second republic. The issue is not just about gender equality; the problem is also evident in relation to groups other than women. Rather, inequality in political participation also reflects the power and economic inequalities suffered by groups such as migrants, people with disabilities and the working class (Barry 2008; O'Connor 2008). This challenge of addressing equality of political representation and participation is further discussed in Chapter 9.

SOCIAL PARTNERSHIP: CO-OPTING DISSENT

Mair (2010) argues that Ireland has a passive citizenry with relatively low voter turnout of 65 per cent and low levels of political party membership (2 per cent). This is paradoxical in a state that was founded out of a rich tapestry of activism by a wide and varied range of civil society organisations (Kirby 2002). Following independence, civil society settled into a very dependent relationship on the state. After the accession of Fianna Fáil to power in 1932, the party proved adept at co-opting dissent whenever it showed the potential to mobilise significant support, and at marginalising and repressing it on the rare occasions when co-option failed. Social movements did emerge that gained significant support at particular moments, especially the workers' and the women's movements (Connolly and Hourican 2006). However the state always proved able to satisfy enough of the aspirations of the main currents of opinion within these movements to ensure that they never became a threat to Fianna Fáil hegemony. All of this contrasts strongly with what was happening in Northern Ireland with the emergence of the civil rights campaign in the late 1960s and the abject failure of the northern state to respond to its demands (Smyth 2006). Furthermore, the increasing dominance of the Irish economy by multinational capital over the period since the 1960s further weakened the trade union movement, whose base of support was more and more restricted to public sector workers, while increasing the power of the international capitalist class. This created a context that further blunted more radical developmental aspirations.

However, from the late 1970s onwards, radical critique of the state's developmental direction began to come more from a growing sector of grassroots activism, what came to be called the 'community and voluntary' sector. While Ireland has had a vibrant sector of voluntary organisations since the early nineteenth century, largely based on the churches and running most of the social services in the country, this was joined from the late 1970s by a more secular, critical and at times militant community sector running social projects with the poor and marginalised, with funding primarily from the European Economic Community (EEC) and inspired by the ideals of community empowerment. The growth of the sector in the 1980s led Daly, in her mapping of Irish civil society, to write that the 'analysis of voluntary and community organisations is key to understanding civil society in the Republic of Ireland' (Daly 2007: 162). Yet, while their commitment to developing a more just society and a more participative democracy held much promise in the mid to late 1980s, this faded as, from the mid 1990s onwards, they were drawn into a tight embrace by the state through the institutions of social partnership.

Social partnership originally developed from an initiative by the incoming Fianna Fáil government in 1987 to draw the main economic organisations – the employers' organisations, trade unions and farmers' organisations – into negotiations on the key parameters of economic policy. Though ostensibly aimed at ending unemployment, these talks actually involved – as one of Ireland's most senior trade unionists, the secretary general of the Irish Congress of Trade Unions, David Begg, retrospectively observed – giving 'business ... virtually anything it asked for – low corporation taxes, low capital taxes, low social insurance contributions and a virtually unregulated labour market' (Begg 2005). The apparent economic success that followed convinced government that these agreements were key to maintaining it; and so tri-annual negotiations were institutionalised on the broad thrust of economic and social policy under the title of social partnership, forging a consensus among the social partners and giving expression to this in detailed agreements to which all sides signed up.

In the early 1990s, social partnerships were established in places with acute social problems, drawing the state, business and social organisations into establishing area-based partnership companies to address these problems. The principle was further extended to the establishment of city and country development boards, and to numerous initiatives focusing on specific areas of social policy. In these ways, therefore, members of the community and voluntary sector soon found themselves deeply involved in a wide range of bodies alongside state and business representatives. In a novel development, the community and voluntary sector was named a social partner in 1996 and given a seat at the negotiating table; the same happened with environmental NGOs in 2009. Furthermore, the principle of social partnership came to dominate the state's approach towards policy deliberation, with the establishment of a large variety of forums through which to reach a consensus on policy in specific domains, particularly on social issues.

Business organisations, trade unions and farmers' organisations have always entered social partnership with power resources and used it as a form of corporatism for economic planning rather than as an exercise in deliberative democracy. Initially, social partnership was broadly welcomed by leaders of the community and voluntary sector, since it gave them a seat at the table of policy making and a voice in influencing the direction of state policy. However, doubts soon began to be voiced by some of those most involved, who had high expectations of exercises in deliberative democracy. By the mid

2000s, Meade could report 'a palpable sense of frustration among members of the sector who have come to doubt the effectiveness of their own participation in the process and yet who are at a loss to identify alternative approaches to political mobilisation' (Meade 2005: 364). Analysing what had been achieved by social partnership, Teague and Donaghey wrote that 'considerable effort has been made to deepen deliberative democratic practice in Ireland during the social partnership era' (Teague and Donaghey 2009: 60). However, in examining the practice of two kinds of institutional arrangements to deepen deliberative democracy, they found that they fell far short of the promise: the establishment of numerous working parties resulted in 'few successful policy initiatives' (ibid.: 63) while local area partnerships 'have not advanced local civic participation or empowerment to any significant extent' (ibid.: 65). Yet, important as it was, the failure to influence policy in the direction desired was compounded by an arguably more serious problem: the cost to the community and voluntary sector's independence as a critical voice for alternative policy directions.

Since 2002, analysts have identified in state policy towards the sector an ever greater determination to limit the role of civil society to that of providing services, greatly restricting its ability to criticise policy and lobby for social change. Harvey offers evidence of an ever more restrictive and controlling regime being imposed on charitable organisations, summed up in the sinister phrase 'non-adversarial partnerships', used by the National Economic and Social Council in 2005. As he put it, 'that the Irish state fears a civil society that might dare try, in its words, to "persuade", speaks volumes of its multiple insecurities' (Harvey 2009: 32–3). Geoghegan and Powell argue that through this reining in of the community and voluntary sector, the state has achieved the 'reinvention of community development as consumerist welfare provision rather than developmental active citizenship'. The managerialist logic of social service provision, they write, orients active citizenship away from political activism and points it towards 'more socially conservative conceptions of active citizenship that emphasise "self-reliance"', thereby reasserting not only the pre-eminence of the state within social partnership, but also the dominance of a neoliberal paradigm (Geoghegan and Powell 2009: 106). Ó Broin concludes, therefore, that through social partnership, 'in essence, the state has engaged in a process of bureaucratising potential vehicles for dissent'. By involving in the process groups that might obstruct the future implementation of public policy, the state severely limited 'their options to advocate alternative positions outside the process' (D. Ó Broin 2009: 123–4).

Twenty years of social partnership, therefore, have shown its success in facilitating, not the emergence of an activist civil society able to move public policy towards the achievements of its goals, but, rather, the taming of civil society, the severe restriction of its sphere of activity, the effective silencing of alternatives to the dominant neoliberal policy paradigm, and the development of a stultifying narrow consensus that has allowed elites to inflict severe damage on Irish society with few critical voices being raised. Those groups able, wholly or partially, to criticise government policy either within or outside the social partnership framework generally had access to resources independent of state funding. Many of the more vocal actors were from religious orders or worked for church-funded organisations. Even then monopoly ownership of the media meant that few media outlets aired debate about alternatives to the hegemonic common sense. While Connolly and Hourigan (2006) clearly identify a rich history of social movements in Ireland, their nature became more muted over the last decade as the state took a more proactive role in co-opting civil society and shaping its direction to suit the needs of a populist state (L. Cox 2010). This included discouraging the political capacity of civil society to be the public sphere necessary in a healthy and functioning democracy and encouraging a neutral stance in the relations of social movements with political parties. There has been significant public comment on the absence of civil society protest against austerity, compared to what has been seen in Greece, France and Iceland. The historical trajectory of a deeply controlling populist state has muted civil society's capacity to be socially transformative. This discussion is further developed in Chapter 10, which reviews the possibility that civil society might play a more transformative role in Irish society, imagining alternatives and engaging in the political battle of ideas about the direction to be taken by society at this critical juncture.

THE PUBLIC SPHERE: IDEAS IN A POPULIST STATE

Ideology can appear to be absent in the Irish state (Coakley 2004: 53). This, of course, is not equivalent to saying that Irish politics is non-ideological, since clear conservative economic and social stances tend to predominate among Irish policy makers. Furthermore, the Irish state has always seen itself as subservient, firstly to the power of the Catholic Church, which ran most of its educational and health services for it and, more recently, to the power of global capital, which runs most of its economy. Instead, Irish politics tends to be cloaked in a populist discourse that rarely acknowledges its ideological content. Absence of debate about ideology has allowed neoliberal ideology to gain hegemonic status over recent decades; not only was this virtually uncontested, but it cloaked itself in a benign discourse about 'partnership', 'combating poverty' and 'fostering equality' that obfuscated what was really happening. This ideology found strong expression in the Irish response to the global economic and banking crisis, as outlined in Chapter 4 – a response that served to deepen and prolong the crisis compared, for example, to the response in Iceland (see Chapter 8). The absence of a clear left–right divide between political parties and, for much of the last two decades, a consensus about policy that predominated in social partnership, suggests a pragmatic, flexible state and bureaucracy, marked by the absence of critical debate about alternatives and dominated by a narrow range of voices, usually those of (male) professional economists (mostly employed in financial services) promoting neoliberal responses to the crisis.

Why is this so? There are many explanations for the absence of a counter-discourse in Irish society. These include monopoly ownership of the media, co-option into social partnership processes and the creeping state control of civil society, the absence of radical critique by cultural writers and artists who are supported by the state and often dependent on its funding, and a diminution of the role of political satire and robust debate in public broadcasting. As academics, we are only too aware of the lack of a 'public sociology' and a relative absence of an academic voice in public discourse. An already weak public intellectual tradition in Ireland is being further impeded by an increasingly managerialist culture in Irish third-level institutions. As Lynch (2006:8) rightly observes, marketisation is a threat to critical voices. Muting of dissent has a long history in the Irish populist state. Foster (2008) describes how, from its foundation, Fianna Fáil was a dynamic populist party that married traditional clientelistic Irish political techniques with modern forms of manipulation of political opinion. O'Brien (2001) noted the Fianna Fáil founder Eamon de Valera's almost Machiavellian use of the family-owned Irish Press newspaper group to mould public opinion and discourse. Joe Lee (1989) highlights a deeply anti-intellectual Irish culture in his magisterial study of politics and society throughout the twentieth century. Furthermore, the Irish bureaucracy and key Irish public agencies are characterised by a dominant technocratic ideology that is rarely challenged by other ideological perspectives. The state, explicitly and implicitly, set boundaries for what is considered plausible discourse about policy change in Ireland. In the absence of a wide range of think tanks, the Economic and Social Research Institute (ESRI) and the National Economic and Social Council (NESC) are the only epistemic communities, and they monopolise ideological discourse. Kirby (2002) argues that the ESRI analysis is epistemologically rooted in neoclassical economic theory and orients debate in a technical direction focused on statistical measurement rather than, for example, on the promotion of values. Within social partnership, state actors and others were required to 'leave ideological differences outside the door and problem-solve in the context of a shared understanding' (McCarthy 1998). However, the shared understanding is developed within the current hegemonic ideology and is already 'cognitively locked' into a neoliberal agenda (Connolly 2007). External ideas are diluted as they become processed through domestic political institutions and a populist political culture that is immune to 'radical' policy prescriptions (Smith 2005:183). Ferriter (2004: 337) described Irish ideology as originally Catholic, conservative and patriarchal, somewhat softening socially and culturally, but hardening economically in the context of a global neoliberal hegemony. Higgins (2007: 323) argues that elites controlled the development of new discourse to justify and legitimate the economy's disservice to society. All this serves to illustrate the strength of hegemonic thought and the difficulty of breaking through 'common sense' with alternative arguments or 'good sense'.

Where debate happens is crucial. Change is less likely when policy debate happens among a narrow subgroup of policy actors in a tightly controlled coordinative technical discourse in social partnership committees, closed expert groups and interdepartmental committees. This limited form of discourse leads to reform that is incremental rather than transformative and structural. The most successful countries have coherent coordinative *and* communicative policy discourse, which appears capable of creating more sustainable outcomes. The filtering of international ideas and the dampening of domestic policy discourse through coordinative policy processes has implications for the type of policy change possible in Ireland. Political economist Scharpf (2000) argues that more substantive change requires that ideas be processed in a wide, communicative political discourse that enables social learning and attitudinal change. Schmidt likewise concluded that countries manage adjustment to the external economy, 'not only because of their greater or lesser economic viability, their greater or lesser institutional capacities and better or worse policy responses but also because of their more or less convincing legitimating discourse' (Schmidt 2000: 306).

If policy is to be effective in moving Ireland towards becoming a capable society and economy, it will require more processes of 'communicative discourse' that are capable of promoting social learning leading to a change in values, which can in turn support a fundamental restructuring of policy and institutions. In Ireland we are more likely to find 'coordinative discourse' in which change is managed through a closed elite-level policy process confined to problem solving or lesson drawing. In Habermasian terms, what is missing is a public sphere. Some civil society-led responses to the current crisis, recognising the limits to political discourse in tightly organised state-controlled spaces, have opened up new spaces to promote wider imaginative discourse on alternatives, but with limited success. These responses are surveyed in Chapter 10.

NORTHERN IRELAND

This chapter ends with a review of the politics of Northern Ireland, concentrating on recent political and institutional changes. This is done in recognition of the present constitutional aspiration for consensual unification; later chapters continue this focus on the island as a whole, discussing the prospects for political unification. The 1920 British Government of Ireland Act established the six counties in the north-east of Ireland as a statelet under British rule, but with devolved powers. Following the War of Independence and the 1921 treaty negotiations, this two-state situation became permanent. An immediate electoral reform from a proportional to a plurality voting system consolidated unionist majority power; subsequent manipulation of electoral boundaries further reinforced that power. With little oversight from Westminster, the permanent unionist majority governed the Northern Ireland state and historically discriminated in favour of the unionist population. Adshead and Tonge (2009) describe how ensuing discrimination fuelled a 1969 civil rights movement and civil unrest which culminated in an armed Irish Republican Army campaign beginning in 1971. Direct UK rule was introduced in 1972. Processes between the Westminster and Irish governments (1985 Anglo Irish Agreement and 1993 Downing Street Declaration) opened a political space which led eventually to a full IRA ceasefire. The negotiated 1998 Good Friday Agreement established the contemporary constitutional structure of Northern Ireland. On 22 May 1998, voters in Northern Ireland voted 71.12 per cent in favour and voters in the Republic 94.4 per cent in favour of devolved new political institutions in Northern Ireland. The Republic's referendum included a fundamental provision deleting the claim to the North's territory in the Irish Constitution; this reflected southern public opinion that a united Ireland can only be achieved through consensus. After a rocky start to self-government and renewed paramilitary activity the new devolved political institutions were suspended in October 2002, but were fully established in 2009. Policing and criminal justice were fully devolved to the Belfast executive in 2010.

The agreement was structured into three strands. Strand One, dealing with the internal arrangements for Northern Ireland, created a consociational executive within a democratically elected assembly with 108 MLAs elected from 18 Westminster constituencies under the same PR-STV electoral system as used in the Republic. The first minister and deputy first minister are nominated by the largest and second largest parties respectively and act as chairmen of the executive. Crucial conflict-resolution institutions include the Bill of Rights, the Equality Commission and Inter-Communal Reconciliation processes. Under Strand Two of the agreement, the North–South Ministerial Council was established to develop consultation, cooperation and action within the island of Ireland on matters of mutual interest. A north–south civic forum was also anticipated but has not yet been implemented. Strand Three deals with east–west arrangements and the creation of a British–Irish Council bringing together representatives of the British and Irish Governments, members of the devolved institutions in Scotland, Wales and Northern Ireland, and representatives from the Isle of Man and Channel Islands. The British–Irish Intergovernmental Conference brings together the British and Irish Governments to promote bilateral cooperation on matters of mutual interest.

It is too early to speculate about the effectiveness and levels of trust in these institutions. Hayes and McAllister (2008) note the importance of political leadership in shaping the emerging consensus about political reforms. Sinn Féin and the Democratic Unionist Party, the two largest parties in the Northern assembly, had originally resisted the institutions longest, but have since achieved the greatest electoral gains from the reforms and are now embedded in these institutions. The May 2011 elections reinforced this pattern of DUP and SF dominance. O'Dochartaigh (2008) reflects on the fact that the electoral shift to these parties was a logical outcome of the sectarian logic of the consociational institutions which inevitably embed, deepen and institutionalise those divisions. This weakness of consociationalism has been well aired in political debate. Tonge (2005: 255) reflects how some argue that societal reconciliation is possible, but that it is less likely to occur under the compartmentalised ethnic elitist blocs associated with consociationalism. Others argue that consociationalism merely reflects the political reality of a sectarian society, but does not rule out the scope for political parties to shift and change. Gormley-Heenan and Devine (2010) report that there is relatively little difference in levels of trust in Northern Ireland institutions along sectarian lines, and that age and party affiliation provide greater grounds for differences than the traditional Catholic–Protestant division. However, they note that specific groups of people have higher levels of disinterest, disaffection and distrust; these include women, young people and older people. If such distrust were to continue, this could challenge the legitimacy of the revived institutions. The lack of progress and engagement with the north–south civic forum is a real concern in this regard. Furthermore, the political challenges facing Northern Ireland need to be understood in the context of the economic challenges outlined in Chapter 4. The recession put extra pressure on an economy that is already over-reliant on public-sector employment. A reduction in EU funds for the peace process, as well as the withdrawal or spend down of US philanthropic bodies, compounds recession-fuelled unemployment. There are very divergent views on what the peace process means for the prospects of Irish unity. On the one hand, key ingredients, including cross-border institutions and confederal governance arrangements, point one towards reunification. On the other hand, the agreement includes key political safeguards for the unionist community. Tonge (2005) describes the bi-national aspects of the agreement as weak. O'Dochartaigh (2008) points to the possibility of unification being naturalised through embedded cooperation, but recognises that unionists will resist 'creeping integration' and that cross-border institutions may reinforce rather than weaken the border. Much of the answer will lie in the convictions and leadership of the key political parties and civil society. Adshead and Tonge (2009: 139) point to Northern Ireland's civil society as being conditioned by the complete domination of sectarian division and sectarian groups up to the 1970s, but recognise the emergence since devolution of a still marginalised and weak, but more universal, civil society. While all of the above is still fragile, progress to date has nevertheless been impressive. The degree to which the developments above represent a reversal of partition and a move towards unity on the one hand, or a deepening of that partition and a move away from the possibility of an all-island political community on the other, is further discussed in Chapter 10.

CONCLUSION: AN ARGUMENT FOR A SECOND REPUBLIC

The crisis has exposed the deficiencies of Irish political institutions. Cox (in Mulholland 2010: 18) refers to the fact that 'naturally dense networks of family and community which bind us together in Ireland have been accentuated by a whole political and business ecosystem of mutually interdependent cronyism'. However, he argues that this is not inevitable and that comparable states, including Finland, Austria, Belgium and the Netherlands, came out of the recession more quickly and more successfully than Ireland. Farrell (in Mulholland 2010) argues that this political system is now at a point of disequilibrium, and that the crisis has been the catalyst for a coalition of disparate views about how to overhaul the political system. The core problem of policy making derives from the relationship between the institutions of the existing political system and the political culture they create, the political and economic elites which have such influence within them and the ideological configurations that underpin them. This chapter has highlighted how various elements of the political system arose historically and came to constitute a system that reinforced its own inertia. The following chapter continues that theme, examining the nature of Irish bureaucracy. What this chapter has demonstrated is the weakness of parliament in holding elites to account, a weakness intensified by the localist and personalist outcomes of the PR-STV electoral system, which in turn reinforces a political culture and a relatively passive civil society and public sphere. Addressing these issues will necessitate such fundamental institutional reform, political party realignment and fundamental changes in public culture and values that it requires no less than the refounding of the institutions of the Republic. An Oireachtas Committee on Constitutional Reform (2010) made a series of recommendations. That year saw a range of civil society-led organisations campaigning for various political reforms and the Fine Gael–Labour coalition government elected in early 2011 committed in its Programme for Government to a citizens' convention to develop a series of proposals for political reform and to act on its recommendations in 2012. There is a danger that momentum for reform precipitated by the crisis will be forced into a problem-solving coordinative process rather than a communicative process capable of changing values and culture. The future of Northern Ireland in any new republic is unclear. The new cross-border institutions contain the seeds of north–south cooperation; but this can only happen in a context of political consent and compromise that is not always present. Chapter 10 returns to these issues.

3
The Irish State Bureaucracy

The civil service of the Irish Republic, as with other countries, has been justifiably described as the 'permanent government'. Civil service power is neglected in most studies of political systems, which focus on the elected state while leaving the unelected state unexamined. Barry Desmond (2011), a former Irish Labour politician who served as a government minister, colourfully described how civil servants viewed politicians as 'defecating birds of passage flying overhead on their journey home'. Pye (2011:16) describes in even more vivid fashion how the Department of Finance regarded 'its statutory role as the last line of defence against the predations and venality of a self-serving political caste'. Mair notes a lack of control, accountability and responsibility on the part of the Irish political class. He describes Ireland as a political system that has been governed at one remove, in which politicians allocated 'to the bureaucracy the role of principal initiator and designer of policy rather than simply the executor of policy' (Mair, in Mulholland 2010: 68). This chapter analyses a neglected feature of the Irish political system, namely the power that inheres in the civil service, and the traditional weakness of political party control over the decisions and actions of that civil service. But it also explores how over the last two decades power has shifted towards the political system, with Fianna Fáil ministers increasingly overriding the advice of civil servants in framing budget policy. The political choice to ignore the more conservative civil service fiscal advice has contributed towards budgetary decisions that have served to increase the budget deficit and partially fuel the crisis. The power that inheres in bureaucracies is seen as a problem by critical observers of government and politics in most countries, and Ireland is no exception. However, in the Irish case, the combination of secretiveness and unaccountability that characterises most bureaucracies is compounded at all levels by both a remarkable weakness in overall policy-making capacity and a poor record of policy implementation. The chapter concludes that a second republic would need to address two key concerns: the uneven but relatively weak overall policy capacity and implementation record in public administration at national and local authority levels, and issues of accountability and transparency in many arms of the Irish bureaucracy.

The chapter first examines the evolution of the Irish civil service from British colonial rule to the Irish Free State. The second section outlines the central and powerful role the Department of Finance plays in the Irish bureaucracy; the following section outlines the traditional political culture of the Irish civil service, marked as it is by populism, patriarchy and a deep conservatism associated with an insular Catholic Irish state and society. The fourth section reviews the changing role of the civil service, drawing attention to its engagement with new public management, and the transfer of power and functions to quasi-autonomous non-governmental organisations (quangos). The next section reviews decentralisation, devolution and developments in local government. The sixth section is a brief assessment of bureaucracy in Northern Ireland, while the penultimate section changes tempo and draws out some key tensions and ambiguities in the Irish bureaucracy, including the relationship with politics and society and a tendency towards weak policy and implementation capacity. The concluding section addresses the dangers of cosy consensus.

THE COLONIAL LEGACY

The new Irish state inherited both the fundamental machinery of the British Westminster model of politics and the British Whitehall model of civil service and public administration. The nature of the modern Irish civil service is still, almost 90 years later, very much influenced by this colonial inheritance. The Irish bureaucracy inherited a structure based on strict hierarchies of power and, following the British Treasury model, on the structurally dominant role of the Department of Finance. In the transition to the Free State in 1921–22, over 98 per cent of the 20,415 Irish civil servants remained, which resulted in a remarkable continuity of culture. Indeed, there was little radical restructuring of Irish institutions until the 1970s, when Ireland joined the EEC. A relatively strong state framework was legislated for by the Ministers and Secretaries Act (1924) and later in the 1937 constitution. Central to the Whitehall system was a strong principle of 'corporation sole', or full and total ministerial accountability for the actions of civil servants. This ministerial responsibility distorts the degree of bureaucratic power and leaves civil servants' actions largely hidden and unaccountable.

The Whitehall culture resulted in a strongly conservative bias to policy and administration, and a culture of secrecy (Adshead and Tonge 2009: 51). While ministers had the legal responsibility of 'corporation sole' and a political power base, the bureaucracy had a power base of information, resources, longevity, experience, expertise and rational rule making among civil servants. Traditionally ministers did not play a 'direct role in the internal management of their departments' (Connolly and O'Halpin 1999: 263) and they tended to leave this to civil servants (the 'permanent government'). A co-dependent relationship has developed between the political civil service or 'permanent government' and the politician. There is tension certainly, but also a cosy consensus whereby both are protected behind a culture of secrecy and a well-documented lack of accountability and transparency. A contemporary consequence is the lack of a clear division between the minister and the civil servant, a consequent lack of direct accountability, and also a tendency towards blame avoidance and risk taking.

THE DEPARTMENT OF FINANCE

As in other states there is a clear hierarchy of functions and status in the Irish civil service. One department stands out above the others in terms of status, dominance and power: the Department of Finance (like the Treasury in the British system) dominates the civil service. The consequent primacy of expenditure control, with expenditure being the first item on all cabinet agendas, means that the DOF mediates all other departmental expenditure decisions. Relatively strong expenditure-monitoring institutions include the Audit and Accounts Department and the Comptroller and Auditor General and, in the legislature, the Public Accounts Committee. Three principles dominate the strict controls on expenditure: monies can only be spent for the purpose allocated, there can only be one single fund, and all expenditure can only be met from current annual receipts. Over time, this preoccupation with expenditure has entrenched a fiscal anorexia in the Irish state (Boyle 2005) and a reluctance to invest in expenditure, especially social expenditure. This has had far-reaching consequences for the social cohesion and development of the Irish state and society; the more senior department, Finance, is both ideologically and pragmatically associated with low public expenditure (Lee 1989). Later in this chapter we see how such reluctance to spend was tempered by an increased tendency by

Fianna Fáil-led governments to frame budgetary policy in the context of electoral cycles.

Historically, the statutory role of the Department of Finance has meant a highly centralised approach to economic and social planning, human resource management and public administration between Finance and line departments. The Public Expenditure Unit (PEU), which links each line department to the DOF, is conservative about public spending and has a reputation for 'pouring cold water' over policy innovation and for vetoing spending. This culture is then reflected in highly centralised line departments in which most resources are dedicated to service delivery and implementation rather than to policy planning or evaluation. There are traditionally tense relations between Finance and line departments. At various times in the 1960s and 1970s, initiatives were made to devolve government spending, but there was a reversal of that devolution in the more tightened circumstances of the late 1980s. In the 1990s, key policy priorities of Economic and Monetary Union (see Chapter 4) meant that generating economic growth and avoiding borrowing dominated the DOF agenda. After entering the euro in 1999, governments largely respected the three criteria of the Stability and Growth Pact: low inflation, a 3 per cent limit on government current deficits, and a 60 per cent threshold on government debt. While largely focused on tasks rather than on policy, the DOF was comfortable with this monetarist approach, which was consistent with its clear pro-market ideological policy agenda, associated with a preference for low social expenditure and low taxation. Cousins (2005) sees the different approach of the British Treasury, driven in the 1990s by an overt policy agenda particularly focused on jobs and employment, as illustrating that change can happen even in such entrenched bureaucracies.

THE TRADITIONAL POLITICAL CULTURE OF THE IRISH CIVIL SERVICE

The political system and political culture outlined in Chapter 2 reflect characteristics that have been identified in the small states literature – most notably in the personalism that marks the political system and the more informal style of policymaking that has tended to predominate (Connaughton 2010). In Ireland the political culture of the civil service is further marked by a strongly populist culture. As discussed in the previous chapter the Irish state is also a patriachical state. Article 40 of the 1937 constitution recognised 'the special role of women in the home', which was reflected in the 'male breadwinner' model accommodating wifely labour (Shaver and Bradshaw 1995). This finds expression in various social welfare payments, home-care tax credits, a household-based tax system, and a universal child benefit supporting women caring in the home. Up to 1995, when the clause was removed by referendum, there was a constitutional ban on divorce. Furthermore, legislation was in force up to 1972 requiring female civil servants to leave state employment upon marrying. Consequently the Irish civil service was predominantly male. While the workforce in the civil service is now of more mixed gender, the legacy of the marriage bar is still evident. The absence of women at senior levels is notable and the culture of the senior civil service is strongly masculine (O'Connor 2008; McGauran 2005). The remarkable cultural overlap in nature and composition between the early civil service and the political class follows through to the contemporary political, social and economic elite (Collins and O'Shea 2003). This is reflected in a largely consensual and cooperative relationship between the political and bureaucratic elite and their shared project of a conservative nationalist Catholic Ireland. Despite the homogeneity of the civil service when viewed from outside, there are nonetheless considerable cultural and ideological differences and a clear hierarchy between key government departments. Taking social policy as an example, Murphy notes that the Department of Social Protection (DSP) has an importance for overall government policy and a large budget, but finds the Department of Enterprise, Trade and Employment (DETE) (now renamed the Department of Enterprise, Jobs and Innovation) and the Department of Finance (DOF) are institutionally stronger, while the Department of the Taoiseach plays a coordinative role (M.P. Murphy 2006: 127). Turf wars and power struggles between departments are not uncommon. The localist and non-ideological nature of Irish politics has resulted in a state which has relied heavily on the role of professional civil servants in administration and in policy development. However, civil servants use this power discreetly and subtly, preserving the status quo and avoiding radical change. Retired senior civil servants stress the incremental nature of policy change and civil servants control that process and exert their greatest influence 'not only through their preparation of information and the evaluation of policy alternatives, but also through their ongoing contact with a wide range of interest groups' (Connolly and O'Halpin 1999: 263). While this could be said about practically any country, as Mair (2010) notes there has been an extraordinary lack of control, accountability and responsibility on the part of the Irish political class.

Inaction and ineffective monitoring by the Financial Regulator, the Central Bank, the Department of Finance and the Oireachtas Joint Committee on Economic Regulatory Affairs were found to be key weaknesses contributing to the current crisis in the trilogy of reports analysing the causes of the crisis (Wright 2010; Nyberg 2011; Regling and Watson 2010). Absence of accountability is a clear feature of Irish power relations. Martin (2010) points to a range of formal and informal mechanisms in the Irish political system that can hold bureaucratic power to account; these include junior ministers, coalition governments, parliamentary questions, the media, tribunals of investigation and the parliamentary parties. He assesses some formal bodies like the Comptroller and Auditor General as highly effective but, as Mitchell (2011) concludes, their role is limited to expenditure efficiency rather than policy effectiveness. The 1997 Freedom of Information Act did much to challenge the culture of secrecy within government, but was diluted in 2002 (Zimmerman 2008).

THE CHANGING ROLE OF THE CIVIL SERVICE

Reforming and modernising are not new agendas for the Irish civil service. The largely unimplemented 1969 Devlin Report had previously heralded the need for public sector reform and modernisation. Reforms after 1985 devolved some power to manage government departments to the renamed 'Secretaries General' of civil service departments and heralded a long series of government policy initiatives and legislative processes which aimed to improve accountability, policy making and service delivery in the Irish civil service. They did not, however, remove the legal principle of ministerial accountability, what is called 'corporation sole'.

The most recent review of the Irish public service highlights change over the last two decades (OECD 2008). Some of this change is consistent with broader experience across western liberal states, where new-right ideologies followed the 1970s oil crisis, introducing austerity programmes as a response (Adshead and Tonge 2009). New public management (NPM) is a management philosophy used by governments in public sector reforms since the 1980s (Duncan and Chapman 2010). NPM agendas focused on adapting private-sector management language, techniques and tools into the public sector and brought a greater focus on efficiency and the measurement of outcomes. Adoption of NPM led to changes within the structure and operations of the state bureaucracy. The 1980s and 1990s saw the establishment of the Ombudsman's Office, the Data Protection Act, the Public Offices Commission and the Information Commissioner, all of which were designed to open up the traditional culture of secrecy in public administration. An important modernisation agenda was heralded in the 1994 Strategic Management Initiative. Various initiatives in regulatory reform included the Ethics in Public Office Act in 1995 and the related Public Services Management Act in 1997. These stress guidelines for preparing strategy statements, performance management systems, financial management systems and an information technology framework. The 1990s also saw various customer services quality initiatives, including customers' charters, information campaigns and investment in citizens' rights and information services.

The challenge of combining the traditional role and culture of the civil service with 'new public management' roles and practices opened up a new type of mixed economy and a shift in the role of the public service from providing services to regulating or enabling them. While the NPM did not fundamentally change the nature of the civil service in Ireland to the extent it did in other liberal regimes, there has been some impact. The Irish bureaucracy has grown more fragmented, complex and multi-level, and this has had an impact on corporate governance, accountability and transparency as well as on the capacity for policy making and implementation (Connolly 2004: 348). Pollit (2005) writes that NPM appears to be less embedded in Ireland than elsewhere, and has had little impact on Irish public-sector reform processes. Boyle (2009) argues that while the NPM may have brought some positive reforms it has also led to a more fragmented and complex public service with more separation between policy development and implementation. This has made accountability more rather than less complex. One impact has been the sheer scale in the growth of the number of senior civil servants (that is, those with resource allocation or substantive decision-making and policy-making powers) (see Figure 3.1).

The Irish state has always been described as a mixed welfare state (Cousins 2005; McCashin 2004). For ideological, pragmatic or cultural reasons the British state had ceded control of large areas of decision making to societal actors, in particular to the Catholic Church, which designed and implemented many health and education services. This is consistent with other colonial societies and accounts for the strength of religious forces in Ireland, although over

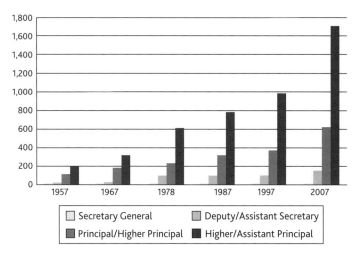

Figure 3.1   Profile of the civil service grade structure, 1957–2007

Source: Hardiman and MacCartaigh, in Hardiman (2009: 33)

time these services have increasingly been delivered through non-governmental organisations (NGOs) in the increasingly secularised community and voluntary sector. In the 1980s many state functions were either privatised or devolved to new state agencies and a new type of largely unaccountable state agency became a key feature of the Irish state (see Figure 3.2). The OECD (2008: 295–8) argues that motivation for the establishment of these agencies varied: some were initiated as a way around the slow and cumbersome machinery of the civil service; some were established to avoid ministerial responsibility and/or public accountability; some were pragmatic responses to public sector recruitment embargoes; and some were the outcome of power games or were created by ambitious political or bureaucratic actors during the economic boom. Growth in such agencies was consistent with the general trend towards NPM in western liberal economies, as was a focus on privatisation of state enterprises (in Ireland this applied to steel, sugar and coal, and to post and telecommunications). Transport functions, including air, rail and sea, were either re-formed into semi-state agencies or privatised. In 2002, the government centralised a regional structure of eleven politically appointed health boards into a centralised Health Service Executive. This has proved to be an exemplar for a new public management obsession with management systems, indicators and targets, the combined result of which has been a highly ineffective and unaccountable health system.

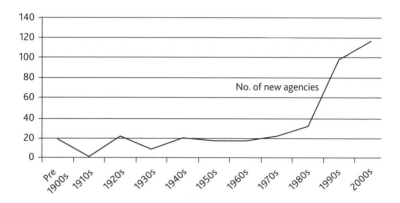

Figure 3.2   Number of state agencies in Ireland by decade, 1900s–2000s

Source: 'Mapping the Irish State'database, http://geary.ucd.ie/mapping (Hardiman 2009: 35)

Hardiman (2009) observes that the number of new agencies in the state rose from an average of 20 per decade in the period between the foundation of the state and the 1970s to over 100 in each of the last two decades. These newer agencies are advisory, regulatory or temporary in nature and less subject to legislative controls or, in some cases, to any standards or accountability (OECD 2008). Clancy and Murphy (2006) identify one state body for every 5,000 Irish people and over 450 diverse executive and advisory bodies at national level. Ó Broin and Waters (2007) mapped 491 bodies and 22 distinct types of body across local and regional authority administrative areas, amounting to one for every 4,000 citizens. Locally subregional or devolved governance appears to have developed without reference to existing national or regional spatial strategies. The early 2000s also saw a process of Irish local government reform and a 'cohesion' process within the local development sector, in which local development and community development agencies were required to merge. As Harvey (2009) argues, since 2002 many local area-based partnerships, community development programmes and local drugs task forces have been obliged to work within more bureaucratic and inflexible processes and have effectively been re-engineered from transformative locally driven projects to cheap, or at least cost-effective, service delivery agents of the state. Cerny's larger political understanding of this proliferation of agencies is to see it as the state, in the context of managing a more competitive form of globalisation, seeking to steer rather than row. This strategy is also consistent with the co-optation of NGOs as a political containment strategy.

Regardless of this growth, the OECD (2008) found the Irish civil service to be relatively modest in size. This was consistent with the colonial legacy of conservative expenditure and reliance on the church to deliver health and education. While growth in public spending and in public sector numbers has been relatively high in Ireland compared to other states over the last decade, this needs to be understood in the context of playing catch-up from historically low levels. In 2005 total Irish government expenditure at 34.4 per cent of GDP was the third lowest in the OECD (only Korea and Mexico spent less with 28.9 per cent and 19.5 per cent respectively). Irish expenditure is also low compared with other small states (Finland 50.5 per cent; New Zealand 40 per cent; Norway 41.9 per cent). The OCED assessed employment in the Irish general government sector, including voluntary schools, hospitals and universities to be approximately 15 per cent of the total labour force, similar to mid-ranking countries including the USA, Poland, Spain and the Netherlands (OECD 2008: 64). While the core civil service still comprises a small percentage of overall employment within the public service, there has been a considerable increase in the number of senior civil servants, reflecting investment in management and senior administrative roles associated with a NPM culture. However, most of the 50 per cent increase in public service employment over the last decade has been in functional or front-line sectors, such as health and education; even in the context of significant public sector reform it is difficult to see how the numbers of public services can be reduced without impacting on the delivery of front-line services.

DEVOLUTION AND DEVELOPMENTS IN LOCAL GOVERNMENT REFORM

Ireland is a unitary state in which power is constitutionally centralised. Local government is limited to functions relating to physical infrastructure and public recreation, as well as some public services relating to environmental and planning issues. Many of these functions are more the executive function of centrally appointed county managers than the direct function of directly elected councillors. This managerial system of local administration has grown rather than receded over the years, rendering weak democratic accountability for local government (Adshead and Tonge 2009: 160). The main local government infrastructure is based on 29 directly elected county councils and five urban or city councils representing the cities of Dublin, Cork, Limerick, Waterford and Galway. Dublin city and county is divided into four councils. A lower tier of urban district councils and town commissioners survived a 1920s reform that abolished rural district councils.

These county-level administrative areas coexist alongside a number of state-sponsored regional bodies with functional responsibility for health, education, policing, environment and cultural services. These bodies have often developed their own administrative regional boundaries, which cause significant overlap and confusion. They also fall outside the remit of regulatory and Dáil supervision and are democratically unaccountable. The 1990s saw the development of sub-county-level local-area development 'partnerships' of voluntary, statutory and private-sector actors (Sabel 1996). While often innovative (and a useful vehicle for drawing down EU structural and social funds) these partnerships also added to the layer of sub-national administrative infrastructure. A White Paper on local government (1996) introduced NPM concepts to local government and established new layers of Strategic Policy Groups, City and County Development Boards and Corporate Policy Groups into an already complicated picture. To maintain a priority line to EU structural funds available to countries judged to need development aid, government also divided the country into two largely symbolic administrative areas, one of which, the Border Midland and West, was considered eligible for EU Objective One funding status. This added to the overall administrative complexity and confusion of sub-national government.

Given the fragmented and incoherent nature of Irish local government reform, it is difficult to see where power lies in Irish local governance systems; but many functions are still located within the administrative function of county managers rather than of elected politicians. This presents difficulties for local popular political action. Moreover, the pace, direction and shape of local government reform remains firmly in the control of central government. Irish local bureaucracy remains distinctive from state bureaucracies in other small states in the degree to which it is still highly centralised, with decision making over many key functions, such as health, education and policing, not being devolved to local level. Without independent local revenue-raising powers, local government will remain the pawn of central government and local participative forms of citizenship will remain difficult to activate. Local government reform therefore needs to be a high priority for a second republic.

The following case study is offered as an example of how Irish policy making was manipulated by short-term electoral agendas and lacked a coherent vision of local government reform. In December 2003 the Fianna Fáil minister for finance, Charlie McCreevy, introduced a decentralisation project under which government departments were to be geographically dispersed to key provincial towns. The plan was to move 10,922 public servants and 48 sections of government departments and semi-state agencies to 58 locations by the end of 2006. This was not a plan for devolution or local government reform; rather, the use of the term 'decentralisation' simply meant transferring outside of Dublin eight of the 15 headquarters of government departments. The decision that decentralised departments would keep a small ministerial office in Dublin highlighted the folly of the decision. Decentralisation diminished the policy capacity of those departments involved, in that it either split the departments into different offices or it caused the departure of key experienced policy staff who, for family or lifestyle reasons, refused decentralisation outside Dublin. By June 2010, only 29 per cent of the original 10,922 jobs had been decentralised and most projects were deferred. Kitchin (2010) observes that the failed project imposed a considerable cost to the taxpayer in human resource planning, land sites, building and fit-out costs. It was developed in secret by four ministers with no wider consultation with affected parties or the general public, no evidence-informed analysis, no cost-benefit analysis, no impact analysis, no assessment of how it would affect workers and their families and no alignment with other government policy such as the National Spatial Strategy. The former taoiseach, John Bruton, described decentralisation as the single greatest act of administrative and political vandalism since the foundation of the state. Thornhill (in Mulholland 2010: 128–31) associates decentralisation with a general decline in standards in the public service, with public services being used as 'playthings' of a populist political system seeking electoral advantage in rural constituencies. Kitchin concludes that this is an example of electioneering and short-term political gain being placed ahead of what is right for the country.

NORTHERN IRELAND BUREAUCRACIES

To what extent is there convergence or divergence between public administrations north and south? Comparison with developments in Northern Ireland highlights the degree of historical divergence between the two jurisdictions. There are differences of governance and policy experiences and challenges in the two bureaucracies, but also some similarities between north and south. Both jurisdictions have their origin in the British civil service, which itself had shown remarkable consistency from its inception in the 1850s to recent changes in the 1990s. The Northern Ireland Civil Service (NICS) is separate from but mirrors the UK civil service. Adshead and Tonge (2009) argue that it is best understood in the context of the sectarian state in which it developed between the 1920s and the 1970s. Discrimination against Catholics in recruitment to the civil service and in the allocation of public goods through the public service was extensive until direct rule in 1972. Thereafter a number of legislative frameworks, including the Fair Employment Act, began to erode the sectarian recruitment practice. By 2000 the proportion of Catholics and Protestants employed by the NICS reflected the broad populations. There was also marked improvement in the gender balance. Adshead and Tonge (2009) refer to the high level of scrutiny of the NICS, a result of monitoring sectarian practice and a more intensive focus on new public management outcomes monitoring than in the Republic. Devolution in 1998 and implementation of the structures of the Good Friday Agreement meant reorganisation from six to ten departments, but perhaps with little significant change in culture and practice. Rather, suspension of the political institutions gave senior civil servants the opportunity to embed these new departments with no political oversight for a number of years, thus reinforcing the power of the bureaucrats.

Local government in Northern Ireland has undergone more systematic reform processes than its southern counterpart. Since its inception in 1920, Northern Ireland local government has been subject to sectarian power imbalances and discriminatory practice. Unionists comprised 66 per cent of the population but, through gerrymandering, controlled 85 per cent of councils. However, since direct rule in 1972, sectarian practice has begun to be addressed. The general consensus that Northern Ireland is over-governed (Adshead and Tonge 2009: 164) was addressed in 1972 with significant reforms; but by the time of the GFA there were still a substantial 582 councillors across 26 local authorities. In contrast however to the slow, selective and politically motivated public sector reform in the Republic, the 2006 Review of Public Administration in Northern Ireland was much more ambitious and objective (Birrell 2006). This perhaps reflects a less populist political culture. Local government reform in Northern Ireland faces the additional challenge of being part of the wider UK jurisdiction, as well as challenges similar to those affecting the south regarding the continued use of quangos and issues of democratic accountability. These were also problems in the United Kingdom. The final decisions of the 2006 review included ambitious plans to reduce the total number of quangos by half (99 to 50), to replace 27 local government agencies with seven and to reduce 15 executive agencies to seven. The clarity of the reform agenda and its specific targets stands in contrast to the vague reform agenda in the Republic. A 2008 decision eventually reduced the target for reform to a more politically acceptable 11 local authorities for the 1.6 million population of Northern Ireland. This change agenda points to some similarities between Northern Ireland and the Republic. On the one hand, both jurisdictions are influenced by new public management theory and practice and have to contend with neoliberalism and cuts that will curtail the scale and scope of the public sector. They share a common concern with issues of governance and accountability, quality and customer service, and coordination and integration, while the use of Information Communication Technology is also shared. Where Northern Ireland uses language of equality and human rights, the Republic has concentrated on inclusion, equality, disadvantage and area-based strategies. On the other hand, the jurisdictions exist in different political cultures. The North's focus has been on efficiency, effectiveness, subsidiarity and cross-community issues, while in the Republic, the focus has been on management and evidence-based policy making (Birrell 2006). This raises the prospect of some common reform agendas, but also of different reform priorities.

POWER, POLICY-MAKING CAPACITY AND IMPLEMENTATION

What does all this tell us about the policy and implementation capacity of the public service? Economic governance and the developmental capacity of state structures are further discussed in Chapter 4. More generally Mitchell (2011) observes that for all the preoccupation of the Department of Finance and the Public Accounts Committee on controlling expenditure, there has been less concern with what money was spent on or whether public expenditure produced appropriate results or outcomes. In examining social policy, M.P. Murphy (2006) sees a lack of policy capacity and a weak tradition of policy making to be defining features of the Irish civil service. Despite some unsuccessful attempts to devolve power, highly centralised line departments are still controlled by the DOF. This strong controlling role comes at the expense of developing a strong capacity for national planning and innovation. To counter this gap in national policy making, various departments or agencies have been established to undertake some of the national planning function; these include the Economic and Social Research Institute (ESRI) in 1960, and the National Economic and Social Council (NESC) in 1973. However, warning signals from such bodies were not necessarily heeded. Cox draws attention to the consistent pattern of ignoring the National Competitiveness Council's red-flag warnings about loss of competitiveness (P. Cox 2010). This lack of policy oversight contributed greatly to the recent crisis. Attention has also been drawn to policy competence; the Wright (2010) and Nyberg (2011) reports point to the absence of trained economists in the Department of Finance.

There is unevenness and even contradiction in the bureaucracy's ambition and capacity for policy; and, as discussed in Chapter 1, there are different historical phases in the development of the Irish state. On the one hand there is evidence of a capable technocratic developmentalism, illustrated by the success of the Irish Development Authority (IDA) in attracting foreign direct investment, by the growth in Irish tourism under Bord Fáilte and, to some degree, by the role of state enterprise agencies in the development of an indigenous software industry (Ó Riain 2004). On the other hand, there are far too many systematic policy failures. Ross (2009) draws our attention to Coras Iompair Éireann (responsible for the national transport infrastructure) and the Health Services Executive as unaccountable agencies whose policy decisions were at times more consistent with localised political agendas than with national policy need. There is systematic failure to achieve effective planning and to maximise synergies between positive developmental outcomes and other national policy goals. Despite the significant presence of world-leading multinational information technology companies (such as Dell, Google and Intel) in Ireland, there has been a failure to develop an infrastructure or knowledge economy in relation to information technology, including a lack of investment in information technology and broadband (O'Toole 2009). Kirby and Murphy (2011) examine the tensions between the dual aspects of the Irish state and stress how the state's contemporary developmental traits, while clearly evident, serve the logic of competition and the needs of the external political economy. State developmentalism seems largely to have been restricted to areas in which state intervention was required to enable competition, so that business – particularly foreign-owned companies – could thrive and profit. Developmentalism took various forms and crossed many policy areas, including national infrastructure, education policy, taxation policy and industrial policy. However, the state failed to be developmental in supporting other infrastructure, for example, broadband infrastructure, and has generally favoured MNCs over indigenous industry. This indicates clear limitations to the Irish state's developmentalism. Boucher and Boyle (2007) show that over the last two decades strong state developmental capacity and outcomes in some policy areas (industrial policy) have coexisted with limited state developmental capacity in others (anti-poverty policy). In other domestic areas, the policy agenda of Irish agencies is driven by short-term populism and the clientelistic ambitions of Fianna Fáil politicians, who have offered political protection to core agencies as long as they delivered locally and on key short-term political objectives. Other policy areas, such as childcare, have seen policy debate pulled in opposite directions by different vested interest groups, so that decisions were caught in a 'policy paralysis' giving rise to the image of a frozen landscape of reform (M.P. Murphy 2006). Often, therefore, political culture meant that public sector capacity was sacrificed for political gain. This culture plays out most powerfully at a local level and permeates local state bureaucracy. The following example clearly illustrates this.

In 2009, the Comptroller and Auditor General (CPAG), John Buckley, published a report on the running of the state training agency, FÁS (An Foras Áiseanna Saothair, the Irish Training and Employment Authority). The report captures perfectly a political culture in which politics and public sector agencies overlapped, and lax financial controls enabled an elite to live a lavish lifestyle funded by public monies. Reports by the CPAG in 2010 reviewing the corporate governance structure of FÁS highlighted an exaggerated macho culture of Irish elites that crossed public sector bodies, cultural groups and the social partners. The resignation of Roddy Molloy as director of FÁS in November 2008, and the continued public controversy surrounding the resignation, focused attention on the lack of accountability of both the FÁS board of management and the relevant ministers for Employment, Trade and Enterprise (Mary O'Rourke, Mary Harney and Mary Coughlan). Subsequent revelations about the handling of Roddy Molloy's pension deal and that of his FÁS predecessor, John Lynch, in 2000 have shed further light on corporate governance issues in state agencies. Further questions about financial mismanagement have necessitated six separate audits and a number of fraud investigations (Comptroller and Auditor General 2009). Ross (2008) colourfully described in his blog how 'a sort of symbiotic relationship ruled. FÁS delivered the loot to the area, schemes sprouted and politicians basked in reflected glory. FÁS and the politicians played ball. FÁS influenced the media with advertising and politicians with local largesse' (Ross 2008). Boyle describes how FÁS devoted great efforts 'to responding to requests from elected politicians on behalf of constituents' (Boyle 2005: 42). FÁS provided an intensive service in local constituencies and in turn FÁS achieved political protection and immunity from scrutiny. Labour Party TD Roisin Shortall suggested evidence of an institutionalised culture of 'sweetheart deals' between Fianna Fáil and people close to that party (Oakley 2009: 1). O'Halloran (2009) describes how there was gross political interference from the top to the bottom of FÁS. While this vignette is of FÁS, work by Allen (2007, 2009) and Clancy and Murphy (2006) highlight that behind the apparent disconnection between government and state agencies is a cosy consensus between key political and policy elites whereby many state agencies and bodies are politically protected. Coras Iompair Éireann and the Health Services Executive are named by Ross as also benefiting from such political protection (Walsh 2009).

All of this has an impact on bureaucratic culture. Molloy describes the failure of Irish institutions to act as an 'implementation deficit disorder', which he likens to a deeply embedded impulse established within the culture of established institutions (Molloy, in Mulholland 2010: 40). The symptoms of such disorder, like those of blame avoidance associated with significant veto points, include denial, obfuscation and failure to acknowledge reality, failure to take responsibility, and the protection of stakeholders. This culture, Molloy argues, is not restricted to the public service, but permeates social partnership and self-regulating bodies. The NESC (2006: 14) also appears to identify this culture when it laments the poor policy capacity of the Irish state and identifies four key weaknesses: lack of decision, weak execution, lack of knowledge about policy impact and implementation paralysis. Arguing that strategic decisions are often delayed or reversed, it sees policy debate as often characterised by a deliberate ambiguity and by tensions between traditional hierarchical government policy making, and implementation as a function of the bureaucracy. The dilution of the Freedom of Information Act and the erosion of transparency make it difficult to assess the quality of civil service advice and the reception by government of that advice (Zimmerman 2008). Horan (in Mulholland 2010) likewise points to the lack of transparency in the policy advice role of the civil service and to the growing problem of the politicisation of advice. This tendency is also a source of concern to the OECD (2008).

The Wright Report's (Wright 2010) examination of the Department of Finance's performance over the last decade bears out the above observations. The report, which was controversially received, found that the DOF provided the government with clear, direct and comprehensive warnings on the risks of pro-cyclical fiscal action, but that this advice was substantially ignored by political actors framing annual budgets. The report lays the blame for the fiscal policy failure on three factors: extraordinary expectations of demand for public spending, the trumping of bureaucratic advice by political and social partnership programmes, and a lack of initiative on the part of the Department of Finance to adapt or make more urgent the tone of its advice. The Nyberg Report (Nyberg 2011) subsequently reinforced this assessment, pointing to a strong culture of consensus and 'groupthink'. Both reports draw attention to serious capacity issues in the Department of Finance. While concluding that it is broadly fit for purpose, they draw attention to a lack of critical mass in technical skills, with too many generalists, insufficient engagement with the broader economic community, limited information sharing, a poorly structured senior management and poor human resource management. There is no reason to believe that other departments perform better on these criteria.

The Wright and Nyberg reports point to the need for more public sector capacity and greater parliamentary oversight to avoid the risks of pro-cyclical fiscal action. Much of the problem however lies not in skills or structures but in political culture and in an increased tendency to frame budgetary policy not in the context of economic cycles but in the context of electoral cycles. This political culture of electoral cycles emerged from the 1970s onwards, when

Fianna Fáil-led governments began to ignore the direction of Finance officials and engage in electoral spending sprees (Leahy 2009). This pattern was first associated with a new FF political elite that had lost the conservatism of the early political pioneers and was more inclined to use spending to win power in elections. Overspending associated with spending commitments in the 1977 general election led to the severe cutbacks of the 1980s. Cousins (2007: 20) argues that political budget cycles can help to explain the recent pattern of social security expenditure increases in Ireland and describes the '2002 and 2007 elections as the clearest examples of a political budget cycle which one could wish to find'. Expenditure rose significantly as the 2002 election approached but dropped immediately after. Subsequently, following poor election results for the government in the 2004 local and European Parliament elections, social security spending increased substantially again as the 2007 election approached. This pattern marks a shift in power from civil servants to the political system and makes it more likely that politicians will ignore prudent fiscal advice (Leahy 2009; Cooper 2009; D. O'Brien 2009). In Pye's words (2011:16), from the early 2000s on, 'whatever the politicians wanted the politicians got'. The shift in political culture and the pattern of pro-cyclical spending is best captured in the infamous 2002 words of then minister for finance, Charlie McCreevy: 'When I have it I spend it' (Leahy 2009). O'Brien (2009), noting the recklessness with which McCreevy used taxpayers' money for electoral purposes, states that he not only loosened the purse strings to win voters' favour, he 'upended the public purse, allowing spending to run out of control'. He also made a series of taxation decisions that benefited rich elites.

This political ideology was reinforced by the Irish Independent newspaper group arguing for 'payback time'(most notably before the 1997 general election when the group supported FF); the group's owner Tony O'Reilly had close social networks with the Fianna Fáil leadership (Cooper 2009). History shows us that pro-cyclical budgets became the norm, fuelling an already overheated economy, increasing inflation and contributing to a culture of excessive consumer spending. While the 2008 recession has brought public expenditure back firmly under the control of key civil servants in Finance and the ECB/EU and IMF, without more lasting institutional forms of specific accountability for spending decisions there is no guarantee that there will not be a reversion to electoral spending cycles.

CONCLUSION: POWER ELITES AND COSY CONSENSUS

The Wright Report (Wright 2010) controversially associated some of the fiscal latitude of the mid 2000s with the pragmatic acquiescence of social partners; but this assessment affords greater power to social partners than they may have had. Fiscal latitude owes most to the longevity in power of an increasingly laissez-faire Fianna Fáil. A near permanent Fianna Fáil government meant that many civil servants worked for almost two decades in an unbroken political regime and culture. While many of the traditional civil servants remained committed to traditional values of impartiality, there also evolved a cultural and ideological overlap between some public servants and politicians. This can be seen most in the politically protected state agencies that stood outside the traditional accountability of the mainstream civil service and that better suited a populist political machine. The apparent immunity of state agencies also impacted on their relations with civil society. The social partnership process, while described as corporatist, in practice afforded a great deal of power and initiative to key civil servants who mediated between the social partners and the appropriate political ministers. In much the same way, civil servants mediated lobbying processes and usually filtered requests from vested interest groups for ministerial meetings. As Crowley 2010 notes, many civil servants used their power to champion equality and progressive social change; other senior civil servants, however, overtly followed more conservative ideological agendas in their dealings with civil society groups and played a role in the marginalisation of dissent. This has led to a policy shift within the civil service whereby policy areas such as gender-based violence, immigration, equality and human rights have been downgraded or subjected to cutbacks. Likewise the reorganisation of local community development programmes was perceived to be overseen by civil servants with agendas consistent with, or aligned to, key political actors. The Advocacy Initiative (2010) suggests that the threat or control of the state may not be as strong as the perception of control, but that the perception is enough to induce self-censorship by wider civil society. The OECD (2008) Report on Public Sector Reform and the government's own expenditure review (McCarthy 2009) focused on reducing the number of public-sector agencies. However, even in the context of fiscal pressure, there has been relatively little reduction in the number of these agencies in recent years. One clear exception is the reform or outright abolition of national and local bodies with functional responsibility for equality, poverty, human rights and community development. An interesting development in the narrative of the recent crisis is the degree to which key features of public debate – ranging from academic grade inflation, pressures on processing passport applications, social welfare fraud and public-private sector wage comparisons – have all found their way into public debate. It seems that this role of spinning, largely the preserve of political actors, is becoming part of the culture of the civil service and quangos.

This chapter has discussed the considerable power base of the administrative elite. A traditionally fiscally and socially conservative culture of maintenance has dominated the public service alongside pockets of technocratic developmentalism that emerged in certain spaces associated with the international political economy. Much of this chapter has discussed how the Irish bureaucracy was given effective free rein by the localist and personalist political system. The political system has effectively ceded much policy formation to unaccountable bureaucratic power and self-regulating professions, and this has exposed Irish policy to the strong influence of other entrenched vested interests, such as bankers, property developers and social partners. Since the 1970s, this free rein on policy has not extended to control over electoral budget cycles, and Fianna Fáil governments in particular have engaged in electoral spending cycles that produced the fatal boom–bust cycles of Ireland's political economy.

The interactions between this relatively pragmatic and unaccountable bureaucratic system and the boom–bust cycles of the political economy are mediated by two key factors. Advice is ignored by political leaders, especially in the run-up to elections (Cooper 2009; Cousins 2007); and there is a degree of political protection of key agencies (Ross 2009). Clifford (2011) observes that crony capitalism became so much the norm that neither political parties nor other power elites even tried to conceal their interactions. Recent changes within the structure and operations of the state bureaucracy highlight the ways it has grown more fragmented, complex and multi-level. Accountability and transparency need now to be extended to state agencies, multi-level governance and relationships between formal public services and more informal governance processes.

Impartiality may have been one of the features that made the early Irish bureaucracy distinctive from state bureaucracies in other small states. However, the populist state under virtual one-party rule has, over time, merged party and national interests. Some aspects of the bureaucracy began in recent decades to suffer the familiar 'groupthink' evident in crony capitalism. There is also a weak policy capacity and lack of openness to ideational innovation and debate. These features both contributed to and have framed responses to the crisis. Bureaucratic capacity will now be further eroded through the scale of cuts in the four-year austerity plan to be implemented under IMF/ECB supervision. Public service reform is now governed under the Croke Park agreement, in which public services unions agreed to a series of reforms in return for pay freezes and job protection. A new senior public service unit will address recruitment and the deployment of senior civil servants. The 2011 Fine Gael–Labour government initiated a significant reform in splitting the Department of Finance into two departments. The minister for finance, Michael Noonan (Fine Gael), takes responsibility for budgets and taxes while a Minister for Public Expenditure and Reform, Brendan Howlin (Labour), takes control of spending and the overhaul of the public sector. The Public Service Modernisation Division of the Department of the Taoiseach will be merged with two divisions in the existing Department of Finance to form the new department. However, as Kelly observes, much of the change required in the public service is behavioural rather than structural (P. Kelly 2011). He notes the enormity of the challenge of implementing a large agenda in the context of significant public sector cuts; instead, in a time of crisis the instinct is to centralise control and to prioritise the immediate obligation to meet IMF/ECB imposed targets. In the absence of pressure from political leaders to determine change priorities, it is unlikely that public service managers will dedicate time to promoting discretionary change. Irish bureaucrats have thrived in a particularly Irish-style co-coordinative discourse dominated by closed task-focused committees. However this configuration of Irish institutions, interests and ideas has led to a narrow, problem-solving approach to policy making, at the expense of a more value-led popular discourse that might create the attitudinal change necessary to support deeper public sector reform. A case study on New Zealand public service reform in Chapter 8 affirms the importance of core public service values. A focus on communicative discourse about values and cultural change is as necessary a part of reform as new institutions and new ministers.

Part II

The Celtic Tiger Model

This part examines the nature, evolution and impact of the Celtic Tiger model of development. Chapter 4 analyses the various phases of the boom, linking these to the nature of politics during each of the phases, and highlights the vulnerabilities inherent in the political choices that were made. Chapters 5 and 6 identify who the losers and winners were from the Irish model, illustrating the fact that it failed to serve the good of Irish society in any broad way.

4
Managing the Irish Boom

As outlined briefly in Chapter 1, the beginning of Ireland's latest and most spectacular boom–bust cycle can be dated back to the incoming Fianna Fáil administration of 1987, which implemented a swingeing austerity budget immediately on taking office to bring the decade-long problem of the country's large foreign debt under control. This turned the economy around much faster than most had predicted, laying the foundations for the boom years that began in 1994 and lasted, with a brief decline in 2002, until 2007. While most accounts of the Celtic Tiger period have focused on the policies that helped bring it about (such as the success in winning high levels of foreign investment, the ways in which EU structural and cohesion funds were spent to support the boom, and the role of social partnership in engineering a consensus between employers and the trade unions), the account here places these policies in their political context, showing how the boom passed through various phases reflecting the parties that made up the governments at the time. The chapter opens by outlining these phases and identifying the contours of what came to constitute an Irish model of development at the height of the Celtic Tiger period. The following section examines in more detail how the changing political priorities of parties in power helped undermine the foundations on which the boom was initially built, focusing particularly on the role that property development began to play from the early 2000s, and how virtually the entire national banking system came to be implicated. The third section turns its attention to what was happening in Northern Ireland over this period and the possibilities opened by the peace process for building links with the economy in the Republic. The fourth examines the broad options now facing policy makers in mapping out the future direction of Ireland's economic development, including the actions taken between 2008 and 2011 to fix the banking sector and address the state's huge fiscal deficit. The final section draws conclusions about the failures of Irish politics and political institutions that this latest boom–bust cycle reveals so dramatically.

PHASES OF THE CELTIC TIGER

The advantage of breaking the period of the Irish boom into various phases is that this allows a clearer identification, not only of the more positive and successful aspects, but also of the weaknesses that eventually led to its dramatic collapse in 2008. A number of analysts have identified three phases, as outlined in Table 4.1. These can be summarised as follows:

- 1987–92: a *growth phase*, in which a right-of-centre political coalition brought the country's fiscal crisis under control and positioned the economy to benefit from wider international developments, such as the completion of the European single market and the beginnings of the US expansion of the 1990s.
- 1992–97: a *developmental phase*, in which a left-of-centre political coalition brought a focus on equality and on the development of a dynamic indigenous software sector.
- 1997–2007: a *competition phase*, in which a right-of-centre political coalition focused on reducing taxes and stimulated a property boom through state subsidies and tax breaks.

A number of aspects are worthy of note in this chronology. The first and most obvious is that politics ultimately determines the mix of policies that configure social and economic outcomes. While this may be an obvious thing to say, the link between policy orientations and the nature of the parties holding power was largely neglected in analyses of the Celtic Tiger throughout the boom years. The second is that what is happening internationally matters hugely, particularly to small countries. This provides the opportunities and constraints to which counties have to adjust if they are to succeed, but, as is evident in Table 4.1, it also provides different sets of ideas that countries can draw on to inform the policies they adopt. So, for example, in the mid 1990s the Delors EU White Paper offered a more social-democratic approach as against the more neoliberal approach of the OECD at the time, while in the early 2000s the European Union had itself adopted a more neoliberal approach in the Lisbon Strategy. Finally, a fundamental difference between policy paradigms relates to how economic and social policies are linked to one another. For example, the 1995 UN Social Summit provided ideas that influenced the Irish government's National Anti-Poverty Strategy (Ireland 1997), thereby bringing a key social objective to the heart of national policy. In the more competition-oriented policy

Table 4.1 Phases of the Celtic Tiger, 1987–2007

Year	Political Regime	International	Murphy	Breathnach (2005)	Ó Riain (2008)	Meaning of Phases
1987–92	Centre Fianna Fáil Fianna Fáil/PD	International recession Monetarism EMU	Growth Coalition	Early foundation phase	Macro economic stabilisation	• Breaking the vicious socio–economic cycle and building a shared alternative future analysis • Foreign direct investment with tax incentives • Welfare characterised by cutbacks and stabilisation
1992–97	Centre-left Fianna Fáil/Labour Fine Gael/Labour/Democratic Left	UN Summit Social Development Delors White Paper OECD Jobs Crisis	Equity coalition	Expansion phase	'Developmental network statism'	• Increased focus on social equality and sharing of benefits • Extension of the partnership model, deepening the innovation system and managing growth and inflation
1997–2007	Centre-right Fianna Fáil/Progressive Democrats	EU Lisbon Strategy Growth Competition Employment	Competition coalition	Transition phase	Growth machine	• Refocuses on economics and a process of narrowing and controlling the agenda • Lower taxes and increasing domestic consumption • Narrowing the development strategy and institutions and a reassertion of central state control

Sources: M.P. Murphy (2006); Breathnach (2005); Ó Riain (2008)

priorities of the 1997–2007 phase, social objectives tended to be made secondary to the objective of maintaining high levels of growth.

International recognition of Ireland's success in maintaining high growth rates, increasing employment and raising living standards focused attention on how these successes had been achieved, and this led to the identification of an 'Irish model'. The term 'model' relates to the discussion in Chapter 1 on different varieties of capitalism, namely the ways in which the productive economy relates to the society – in other words, the relationship of the regime of capital accumulation, whether in private or public hands, to that of distribution. Both accumulation and distribution rely centrally on the relationship of state and market and for this reason they constitute a political economy model. A stable model rests on what Rapley has called 'an implied contract that binds elites and masses in bonds of mutual obligation' (Rapley 2004: 6–7), thus recognising that all such models are underpinned by support from civil society (or, as was often the case in authoritarian states, its repression). While the different phases of the Celtic Tiger highlight the fact that the model evolved over time, the final decade saw it clearly manifesting the features that led to its dramatic collapse.

What interested policy makers and observers abroad in the Irish model – particularly in regions such as central and eastern Europe and Latin America, which had shared many of Ireland's development problems – was that it seemed to contradict key tenets of the dominant neoliberal development prescriptions actively promoted by the World Bank at the time. Viewed from a distance, they saw the Irish state as having played an active role in winning high levels of foreign investment in cutting-edge high-tech sectors, thereby upgrading the industrial and services economy and coordinating policy making between the main stakeholders through social partnership, resulting in a spectacular increase in living standards and employment. This appeared to offer a new state-led road to successful development, one able to manoeuvre deftly amid the pressures and threats of globalisation. They wanted to learn more about this seemingly successful 'Irish model', and Irish policy makers and academics were much in demand to explain what constituted it. As Casey has written:

> When Ireland was booming we had a more important voice in international fora. At meetings in the European Union whenever structural reform was being discussed, the Irish delegation would

usually be asked to explain the flexibility of our labour market or the beneficial effects of low taxation. How had we done what the rest of Europe – still in the throes of Eurosclerosis – could not do? … It was heady stuff. Instead of being ignored as we were in the 1970s and 1980s, we were now the talking point and an oracle to be consulted. (Casey 2009: 13)

Yet the model that from a distance seemed so successful turned out to be much more ambiguous on closer examination. Three main weaknesses can be identified. The first relates to the model of capital accumulation as the motor of growth, which did not come from capabilities developed within the economy, but rather was by and large an extension of the success of the US economy, since it depended on the growth and innovation generated primarily by US multinationals attracted to Ireland. As Bradley has written, Ireland inverted the normal process of development – instead of generating a wealth-building strategy for the Irish nation, the state simply adapted to the needs of the firms in the global corporate environment (Bradley 2002). The same reflexive dependence on multinationals was shown to exist in the one area of state policy that is seeking to build innovative capacity in Ireland, namely state spending on research and development (R&D). While this may have had some successes, it fails to build resilient capacity in the Irish economy and perpetuates the vulnerabilities that are partly responsible for the deep recession in which Ireland now finds itself, since its successes are largely commercialised by multinationals rather than resulting in strong indigenous companies (Kirby 2010). This, then, is the first core feature of the Irish model – its regime of capital accumulation is largely a foreign one: the capital is accumulated by foreign firms and substantial amounts of it are repatriated out of Ireland.

A second weakness of the Irish model concerns social outcomes, namely the weak links between the growth generated in the productive economy and investment in social services. While the increased living standards and improved employment opportunities generated by the Irish model improved the lives of many, less attention was focused on the increases in relative poverty and in inequality that characterised the boom years in Ireland or on the failures to invest adequately in quality social services, especially for the most marginalised. As former taoiseach the late Dr Garret FitzGerald has written:

Why is it that, with a level of income higher than that of 22 of the 27 EU states, our public services fail to look after children in need or to care for the ill and the old; fail to make any serious attempt to rehabilitate our prisoners; and fail to ensure access to clean water – not to speak of failing to provide efficient competitive public transport, just to mention a few of our more obvious public service deficiencies? After all, over the past half century our political leaders were remarkably successful in securing much faster economic growth than anywhere else in Europe, moving Ireland from the poorest of the dozen countries in the northern part of Western Europe to becoming one of the richest. Given this success, why have our governments failed so miserably to deploy the vast resources thus created in such a way as to give us the kind of public services we can clearly afford and desperately need? (FitzGerald 2008: 14)

As Chapters 5 and 6 reveal, Ireland's economic boom dispro-portionately benefited new groups of technical professionals and self-employed small business entrepreneurs, while 'the bulk of Irish society has … acquiesced to the increasing gap between themselves and the rising professional and business classes' (Ó Riain and O'Connell 2000: 339). The Ireland of the Celtic Tiger has also been shown to have 'diverged from the European pattern of welfare effort', as the ratio of social security spending to GDP fell markedly in Ireland, while it was maintained or increased in most European countries (Ó Riain and O'Connell 2000: 331; Kirby 2008: 28). This raises critical issues about the weak regime of distribution that characterised the Irish model; two interlinked features need to be emphasised. Firstly, as was proudly proclaimed again and again by government ministers during the boom, this was a low-tax model, and all the main parties came to compete with one another as to which could cut taxes the most. Following the collapse, this feature became the subject of attention by EU leaders, who emphasised that Ireland had to return to normal European levels of taxation. Ireland's low tax of 12.5 per cent on corporations was a particular object of EU annoyance, as it was widely seen as undermining the efforts of other member states to attract foreign investment. Secondly, the consequence of being a low-tax model was the low level of investment in social services and infrastructure, something constantly complained of by Irish citizens, most of whom never seemed to make the connection that this was the inevitable result of the low-tax route to development.

A third weakness of the Irish model concerns the role of the state. Examining the capability and effectiveness of the Irish state in the sphere of welfare and of regulation, it can be concluded that it tended to seek low-cost solutions that weakened its effectiveness to achieve the goals it set itself (Boyle 2005). These features of the Irish state have been actively debated between proponents of Ireland as a developmental state (Ó Riain 2004) or as a competition state (Kirby 2009). From this debate, it has been concluded that while pockets of developmentalism have been evident in the Irish state, the overriding logic that can be identified in the uneven nature of its actions is one that gives priority to the maximisation of competitiveness and profitability over investment in the welfare of society (Kirby and Murphy 2008a). While the state has remained a central actor in Ireland's development, what it has shaped is a deeply dualistic economy and a weak welfare state. Therefore the state has configured both the regime of capital accumulation and the regime of distribution in such ways that they respond much more to the needs of corporate capital than to those of its own citizens. That said, as Chapters 2, 3 and 6 all show, both developmental and competition logics were sometimes subservient to the political logic of clientelism and cycles of state spending motivated by electoral considerations.

IDEOLOGY UNDERMINES THE BOOM

The danger in outlining the contours of the Irish model, as has just been done, is that this may distract attention from identifying those who made it so. Thus, too much of a focus on the state neglects the fact that the nature of the state and how it operates is caused by many factors – key among them are the political parties who control the state, the civil servants who run it, and the organised lobby groups and movements of civil society who press their demands on it. Chapter 2 has analysed the political parties who run the Irish state, particularly Fianna Fáil, which has dominated Irish politics since 1932; it is not an exaggeration to describe the Irish state today as a 'Fianna Fáil state', since it has come to take on many of the features of that party. Chapter 2 has also discussed the role of civil society during the boom years. Chapter 3 has examined the Irish bureaucracy and its role in making the state what it is. In this section, the collapse of the Celtic Tiger is linked to the ideology and policy priorities of the two parties that ran the Irish state between

1997 and 2007, Fianna Fáil and the small but highly influential Progressive Democrats.

While international factors acted to trigger the Irish collapse by shutting off liquidity to the Irish banks, the causes were very much local. As described by two international financial experts, Klaus Regling and Max Watson, in a report commissioned by the Irish minister for finance: 'Ireland's banking crisis bears the clear imprint of global influences, yet it was in crucial ways "home-made".' They uncover in forensic fashion the multiple governance and policy failures that led to the crisis, and summarise them under three headings: 'Fiscal policy, bank governance and financial supervision left the economy vulnerable to a deep crisis, with costly and extended social fallout' (Regling and Watson 2010: 5). Each of these reflects the ideology and character of the two parties in government at the time. On fiscal policy, Regling and Watson examine both the expenditure and revenue sides. On expenditure they find that current expenditure grew faster than nominal GDP in each year from 2001 to the onset of the crisis (though, as Whelan points out, the share of public spending in GDP was by 2000 well below the European average) (Whelan 2010: 246). On revenue, they chart the ways that the composition of tax revenue had shifted gradually from stable sources of taxation, like personal income tax and VAT/ excise taxes, to cyclical taxes, such as corporation tax, stamp duty and capital gains tax. The share of these cyclical taxes reached 30 per cent of tax revenue in 2006; in the late 1980s it had amounted to only 8 per cent. This created two problems: it made it difficult to assess the underlying structural situation of the budget, and it made the budget more vulnerable to a recession. When recession did hit in late 2008 the state's revenue stream collapsed, with tax receipts of €33 billion in 2009 falling from €40.7 billion the previous year and being equivalent to the receipts for 2003, and the exchequer deficit growing from €12.7 billion in 2008 to €24.6 billion at the end of 2009 (Slattery 2010a). As FitzGerald, has written: 'The idea that when the boom ended our public and social services could be maintained with such a minuscule level of income tax payments was patently absurd, although clearly many people fell for it – including our economically unsophisticated business community' (FitzGerald 2008: 14). What Regling and Watson could not state, of course, is that this shift also reflected the ideology of the parties running the state. They were explicitly committed to a regime of low taxes but, as is clear from the shift in the origins of tax revenue, what they most believed in was a regime of low taxes for the wealthy, since the most significant reductions came in taxes on capital gains and on high incomes, while value added tax on all goods and services at 21 per cent remained high by EU standards and tended to have a disproportionate impact on those on low incomes.

On state regulation of the banks, Regling and Watson found multiple failures. They write that the response of government supervisors 'was not hands-on or pre-emptive', in contrast with the experience in some countries where supervisors 'acted to stem the tide' when faced with evident risks (ibid.: 6). They identify four key problems with government supervision:

(1) supervisory culture was insufficiently intrusive, and staff resources were seriously inadequate for the hands-on approach that was needed;
(2) governance failures were not addressed sufficiently toughly;
(3) macro-financial vulnerabilities were underestimated;
(4) key facts that should have been of central interest to supervisors were not available to policy makers in a timely manner at the point at which the crisis began to unroll (ibid.: 36–42).

The report notes the absence of forceful warnings from the Central Bank of Ireland on macro-financial risks 'in which financial stability analysis should have sounded the alarm bells loudly'. With reference to IMF, OECD and ECB reports on the Irish banking sector, they add that 'in fairness external surveillance sources fared little better'. Overall, they point to the fact that, unlike in other countries, bank regulators were not being asked to deal with technically complex problems. 'Ireland's banking exuberance indulged in few of the exotic constructs that caused problems elsewhere. This was a plain vanilla property bubble, compounded by exceptional concentrations of lending for purposes related to property' (ibid.: 6). Again, the nature of regulation was directly caused by the FF–PD coalition, which reformed the financial regulatory system, putting in place a principles-based regulatory system under which banks and financial firms would abide by agreed codes of behaviour rather than having these imposed on them and supervised by regulatory authorities. However, as Carswell has written, 'the emphasis of the regulator's focus was primarily on issues affecting consumers rather than on prudential matters such as liquidity and funding affecting the banks and their lending practices' (Carswell 2009: 5). For McManus, the problem lies in the suitability of a principles-based regulatory system for the Irish banks. Reflecting the nature of the low-tax development model, McManus writes: 'Light-touch regulation is low cost, because the regulator is lean and, ideally, nimble. It is also responsive to industry needs.' He adds that this form of regulation is 'unfortunately completely unsuited to the culture of Irish banking', as some banks were willing to circumvent the agreed rules (McManus 2009: 18). The Wright Report on the performance of the Department of Finance (2011) over the previous decade also concludes that the department should have intensified the tone of its warnings to government about the danger of its pro-cyclical budgetary policy.

The failings of internal bank governance, as identified by Regling and Watson, point up the triggers of the Irish collapse. They write:

> Errors of judgement in bank management and governance contributed centrally to Ireland's financial crisis. It seems that there were key weaknesses in some banks' internal risk management in areas such as stress-testing; the assessment of credit risks; and in some cases major lapses in the documentation of loans – and that these were factors that allowed vulnerabilities to develop. (Regling and Watson 2010: 29)

The authors identify four indicators of exceptional financial exuberance: a growth in credit whose rate of expansion and rise in asset and funding risks 'should have rung alarm bells' (ibid.); the concentration of lending on assets in property, particularly commercial property, and on a limited number of key developers; high loan-to-value ratios; and a high exposure to funding risks, which was system-wide. They speak of 'a collective governance failure', which in part 'reflected an uncritical enthusiasm for property acquisition that became something of a national blind-spot' (ibid.: 33–4). The role that property development took on as the engine of growth in the Irish economy in the 2000s reflects both the priorities of government policy (subsidies and tax breaks, as well as Fianna Fáil's traditional close links with property developers dating back to the 1960s), and also the lack of substantial alternative investment opportunities in indigenous industry and services, reflecting the extreme dependence of the Irish economy on multinationals. By 2006–07, at the peak of the bubble in house prices, construction accounted for 23 per cent of Irish GDP and Ireland was building 21 housing units per 1,000 population, four-and-a-half times as much as in Britain; one employee in eight in the Irish economy was directly employed in construction (A. Sweeney 2009: 23, 24). As Adshead and Robinson have argued, government policies that helped fuel the housing boom actively diverted economic resources from more productive investment, especially in small and medium-sized enterprises (SMEs) (Adshead and Robinson 2009: 14).

If Ireland's model of development created vulnerabilities to which it eventually succumbed, among these was a greater environmental vulnerability as state policy paid little more than lip-service to curbing carbon emissions. During the boom, the state's Environmental Protection Agency (EPA) warned that economic growth was putting added pressures on the environment and that Ireland's record in achieving emissions reductions was 'not good compared with most European countries' (Stapleton, Lehane and Toner. 2000: 39). By 2008, the EPA was reporting that Ireland's greenhouse gas emissions had increased steadily from 55.5 million tonnes to 70.7 million between 1990 and 2001, though they had then decreased slightly to 69.8 million in 2006, representing just under 17 tonnes per capita, 'the second highest in the EU' (EPA 2008: 30). The agriculture (27.7 per cent), energy (22.3 per cent) and transport (19.7 per cent) sectors of the economy were the major sources of emissions, with the industrial and commercial sector accounting for 17.2 per cent and the residential sector 10.4 per cent. The increase in car traffic alone between 1990 and 2006 accounted for a 170 per cent increase in carbon dioxide emissions. The country's climate had warmed by 0.42 degrees Celsius per decade since 1980, a rate about twice as fast as the rest of the world, and the EPA stated that Ireland 'will continue to warm with possible increases of 3 to 4 degrees Celsius towards the end of the century'. While the economic collapse helped avoid this catastrophic outcome, these data indicate the carbon intensity of the Irish growth model, a further indication of just how unsustainable it was.

In essence, therefore, the speed and depth of the Irish collapse reflected vulnerabilities inherent in the Irish model of development, a model honed by the ideological priorities of the two parties that ran the state at the height of the boom, Fianna Fáil and the Progressive Democrats. As Justin O'Brien, a professor of corporate governance in Canberra, has written:

> The rash of banking failures reflects the deleterious combination of boardroom hubris, defective operational risk management systems and uninformed regulatory confidence. It could not have happened but for the inculcation of an ideological worldview that privileged innovation over security ... While this model was most

extreme in the US, its rationale was inculcated across the globe, particularly in Ireland … While it may be inopportune to engage in structural reform in the midst of a crisis, the advantages of ceding control to a self-serving, self-policing marketplace model have been falsified. Ireland has gone from poster child of globalisation to the symbol of corporate, regulatory and political failure. It is a fitting epitaph for the Celtic Tiger. (J. O'Brien 2009: 11)

It is almost certain that, had the parties that made up the left-of-centre coalition from 1994 to 1997 been re-elected in the general election of 1997, very different policy priorities would have shaped the Irish model, with greater emphasis not just on market regulation, but also on social investment, with the goal of greater social equity. Not only would this have helped avoid the collapse of 2007, but it would have created a very different Irish society, one less obsessed by growth for its own sake and more attentive to the need to manage growth carefully. The choice made by the electorate in 1997, confirmed in 2002 with the re-election of the FF–PD coalition and partly confirmed in 2007 with the re-election of FF as the largest party but the rejection of the PDs, places the focus on the third dimension of any political economy model, the role of civil society, which was discussed in Chapter 2 and is further discussed in Chapter 10.

DEVELOPMENTS IN NORTHERN IRELAND: TOWARDS AN 'ALL-ISLAND' ECONOMY?

Expectations that the signing of the Good Friday Agreement (GFA) in 1998 would lead to a period of economic revival for Northern Ireland have only been partially realised. While the region did not experience the boom of the Celtic Tiger, its growth rate in the mid 2000s was higher than in the rest of the United Kingdom, and unemployment decreased substantially over that period. As elsewhere, the North's economy suffered from the recession of 2008, shrinking by about 4.5 per cent in 2009 and with unemployment reaching almost 8 per cent by late 2010. However, much of the growth of the 2000s was due to major urban regeneration projects in the greater Belfast region rather than to any transformation of its productive economy, and the region remained heavily dependent on the British exchequer subsidy. Policy was oriented towards winning foreign investment, but the region's ability to compete was hampered by the fact that the Republic's corporation tax at 12.5 per cent was about half that of the British rate of between 21 per cent and 28 per cent, a rate which applies in Northern Ireland. Results were at best modest, with some growth in chemicals and engineering; but this hid an economy that has continuing 'difficulties in modernizing its manufacturing base away from its traditional specialities, such as textiles and clothing, towards higher value-added products' (Bradley 2006: 16). By the late 2000s, the public sector still accounted for over 30 per cent of the labour force, compared to a figure of just under 20 per cent for the United Kingdom as a whole.

Economists point to two major difficulties facing Northern Ireland. The first is the level of dependence on Britain, not only on the annual subsidy from the exchequer, but on the fact that it remains tied to the British economy as Britain remains the main destination for its exports. The second is the narrow range of policy instruments available to policy makers in the North, as they have to operate within a policy environment set in London. Bradley identifies a dynamic whereby the North attracts low-profit labour-intensive manufacturing and services from Britain; but he sees this as a sign that the North is a peripheral region within the British economy, which will eventually shed these to low-cost regions in eastern Europe and Asia, and not as a sign of a sustainable developmental dynamic (Bradley 2006: 12). Improved north–south links following the GFA opened new possibilities of addressing these weaknesses. Cross-border trade improved dramatically, rising from 7 per cent of the North's manufacturing exports in the early 1990s to nearly a quarter by the late 2000s (Adshead and Tonge 2009: 191). More importantly, the agreement established a North–South Ministerial Council with six cross-border implementation bodies with executive powers covering food safety, inland waterways, trade and business development, language, aquaculture and marine issues, and special EU programmes. Cooperation in agriculture, education, environment, transport, health and tourism was also agreed. While this institutionalises meetings between Ministers from north and south and therefore helps to break down traditional hostilities, it has not led to any major moves towards an all-island economy, as had been hoped for by some of its architects.

Paradoxically, the economic downturn of the late 2000s may give added impetus to moving towards a more integrated economy. Severe cuts in the British budget in 2010 have forced the North's executive to agree to spending cuts of £4 billion for the period 2011–15, including a reduction of up to 40 per cent in the capital budget that may lead to the abandonment or postponement of some capital projects, and a pay freeze for thousands of civil servants. It is interesting that these cutbacks have again renewed discussion in the North of reducing the region's corporation tax to the level in the Republic; this had been refused by the Labour government under Gordon Brown, but the new prime minister, David Cameron, re-opened the question after he took power in May 2010. While there remains a great deal of opposition to this, particularly among unionists, it does focus attention on the need for the North to expand the range of policy tools available to it if it is to lay the foundations for more sustainable long-term economic development. Furthermore, the much more severe recession and banking crisis in the Republic has led to a new openness to examine every opportunity for economic regeneration, among which, of course, could be closer ties with the North.

OPTIONS FOR THE IRISH MODEL

This chapter has mapped out in some detail the specific sets of relationships between state, market and society that helped constitute what came to be known as an 'Irish model', namely an Irish variety of capitalism. While this model has entered into deep crisis since 2008, this by no means guarantees the emergence of a new model. The dominance of transnational economic and financial elites over domestic policy may paradoxically be reinforced by this crisis, which has seen the EU, the ECB and the IMF take unprecedented roles in Irish policymaking. The role of the EU will be considered in Chapter 7, which examines the options for the Union to play a more progressive role in contributing to the emergence of a new and more sustainable model for Ireland. However, what is crucial in the emergence of such a model is domestic politics; the focus on a second republic around which this book is organised is designed to counteract the narrow focus on economic policy (particularly budgetary and banking policies) that characterises much of the public debate in Ireland. Chapters 9 and 10 examine in greater detail the range of political reforms that are required to help establish that second republic. However, the analysis of the Irish growth model in this chapter would be incomplete if it did not identify the options now facing Irish society as to what political economy model can best deliver a better social future for the country. The role of political actors and institutions in delivering these options will then form part of the discussion in the book's final two chapters.

The trajectory of the crisis from 2008 up to the general election of early 2011 was dominated by attempts to find a way out of the banking crisis and put in place a strategy to deal with the fiscal crisis. Each is dealt with in turn here. Firstly, the Fianna Fáil–Green coalition government took an approach to the banking crisis that served to deepen rather than resolve it. It began with a blanket guarantee of the whole banking system, including international bondholders, announced early in the morning of 30 September 2008 by the government, which feared a run on the banks once markets opened that day. Covering customer deposits and banks' own borrowings to a total of €440 billion and called the cheapest banking bailout in history by the then minister for finance, the late Brian Lenihan, it effectively handed Irish taxpayers the bill for the reckless practices of the Irish banking sector during the economic boom, a bill that grew exponentially over the 30 subsequent months. Five different attempts were made to estimate the final bill for bailing out the Irish banks, which grew from €5.5 billion in December 2008, to €11 billion in February–March 2009, to €35 billion in March 2010, and €46 billion in September 2010. Meanwhile, in April 2009, the state established the National Asset Management Agency to manage the sector's non-performing loans. Altogether it expected to buy €73 billion worth of non-performing loans from the five banking institutions and for these to pay around half the original value of the debts. However, instead of helping resolve the crisis, NAMA's decisions were seen by some to be making matters worse, as they further undermined the solvency of the banks; the Fine Gael–Labour coalition decided there would be no more transfers of property to the agency.

The slow and painful revelation of the depth of the crisis progressively eroded the state's credibility and creditworthiness among international investors and eventually set alarm bells ringing in Brussels, which forced Ireland at the end of November 2010 to accept what was widely seen as a humiliating bailout package from the EU, the ECB and the IMF (see Chapter 7). Meanwhile, with the Irish banks haemorrhaging deposits, the state was forced progressively to nationalise the whole banking sector, which had come to rely on ECB support of some €140 billion to keep it afloat. One of the early acts of the Fine Gael–Labour coalition was to announce the results of new and extremely onerous stress tests of the Irish banks at the end of March 2011; this increased the final bill for fixing the banks to €70 billion, but it was widely welcomed as at last coming up with a figure that had credibility among international bankers and investors. Along with the stress test results, the new government also announced a decisive restructuring of the whole banking sector, based on two 'pillar banks', Bank of Ireland and AIB Bank, merged with a smaller building society, the EBS. The closure of the two banks that had most recklessly lent to property developers, Anglo Irish Bank and Irish Nationwide Building Society, had previously been announced.

The strategy for dealing with the fiscal and wider economic crisis was defined by two different options. The first may be called the mainstream option – that put forward by the then governing Fianna Fáil party, by the largest opposition party Fine Gael, by employers' and business organisations, and by most economists and commentators. This was the dominant and strongest option. However, from the beginning of the crisis a second alternative option began to be outlined, particularly by the Irish Congress of Trade Unions, by the Labour party, by civil society organisations such as the think tank TASC, and by some academics and commentators. Beyond that, parties such as Sinn Féin and the Socialist party voiced a more radical critique; but it is not possible to identify in this critique a distinct third option in the form of an alternative set of proposals for a different political economy model, as distinct from a different strategy for dealing with the banking and fiscal crisis. This section therefore briefly maps out the two options that framed debate and then outlines some key principles that will be required if the Irish political economy model is to deliver more equitable social outcomes and is to be more sustainable.

The principal issue that divides the mainstream from the alternative option relates to the issue of austerity versus stimulus. The dominant view is that severe cuts in public spending and increases in taxation will not just restore the state finances to some kind of sustainable footing, but will also restore export competitiveness and so contribute to a return to economic growth – though proponents of this view differ on when this might happen. By the end of 2009 the budget deficit had widened to 14.6 per cent of GDP, but various measures to cut spending (including two cuts in the income of public servants) and some modest tax increases had reduced it to 11.9 per cent by late 2010; however, once the full cost of supporting the banks is factored in, the deficit rose to 32 per cent of GDP in 2010, widely regarded as the highest ever recorded in a developed country in peacetime. The Irish government sought to avoid having the costs of the banking crisis included in the budget deficit, but this was refused by the European Union. Meanwhile, the economy entered into a severe contraction, with GDP declining by 3.5 per cent in 2008, a further 7.6 per cent in 2009, and 1 per cent in 2010; GNP, regarded as a more accurate measure of Irish growth since it excludes the profits of multinational companies taken out of the economy, contracted by 3.5 per cent in 2008, a further 10.7 per cent in 2009 and 2.1 per cent in 2010. As international markets increasingly lost confidence in Ireland's ability to meet its huge debts, the government announced a four-year strategy to detail how it planned to return the budget deficit to 3 per cent of GDP by 2014, as demanded by the EU Commission. The austerity plan, entitled the National Recovery Plan 2011–2014, announced in late November 2010 details cuts in public spending totalling €10 billion and tax rises of €5 billion. Cuts are spread widely and include reducing the number of public servants by 25,000 from the current level of 307,000, cutting the pay of new entrants to the public service by 10 per cent, cutting public service pensions by up to 12 per cent, and cutting spending on health, education and social welfare. One controversial proposal was to cut the minimum wage by €1 an hour. On the tax side, most of the proposals hit low and average-income earners rather than high-income earners, as the central measure was a reduction in the income levels at which people begin to pay tax, from €18,300 to €15,300 by the end of the plan. Value Added Tax (VAT) is to rise from 21 per cent to 23 per cent in the final two years of the plan, a measure that will also hit lower-income households disproportionately.

In contrast to this austerity, the alternative view argues strongly for the need for a stimulus package, to limit job losses and to encourage investment in small and medium-sized domestic enterprises, so as to boost production and stimulate spending in the economy. According to this view, austerity deepens the crisis and heightens the possibility of prolonging it. Closely linked to the question of austerity versus stimulus is the question of cuts versus tax increases. Those espousing the dominant view place the burden of the adjustment on cutting public spending and are prone to maintain as far as possible the commitment to a low-tax economy, while the alternative option sees much more room for increasing taxes, particularly on those who are most well-off in Irish society, as well on Irish tax exiles. Indeed, in the dominant view the need for state reform is effectively equated with cutbacks, so that Fianna Fáil and the main opposition party Fine Gael vied with one another as to the extent to which the public service should be cut back. This, then, marks a third point of fundamental difference – those adhering to the dominant view see economic recovery as coming from the private sector and have little positive to say about the role to be played by the public sector; according to the alternative view the public sector has a vital role to play through, for example, re-skilling workers, intervening in key sectors of the economy to stimulate development (the telecoms sectors is mentioned) and developing greater capacity to manage expenditure. A fourth difference relates to how to restructure the banking sector. From the beginning, the Labour Party was a lone voice among political parties in the Dáil in opposing the government's plans to establish the National Asset Management Agency (NAMA); it advocated a much more hands-on approach by the state through nationalisation to restructure the banking sector. A final and major difference between the two approaches relates to the need for social investment – both the Labour Party and ICTU emphasise the need for using stimulus spending or resources generated by a National Recovery Bond to invest in education, infrastructure and better public services. Overall, the alternative approach sees the need for a much more radical break with the past. Sweeney, ICTU's economic adviser, has written that 'the solution must go far deeper than simply addressing the public finances … We require a fundamental realignment of our economy and society' (P. Sweeney 2009: 15), while Labour has called for an end to 'crony capitalism' and a new code of practice for corporate governance. However, there are some points of agreement between the two approaches. There is wide agreement on the need for property and carbon taxes and on the importance of investment in green activities, though the Fianna Fáil party has proved very reluctant to introduce a property tax.

Broadly speaking, therefore, the mainstream view espouses a continuation of the Irish model of a low-tax economy, highly dependent on multinational investment (and with a vigorous defence of Ireland's low rate of corporation tax) though with some more robust regulation of the financial sector than in the past. However, the model remains highly reliant on the state playing a role subservient to the private sector. The emerging alternative ascribes a much more directive role to the state, recognises the need to develop a more broadly based taxation system that taxes wealth and higher incomes adequately and that can fund high quality and universal public services. It shows more commitment towards supporting small and medium-sized enterprises to develop greater capacity, so that reliance on multinational investment is lessened – though the actual policies to achieve such an aim are not well developed yet.

One way to assess the adequacy of these alternative political economy models is to test them against a set of robust principles. Since the analysis here is guided by a commitment to principles of equality and sustainability, it is essential that the priority given to economic growth in the dominant Irish model be balanced against wider social and ecological principles. Indeed, the increasingly urgent demands of environmental sustainability (particularly the need to reduce greenhouse gas emissions by up to 80 per cent over the coming decades) and the imminence of peak oil raise serious questions about the possibility of continuing to base development on economic growth. In this context, a commitment to sustainability requires that we base development on a model that recognises the impossibility of indefinite growth in a world of ecological limitations. In other words, we begin to plan for social development in a steady-state economy. Jackson has gone some way towards identifying some of the basic principles that this will require (Jackson 2009b). Firstly, it means establishing what such ecological limits are, through mechanisms such as resource and emission caps and reduction targets. These are already beginning to be put in place at an international and a national level. One example was the Climate Change Bill drawn up by the Fianna Fáil–Green Party coalition, but which was never enacted due to that government's collapse in January 2011. This stipulated cuts of 40 per cent in Ireland's greenhouse gas emissions by 2030 and cuts of 80 per cent by 2050 (over 1990 levels). Jackson recommends an ecological tax reform to help achieve this – shifting the burden of taxation from economic goods (for example, taxes on incomes) to environmental bads (for example, taxes on carbon). The second basic principle requires fixing the economic model, as 'an economy predicated on the perpetual expansion of debt-driven materialistic consumption is unsustainable ecologically, problematic socially and unstable economically' (ibid.: 175–6). Jackson recommends the elaboration of a new kind of economics that factors in strict emission and resource-use limits and reframes preconceptions about labour and capital productivities; he also recommends investing in such things as retrofitting buildings, renewable energy technologies, public transport networks, public spaces and ecosystem maintenance and protection. The third principle is that of changing the social logic from one that locks people into materialistic consumerism to one that provides opportunities for sustainable and fulfilling lives through, for example, more flexible working time, tackling systemic inequality so that all can benefit equally, strengthening social capital, dismantling the culture of consumerism, and developing new measures of progress based on capabilities and flourishing rather than on growth in national income (ibid.: 171–85).

Though neither of the two options currently being proposed for Ireland's development comes near to espousing all these principles, and while the dominant model had come to adopt some 'green' principles (such as a carbon tax) under the pressure of the Green Party's participation in government, it is the alternative model that offers far greater prospect of taking these principles seriously and moving towards their realisation. This is because of its commitment to a robust state to direct the market, its understanding of the need to balance economic development with social development, and its commitment to far greater equity than was achieved by the mainstream model. However, to move towards a model of 'prosperity without growth' will prove very challenging.

The Programme for Government of the Fine Gael–Labour coalition that took power in March 2011 cannot be clearly located within either of the alternatives outlined above.

Prominent is a commitment to stimulating the economy, with the promise of a jobs fund within its first 100 days in office, to include 15,000 places in training, work experience or education, additional resources for a national housing retrofitting plan, and the acceleration of capital works, including schools and secondary roads (on gaining office this commitment was quickly downgraded to a revenue-neutral 'jobs initiative'). Broadly, however, the programme accepts the main features of the austerity package for 2011–12 already implemented by the previous government. On the role of the state, it includes key state-led features, such as a strategic investment bank and other new developmental state agencies, particularly in bio-energy; other proposals entail extensive reliance on the private sector, particularly in areas such as upgrading to a new-generation telecoms network, developing Ireland as a 'digital island', with particular emphasis on cloud computing, agri-food, home and renewal energy programmes and financial services (Department of the Taoiseach 2011). Some of this has promise, and it remains to be seen to what extent it lays the foundations for a new model of productive economy to emerge. However, it is still clearly within an economic growth paradigm and is disappointing in the lack of attention it devotes to the twin challenges of peak oil and reducing greenhouse gas emissions.

However, the Programme for Government is dwarfed by the banking and fiscal crisis. The first Stability Programme Update under the new government (published on Friday 29 April 2011) was a sobering assessment of the scale of the challenge and the limited room for manoeuvre for the new government. The forecasts, broadly in line with EU and IMF 2011 forecasts, saw the anticipated growth rate for 2011 revised from 1.8 per cent of GDP to 0.8 of GDP. Public debt is expected to peak at 118 per cent of GDP in 2013 (it was previously expected to peak at 103 per cent). There was a growing acceptance of the reality of a recovery that did not create many jobs, what is known as a 'jobless recovery', with the export sector as the only source of growth and a loss of 30,000 jobs in 2011 and 15 per cent unemployment; this is expected to drop to 10 per cent by 2015 with the creation of 100,000 new jobs between 2012 and 2015. The scale of the crisis is such that M. Kelly (2011:13) argues that Irish insolvency is now only a matter of arithmetic. He expects government debt to exceed €190 billion by 2014, with a further €45 billion being spent on NAMA and €35 billion on bank recapitalisation. Kelly controversially argues that net national debt is likely to be in the range of €220 to €250 billion; the latter figure would amount to €120,000 per worker and over 160 per cent of GDP, well over the 100 per cent GDP benchmark at which default is highly likely.

As discussed in Chapter 2, the 'Irish model', as it came to be known internationally during the Celtic Tiger boom, liked to present itself as a form of negotiated governance using corporatist type mechanisms (labelled 'social partnership') to achieve a broad consensus among the social partners (which included a range of domestic NGOs) on the central tenets of economic and social policy. This was seen as the key to the successful policies that drove the boom (Kirby 2010). It is paradoxical, however, that when the banking sector and the economy collapsed, so too did social partnership, as both the government and employers' groups effectively deserted it. Instead of being seen as a key element of success, a narrative of social partnership evolved according to which it came instead to be seen as part of the cosy consensus that had failed to identify and address the weak regulation of the banking sector and the many subsidies and tax breaks that were fuelling the property bubble. However, this does not necessitate fundamental changes in the Irish model, which still rests on three features: extensive reliance on foreign direct investment as the motor of growth in the Irish economy; commitment to low taxes (particularly a low level of corporation tax) as an incentive to attracting multinational companies; and the maintenance of a remarkably market-friendly competitive state. Reforms currently proposed will not necessarily change these essential features of the Irish model; but the third feature of the Irish model looks most likely to see more significant changes, with the promise of a more capable and efficient political system and the introduction of a more intrusive and better resourced regulatory system, at least for the banking sector. However, while such reforms might provide the state with greater capacity and effectiveness, how it uses these will be crucial to the future of the Irish model. Again the evidence strongly points to the fact that what will emerge will be a more capably managed version of the low-tax Irish model, heavily dependent on capturing and maintaining in Ireland at any cost some of the world's leading multinationals in the ICT, pharmaceutical, medical devices and financial services sectors. For, while the collapse has bankrupted some leading construction entrepreneurs and generated public outrage at the extravagantly paid senior staff of Irish banks, fundamentally, as this chapter and Chapter 6 show, the Irish economic elite has been little damaged and in fact is growing wealthier. Furthermore, despite gains by the left in the 2011 election, it is difficult to argue that there has been a fundamental change in Irish political elites. Fine Gael replaced Fianna Fáil as Ireland's largest party; but not only is it a right-of-centre party, it has also traditionally represented the professional and commercial elites of Irish society. It looks as if the Irish model may well survive the crisis.

CONCLUSION: MISMANAGING IRELAND'S BOOM

This chapter has identified the links between the weaknesses of Ireland's development model and the ideology of its ruling parties at the height of the boom. Chapter 2 showed how social partnership co-opted those sectors of Irish civil society (the community sector and the trade unions) most likely to highlight the failings of the dominant model, resulting in a narrow consensus that failed to notice the looming vulnerabilities. This shows that behind the collapse of the banking sector and the economy lies a deeper problem, namely the political parties and their political ideology that have dominated the Irish state. In outlining the main differences between the two options being developed to deal with the crisis, it was shown that the dominant one remains wedded to the low-tax model, even if it will seek to regulate it more effectively. Yet, in outlining the challenges now posed by greenhouse gas emissions and peak oil, it has also been shown that what is needed for sustainable and equitable development is a capable state able to shape the economy in a way that weans it off a fixation with growth (and being seduced by finance and consumption) and places the emphasis on distribution and on satisfying basic needs. Not only will this require a very new model of development, but it will require a new politics, putting behind us the Fianna Fáil state, which grew so dependent on property developers and on global corporations, and developing a new second republic with a new political culture and values, a renewed political system and institutions capable of the challenges ahead.

5
The Losers

This chapter analyses the distributional outcomes of the Irish boom from the perspective of the real losers in the Irish political economy. It examines the debates and the evidence about what has been happening to poverty and inequality over the course of the boom and looks at the impact of inequality on the living conditions of Irish people. It analyses how tax, welfare and other distributional policies have not only failed to tackle the embedded structural inequality (a long-standing feature of Irish society), but have also caused new forms of income inequality, deepening the divide between those in work and those without, and impacting harshly on migrants, women and people with disabilities. In particular, it highlights the intersection of inequalities, whereby many people experience multiple forms of deprivation and discrimination and so are particularly vulnerable to disadvantage.

The chapter begins by placing Irish poverty and inequality in an international context and highlights the fact that, regardless of which measurement is used, Ireland ranks consistently among the worst in the European Union for both poverty and inequality. Contesting the view of the Economic and Social Research Institute that the boom years represented the 'best of times' for Irish society, the second section reviews past trends to show that poverty and inequality have been consistent features of Ireland before, during and after the Celtic Tiger period and that social mobility remains low and is marked by educational inequality. The chapter then moves on to identify the various groups whose life chances either worsened or did not improve. The third section examines low-paid workers, people who are unemployed, women and lone parents, children, migrants and recent emigrants, and groups of vulnerable people whose needs were never adequately addressed by state policy, those with disabilities and the Traveller community. Given the place housing played in the building and bursting of the Celtic Tiger bubble, the fourth section pays special attention to housing losers: those in 'ghost estates', in mortgage debt and negative equity, and also those on social housing lists and the homeless. The fifth section draws attention to those living in disadvantaged rural or urban communities, drawing particular attention to the spatial distribution of poverty and inequality in Ireland, highlighting how education, housing tenure, gender and other forms of discrimination mediate Irish life chances and social mobility, and determine which are the most vulnerable groups in Irish society. The final section concludes this mapping of the contemporary Irish class structure

IRELAND IN INTERNATIONAL COMPARISON

Comparing Ireland's income distribution with EU and OECD countries shows Ireland to be an outlier in its level of poverty and inequality. Comparing it to 30 countries and using data from around 2000, Smeeding and Nolan write that 'Ireland is indeed an outlier among rich nations. Only the United States, Russia, and Mexico have higher levels of inequality ... Among the richest OECD nations Ireland has the second highest level of inequality' (Smeeding and Nolan 2004: 9). Fahey (2010) uses 2005 OECD data to compare Irish welfare effort with that of other countries and explain why Ireland ranks so badly on international poverty and inequality indicators. The story is simple in some respects. As GNP rose during the period of the Celtic Tiger, welfare effort declined as a percentage of GNP. This lack of welfare effort is reflected in Ireland's place in international league tables, as shown in Table 5.1: using 2008 Survey of Income and Living Conditions data, no matter which measurement of poverty is used, Ireland lies in the worst third of the EU 27 for its performance in tackling poverty and for income inequality.

The Bertelsmann Foundation (2011) found that Ireland had one of the worst levels of social justice of all OECD member states, ranking it 27th out of 31 countries, ahead of just Chile, Mexico, Greece and Turkey. The study defines social justice as a measure of a citizen's participation in society. The indicators rank the measures the state employs to actively include as many citizens as possible. To this end, they use 18 quantitative and qualitative indicators to measure five categories: poverty avoidance, education access, labour market inclusion, social cohesion, and equality and generational equality. Ireland performed badly (4th last out of 31), particularly because of its high poverty levels (poverty is given three times the weight of the other categories); however, even if the weighting for poverty is neutralised, Ireland still comes 22nd out of 31. The best performers (Iceland, Sweden, Denmark, Norway, Finland, the

Table 5.1   At-risk-of-poverty measures in comparative European perspective

Poverty concept	Measurement	Poverty rate in Ireland	Irish ranking in EU
National-at-risk-of-poverty	Percentage of households below 60% of national median income	18.5	17
EU-at-risk-of-poverty	Percentage of households below 60% of EU median income	9.9	13
National consistent poverty	Percentage below 60% of national median income and above a deprivation threshold that identifies an identical proportion of individuals to that captured by a national income measure	8.7	21
EU consistent poverty	Percentage below 60% of EU median income and experiencing enforced lack of three or more of seven deprivation items	5.1	13
Mixed consistent poverty	Percentage below 60% of national median income and experiencing enforced lack of three or more of seven deprivation items	7.1	17

Source: Whelan and Maître (2010: xii, Table 1)

Netherlands, Switzerland, France and Austria) include many of the small states considered to be Ireland's most natural comparators. The United States was similar to Ireland in terms of the impact poverty had on its final ranking, drawing attention to the nature of the Irish political economy and its low taxation, low expenditure formula. The study confirmed the failure to tackle poverty, the lack of welfare effort relative to GNP growth and the failure to invest appropriately in education – deficiencies in early childhood and primary education in particular are significant causes of Irish poverty and inequality.

REVIEWING PAST TRENDS IN POVERTY AND INEQUALITY

There are few estimates available for poverty or income distribution before the 1970s. In 1972 it was estimated that '*at least* 24 per cent of the population have a personal income below the poverty line' (Ó Cinnéide 1972: 397; emphasis in original). A landmark 1981 Kilkenny Conference on poverty drew attention to the 'one million poor': the third of the population who lived below the poverty line. The evolution of poverty over the course of the Celtic Tiger boom proved ambiguous. Different trends were observed depending on which measurement was used: consistent poverty* or relative poverty. Deprivation-based consistent poverty was adopted as the key indicator for the National Anti-Poverty Strategy (Ireland 1997, 2007) and the EU social inclusion strategy, and so has importance both as a policy and politically. This dropped from 9 per cent of households in 1994 to 4.1 per cent in 2001 for the 50 per cent poverty line. The lowest poverty line at 40 per cent of median income, reflecting the most vulnerable, remained quite constant (increasing from 2.4 per cent to 2.5 per cent over this period). Progress can largely be attributed to decreases in unemployment (from a high point of 17 per cent in 1994 to a low point of 4.1 per cent in 2006), but also to real social welfare increases significantly ahead of inflation over the period 2001–07. The rise in unemployment to 13.4 per cent in 2010 translated into a rise in consistent poverty to 5.5 per cent in 2010; successive cuts in social welfare in the 2010 and 2011 budgets are likely to have further increased the numbers in consistent poverty (CSO 2010a; Loftus 2010).

However, trends in relative poverty, measured as the percentage of households falling below certain percentages of mean income poverty lines, give a somewhat more complex picture of what was happening to poverty. This shows the percentage of households below 40 per cent of average income growing from 4.9 per cent in 1994 to 9.8 per cent in 2001; the percentage below 50 per cent of average income growing from 18.6 to 23.8; and the percentage below 60 per cent of average income declining from 34.2 to 32.2. This suggests a steady rise in relative poverty, except at the 60 per cent line, where poverty has remained quite stable (Kirby 2010). Since the initiation of the EU Survey on Income and Living Conditions (EU-SILC) in 2003, data on poverty in Ireland are grouped into somewhat different categories, making them consistent with data across the EU. The 'at-risk-of-poverty' rate (the share of persons with equivalised income below 60 per cent of the national median income) shows poverty in Ireland declining from 19.3 per cent in 2000 to 16.5 per cent in 2007 and to 14.4 per cent in 2008 and 2009

---

* Consistent poverty is a combination of relative income lines together with deprivation measured according to a list of indicators, such as having a meal with meat, chicken or fish every second day, having new rather than second-hand clothes, having a warm waterproof overcoat and two pairs of strong shoes. Absence of these for households falling below the different relative income poverty lines indicates deprivation.

(CSO 2010a). The Combat Poverty Agency attributes this decline to real increases in social welfare rates and progressive budgets in 2006 and 2007.

The overall picture of income distribution is captured in Table 5.2. The picture for consistent and relative poverty is complicated by a methodological change in 2003 in the survey and data collection methods (Johnston 2005). What is worrying is that, despite some progress since the 1990s, there is now a clear rise in consistent poverty over 2008–09; this can be attributed to the worsening income situation for welfare-dependent families. The data for relative income inequality show that the increasing equality often celebrated is illusory; rather, income inequality is deeply embedded, and the Celtic Tiger did little to shift it.

Table 5.2   Indicators of poverty and inequality, 1994–2009

Indicator	1994	1998	2001	2003	2005	2008	2009
Consistent Poverty	9%	6%	4.1%	9.4%	6.5%	4.2%	5.5%
Relative Poverty at 60% of median income	15.6	19.8	21.9	19.7	18.5	14.1	14.1
S80/20	5.1	5.0	4.5	5.0	5.0	4.6	4.3
Gini	33	33	29	31	32	30.7	29.3

Sources: Kirby and Murphy (2008b); CSO (2010a: 20)

Positive change, where evident, can be attributed to increased numbers of people in employment and to political decisions to redistribute income through progressive budgets focusing on social welfare increases. Initial poverty levels of 35.6 per cent in 2001 were reduced to 21.9 after welfare payments were taken into account. By 2007, the increased adequacy of social welfare payments meant that even higher poverty rates of 41 per cent were reduced to 16.5 per cent. Timonen (2003) shows that, relative to its national wealth, Ireland's social expenditure is less than that of comparable countries. TASC (2009: 20) shows that Irish spending on social protection, at 18.2 per cent of GDP in 2006, compared unfavourably not only with high spenders France (31.1 per cent GDP) and Sweden (30.7 per cent GDP), but also with Greece (24.2 per cent GDP) and Portugal (25.4 per cent GDP). There is a direct correlation between the percentage of GDP spent on social protection and levels of inequality. Rising relative inequality can also be attributed to political decisions in favour of regressive budgets focusing on tax breaks for the rich and causing a significant increase in the incomes of the most wealthy.

The TASC (2009) Hierarchy of Earnings, Attributes and Privilege
Analysis (HEAP) uses 2006 SILC data to illustrate how the income
of the top 0.5 per cent rose sharply, causing the average income level
to increase and pushing more people below the relative poverty line.
The lowest 10 per cent of households earned an average €193.15
a week compared to the top 10 per cent, who earned an average
€2,491.21 a week (12.9 times the lowest 10 per cent). To some
degree, this was caused by the nature of the neoliberal market and
an aggressive bonus policy in financial and banking industries; but
this was aided by government policy not to regulate wages at the
top end of the market, not to tax wealth or high income, and to
enable significant levels of tax avoidance through a wide range of
often unproductive discretionary tax reliefs.

Social mobility

McCall (2009) critically compares the experience of the United
States, which decreased inequality in the boom times, with the Irish
experience of stable levels of inequality, measured by a stable Gini
coefficient, and *rising* levels of inequality, measured by the ratio of
the top 10 per cent of income earners to the bottom 10 per cent.
Evidence that real earnings increased at the bottom as well as the
top would, McCall argues, have been more convincing evidence of
positive progress during the boom. Instead what we see is evidence
of the incomes of the richest 10 per cent increasing during the
boom by a significant factor. According to Social Justice Ireland,
just two deciles saw their share of the total income distribution
increase since the late 1980s. The bottom decile's share increased
by a mere 0.11 per cent, while that of the top decile increased by a
very significant 1.34 per cent. They conclude that 'the gap between
the top 10 per cent of households and all the rest of society has
widened over these years' (Social Justice Ireland 2011:1). This gap
is illustrated in Table 5.3.

Table 5.3 Ireland's income distribution by decile group, 2009

Decile	Bottom 10%	2nd	3rd	4th	5th	6th	7th	8th	9th	Top 10%
% of all income	2.28		3.74	5.11	6.41	7.71	9.24	11.6	13.39	16.48	24.48

Source: CSO (2010a)

This shows that the top 10 per cent of Irish households received
almost a quarter (24.48 per cent) of total disposable income, while

the bottom decile received 2.28 per cent of all disposable income. Collectively, the poorest 50 per cent of households received a very similar share (25.25 per cent) to the 10 per cent (24.48 per cent). Overall the share of the top decile is nearly 11 times the share of the bottom decile. Recent decreases in the Gini coefficient measure of inequality and in the ratio of the income of the richest 20 per cent to the poorest 20 per cent (S80/S20 ratio) suggest a very recent decline in income inequality and can be explained by the recession causing a proportionally greater decrease in higher incomes than in lower ones.* In spite of this, the overall income distribution as shown in Table 5.3 is one of deeply embedded inequality; as TASC (2009) shows, the managerial and professional classes are the real winners of the Celtic Tiger.

This is consistent with McCall's (2009) argument that Ireland is still consistently and relatively rigid by international standards and that social mobility has, in fact, changed little over time. Abolition of third-level fees enabled the middle classes to invest in private second-level education and supplementary privately purchased tuition, further reinforcing and maintaining inequality. Ironically, well-paid construction work in the Celtic Tiger period enticed many men away from education and contributed to higher numbers of men failing to complete secondary school, with the consequence that up to a quarter of young men experience functional illiteracy. McCoy et al. (2010) found that the participation of the manual working class in third-level education actually fell over the course of the Celtic Tiger, and that access to education was mediated generally by class, as illustrated in Table 5.4. They found clear evidence that families have differential access to various forms of cultural, social and economic capital and resources and that many children experience alienation from education at a young age. This is particularly serious given that, between 1998 and 2004, the average entry rate to higher education in Ireland increased substantially from 44 per cent to 55 per cent, except for non-manual groups, whose participation rates fell from 29 per cent in 1998 to between 25 per cent and 27 per cent in 2004 (McCoy et al. 2010). Hout (2007) points to the persistence in Ireland of inter-generational educational inequality, which reflects what he terms 'maximally maintained inequality'.

---

* The income quintile share ratio or the S80/S20 ratio is a measure of the inequality of income distribution. It is calculated as the ratio of total income received by the 20 per cent of the population with the highest income (the top quintile) to that received by the 20 per cent of the population with the lowest income (the bottom quintile).

Ireland continues to spend proportionately less on education (4.7 per cent of GDP) when compared to the average spend across 30 OECD countries (5.7 per cent GDP).

Table 5.4 Relationship between education, income and risk of poverty

Highest level of education achieved by household head.	Equivalised gross income median €	Risk of poverty
Primary/no formal	13,489	33.6
Lower secondary	19,742	23.3
Upper secondary	24,933	15.1
Post leaving certificate	26,433	11.6
Third level non degree	31,812	8.7
Third level diploma	45,707	3.2

Source: TASC (2009: 24)

While the crisis has hit all classes, Ó Riain (2009) observes a disastrous collapse in working-class employment. There are growing differences between the position of those with third-level education and those without (Forfás 2010). McCabe (2009) agrees with Ó Riain that the collapse in employment is primarily in industry and construction, then in hotels and retail, and most recently in services to firms (professional, technical and administrative support services, including temporary employment agencies). Within the private sector, employment in some sectors (information and communication) increased over the last quarter of 2009, others remained stable (transportation/logistics and finance). While Ó Riain (2009) expects some sectors (information, communications, retail and producer services) to recover, he does not expect construction and industry to recover to the same degree. This has implications for access to employment across different social classes. Ó Riain concludes that the short-term and long-term effects of the recession on those in manual and service occupations, and households dominated by those occupations, are particularly disastrous. The labour market analysis of Forfás (2010) also highlights this class dimension to unemployment. Young and older males with low levels of education are most at risk of long-term unemployment. Some characteristics are strongly associated with long-term unemployment risk. Males are more likely to remain unemployed if they have a recent history of long-term unemployment, if they have previously participated in labour market work-experience programmes, if they are of an advanced age, have a relatively large number of children, a relatively low education or literacy or numeracy problems, are located in urban areas, or lack personal transport. The jobs crisis will leave a class scar. In the absence of significant government intervention, young men with less than full secondary education will experience lasting unemployment. For women, the probability of remaining unemployed increases with marriage or separation, the number of children, literacy or numeracy difficulties, a history of unemployment or casual employment status (Forfás 2010).

WHO LOSES MOST?

The CSO (2010a) shows income distribution to be highly stratified. Gender, education and housing tenure in particular account for differences in net disposable income. At a deeper structural level, there are clear losers in the crisis who will not just suffer temporary setbacks, but will be considerably poorer over their life course. The CSO (2009: 45) assessment of who is at risk of poverty shows the ultimate losers in the distribution of Irish wealth and resources. Those for whom the principal economic status of the head of the household is home duties (primarily female carers and lone parents), unemployed and low paid workers, comprise almost three quarters of poor households.

Table 5.5   Households below the poverty line classified by economic status of head of household, 2009

At work	22.8
Unemployed	26.0
Students/school attendees	5.4
On home duties	26.7
Retired	6.6
Ill/disabled	10.9
Other	1.6

Source: CSO (2010a)

Workers

The Celtic Tiger period saw a significant redistribution of income from workers to business. Comparing Ireland's adjusted wage share of the total economy as a percentage of GDP with that of the EU 15 shows that while the wage share in Ireland from 1960 to 1990 was above the EU average, during the course of the boom it fell well below the EU average. In the 2001–06 period it fell to 56.4 per cent of GDP, from 78 per cent in the 1960–70 period. In contrast the

EU12 average had fallen from 70 per cent in the 1960–70 period to 64.2 per cent in the most recent period (European Commission 2009). Workers have not only lost out structurally to business over the Celtic Tiger; they have also directly lost income over the course of the crisis. Average weekly gross earnings decreased from €720 a week in the fourth quarter of 2008 to €685.10 a week in the third quarter of 2010. The drop in weekly earnings was a consequence of decreases in average hourly earnings, but was also driven by a drop in hours worked (CSO 2010c). Gross weekly earnings in the public sector also fell by 4.5 per cent, compared with a fall of 0.3 per cent in the private sector over 2008 to 2009. This reflects the decreases in public sector pay rates announced in the December 2009 budget, but does not capture the deduction of the pension levy that was introduced in March 2009. Gross data for public or private sector wages does not reflect the 2010 budget tax increases. This was the first budget in a series of IMF/ECB austerity measures; it introduced a series of tax increases and a new universal social charge which significantly decreased net take-home pay in both the public and private sectors in 2011. While a 2010 minimum wage cut was reversed in 2011, low-paid workers in various sectors have also experienced an assault on minimum wages.

Unemployment

Box 5.1   Philip

Philip Cullen is in his 50s, he had no job and lives alone in a rural house with no indoor toilet. Having moved to Scotland in his 20s he came back in the early days of the Celtic Tiger to care for his mother until she died. He is now working two-and-a-half days a week in the Community Employment Scheme, a labour market programme, but has little hope of getting a full-time job. He says: 'There is a lot of depression and a lot of heavy drinking. Some of the men when you meet them first don't even speak, they are literally a silent people. They have no confidence, no self-esteem' (Combat Poverty Agency 2007:26). Since the recession, unemployment in his county, Leitrim, has grown, and Philip has suffered two cuts in his weekly income; he will find it harder to get a place on a new work experience programme, never mind a job.

The reduction in unemployment to a low of 4.4 per cent in 2006 was the most important and positive outcome of the Celtic Tiger. The increase in unemployment and more recent increases in long-term unemployment have been by far the greatest casualties of the recession. Data from CSO (2011) show a flattening but persistent unemployment rate of 14.7 per cent (one of the highest in the EU 27, with only Spain, Latvia, Estonia and Lithuania higher). In March 2011 there were 435,121 people unemployed (150,968 women and 290,225 men). There is also evidence of an increased number of casual and part-time workers on the Live Register or unemployment count (19.5 per cent, an increase from 12.1 per cent three years earlier). Even with high levels of youth emigration, the unemployment figure for those under 25 years of age was 81,356. By the end of 2010 long-term unemployment stood at 140,400 or 47 per cent of the overall unemployment figure. Kinsella and Kinsella (2011) point to the huge social implications of long-term unemployment, with people working through a cycle of loss similar to bereavement (disbelief, anger, depression, acceptance), eventually adjusting to a life cycle of unemployment. This leaves psychological and economic scarring. Bell and Blanchflower (2009) show how unemployment leaves people stressful and unhappy, the psychological imprint of joblessness leads to loss of self-esteem, fatalism and loss of control over daily life. This is associated with a physical impact on health, including heart disease and poor diet. The longer the period of unemployment, the harder the re-entry, with younger unemployed people carrying forward a 20 per cent 'wage scar' for the rest of their working lives.

Women

Duwurry (2011) uses the concept of 'hecession' to highlight how narratives of unemployment are often gendered, focusing almost exclusively on male unemployment. Women however, having made economic gains during the Celtic Tiger, are the real losers, bearing the brunt of cuts in public services, on which they are more reliant (Smith 2009). While women's labour market participation increased over the period of the Celtic Tiger, they still experience inequality in the workplace. Occupational segregation, lack of flexible working possibilities and inadequate childcare provision all contribute to the gender pay gap. Women's average hourly income was around 86 per cent of men's in 2006. Women also manage household unemployment and ultimately bear the burden of cuts and poverty; they manage debt and bear the stress of household and child poverty. Women also experience a higher risk of consistent poverty than men. Lone-parent households reported the highest levels of deprivation, with almost 63 per cent of those from such households experiencing one or more items of deprivation compared with almost 29 per cent at national level (CSO 2010a). Lone-parent households are the most at risk of poverty, with a rate of 36.4 per cent. It is the cross-cutting nature of disadvantage that really impacts on women's inequality. The intersection of gender inequality with other areas of discrimination renders a double disadvantage for women Travellers, women migrants, women with disabilities and women who are homeless. The position of carers, in what Lynch (2007) has called a 'careless' society, merits special attention. Economic inequality in two-parent households is linked to affective inequality and inequality of care, time and sharing of domestic work. McGinnity and Russell (2007) record that women do 86 per cent of child supervision, 69 per cent of playing with and reading to children, 82 per cent of care to adults, 80 per cent of cooking, 86 per cent of cleaning and 70 per cent of shopping. Barry (2008) explores the complex intersection or relationship with gender and disability and argues that women with disabilities face compounded difficulties, as they often combine both caring roles and disability and are less likely to be recipients of care. Poverty compounds this inequality of care.

Box 5.2   Rachel

The shocking 2010 death of a 30 year-old mother in Dublin City Council social housing illustrates the real vulnerability of poor women parenting alone. Rachel Peavoy was 30 years old when she died of hypothermia in her Dublin City Council-owned apartment in Ballymun. At her inquest in Dublin City Coroner's Court both her family and her neighbours confirmed that Rachel had made several complaints to Dublin City Council about the lack of heating in her council apartment. The complaints to Dublin City Council about their centrally controlled heating system were made between September 2009 and 11 January 2010, when Rachel died. This coincided with the coldest winter in Ireland since the 1940s. A lone parent with two sons, she had asked her family earlier that week to mind her children, fearing that the cold in the apartment had reached dangerous levels. Rachel's inquest was adjourned on 24 February, the evening before Ireland's 2011 general election; in the midst of national preoccupation with the economy her story received little attention (Newenham 2011).

Children

'Doing better for families', the OECD's (2011) report on family well-being, says that families with children are more likely to be poor than in previous decades, when the poorest were more likely to be pensioners. Irish children aged 0–17 remained the most vulnerable age group in 2009, with an at-risk-of-poverty rate of 18.6 per cent and a consistent poverty rate of 8.7 per cent in 2009, up from the 6.3 per cent recorded in 2008 (CSO 2010a: 6–7). The crisis is having a tangible and negative impact on the quality of life of Irish children. The same report showed over 23 per cent of children reported to have experienced two or more items of enforced deprivation in 2009 (an increase from 18.1 per cent in 2008). Being in poverty also causes adverse effects on a child's education and health: 15 per cent of young people leave school without a Leaving Certificate (the final state qualification in Ireland's secondary school system), 3 per cent leave without any qualification, and almost 1,000 children do not transfer annually from primary to secondary school; 10 per cent leave primary school with serious literacy problems and up to 17 per cent of young males have inadequate literacy capacity. Educational disadvantage means that children from poor backgrounds and early school leavers are at subsequent risk of unemployment and, when employed, earn considerably less than average wages. Poverty affects not only the health status of children, but also their access to health care. Children reliant on the public health system experience much longer delays in accessing

---

Box 5.3   Sharon

Sharon lives in Coolock, a working-class area of Dublin, with her three children, Robert (16), Sean (13) and Jamie (4). The oldest two children are deaf. Sharon left school at 16 and was pregnant by 17. She split up with the father of her first two children when she was 21 and has been alone since. She has struggled hard to go to third-level education to train as an interpreter for the deaf at Trinity College Dublin. 'All I would do is worry, worry, worry', says Sharon. 'Everything that comes up, where are you going to get the money? Financially my situation is just desperate. If I pay my bills I can't buy my messages, if I buy my messages, I can't pay my bills'(Combat Poverty Agency 2007: 22–3). Since 2007, Sharon has seen her own weekly social welfare reduced, her child benefit cut substantially and now also copes with reduced community and public services.

out-patient and in-patient care than those covered by private health insurance. Many children and young people are homeless or at risk of homelessness.

Ireland has a shameful historical record of institutional abuse of children in state-funded but church-administered institutional care (Murphy Report 2009; Ryan Report 2009). Sadly, failing vulnerable children is not just a historical feature of the Irish state. The most vulnerable of all children rely on the state for their care. In the last two decades, over 109 children in HSE care died of unnatural causes, including unlawful killings, suicides, drug overdoses and traffic accidents. Over the last decade 501 unaccompanied minors (migrant children under 18 and seeking asylum) have disappeared from HSE care. Only 67 have been traced, and many are still missing; girls in particular are feared to be victims of sex trafficking (Kelleher, O'Connor and Pillinger 2009). However, it is not just in state care that children are vulnerable. Some of the most vulnerable children suffer abuse in the family home. The state has failed to put in a place an adequate legislative and support infrastructure to protect the rights of children at risk of parental or domestic abuse.

Disability

People with disabilities fare badly in the key areas of education, earnings, poverty and social life, compared to other people in their age groups. Gannon and Nolan (2004) found that people have lower earnings and more restricted social lives as a result of disability. People with chronic illness or disability have substantially lower levels of educational qualifications than the others in their age groups. These disparities are stronger among younger people, and are stronger where disability restricts daily life. People with a chronic illness or disability aged 25–34 are four times more likely than others to have no qualifications beyond primary level, and only half as likely to reach third level. Those aged 55–64 are just under 40 per cent more likely to have no qualifications beyond primary level and about 40 per cent less likely to have reached third level. This is mediated by the date at which the disability was acquired and other background factors, such as social class, which affect both education levels and health or disability risk. Only a minority of people with a chronic illness or disability are in work, and chronic illness or disability is associated with significantly lower hourly earnings. This, combined with lower average hours of work, means lower weekly earnings. Little wonder then that people with chronic illness or disability are more than twice as likely to be at risk of poverty, and more than twice as likely to be poor. In 2008, those not at work due to illness or disability had a 21.6 per cent risk of poverty compared to a 13.8 per cent risk nationally. People with a chronic illness or disability are less likely to be in a club or an association, to talk to their neighbours most days, to meet friends or relatives most days, or to have a social afternoon or evening out. Disabled people saw increases in social housing need, with a rise from 423 in 2002 and 480 in 2005 to 1,155 in the 2008 housing assessment (a 140.6 per cent increase in housing need over that period).

Migrants and emigrants

In some respects the Celtic Tiger period can be characterised by a relatively successful and quick integration of up to 160 different nationalities into the Irish workforce. However, these migrant workers are a significant casualty of the recession. CSO data (2010b) show a significant decrease in the numbers of migrants applying for or successfully finding work. Unemployment figures confirm that migrants are in more vulnerable employment positions and are losing jobs at a faster rate than indigenous workers. Once unemployed, unless covered by social insurance, a habitual residence rule means that many migrants are ineligible for social assistance payments and are more likely to find themselves destitute. This shows quite clearly in the numbers of migrants leaving the country, but also in an increase in those who are homeless and sleeping on Dublin streets, with migrants now comprising 50 per cent of street homeless. This vulnerability is compounded for women migrants, many of whom have their own domestic caring responsibilities, but are also more likely to be employed in informal domestic care employment and less likely to be covered by social insurance (Pillinger 2007). This vulnerability is most exposed in intensified trafficking of women into and through Ireland for the purpose of sexual exploitation (Kelleher, O'Connor and Pillinger 2009). Within Ireland's migrant population there is a hierarchy of inequality, with asylum seekers suffering the severest form of segregation and isolation from Irish society. Denied the right to work, over 4,000 men, women and children are restricted to direct-provision accommodation in hostels and a paltry €19.60 cash payment per week (frozen since 2000); 4,000 vulnerable men, women and children are living in 52 overcrowded, unsafe and inhumane centres for asylum seekers across the country. Families are made to sleep in single rooms and share bathrooms with other residents, while female residents regularly face abuse and sexual harassment.

Forced or involuntary migration is again a feature of Irish social and economic life. Many now emigrating are foreign national migrants returning to their countries of origin or moving elsewhere to find work. A growing number of Irish nationals are also emigrating. Net outward migration rose from 7,800 in 2009 to 34,500 in 2010 and is expected to be over 100,000 over the years 2011 and 2012 (CSO 2010c). The reasons for emigration are not always economic, but those who talk up emigration and economic mobility as offering a good opportunity for young people ignore the real pain for many families and communities as young people are forced into involuntary emigration. This traditional Irish safety valve also diminishes a political response to the crisis, as those who suffer unemployment and poverty find their own unsatisfactory solution to the crisis.

Travellers

Box 5.4   Helen and Biddy

Helen Stokes lives with her husband Martin on St Margaret halting site near Ballymun, Dublin. Her caravan is small and draughty and she is on a waiting list for social housing: 'Our names are down for ten years for a house. Imagine that I have reared 12 children in two caravans and now I am sick. I've arthritis and high blood pressure. I've to go out to go to the toilet and the shower has not worked in years.' Biddy McDonagh is 32 and has seven children. She lives in the same site as Helen, but in a larger caravan, having been moved from an unofficial site. She was recently five weeks without electricity and four months without hot water. Biddy says she is happy enough to stay where she is: 'I've no more choice anyways,' she says, 'I've nowhere else to go, me husband is on the dole, none of us works, what can you do?' (Combat Poverty Agency 2007: 14). Since 2007, Biddy has seen her weekly social welfare reduced, her child benefit cut substantially and now also copes with reduced community and public services.

The Equal Status Act 2000 defines the Traveller community as a community of people identified by a shared history, culture and tradition, who historically had a commercial nomadic way of life and whose culture places distinctive value on extended family. The 2006 census recorded 22,435 Travellers. Over 40 per cent are children aged between 0 and 14 (double the figure for the Irish population) but only 24 per cent of Travellers are aged 35 or over (half that for the Irish population). Only 3 per cent of Travellers are 65 or over (compared with 11 per cent for the population). Behind this story of low life expectancy lies unemployment, poor health, disability, low educational attainment, inadequate housing, premature mortality and distinctively high levels of poverty and deprivation (Office for Social Inclusion 2009: 62). Only 14.4 per cent of all Travellers are in work, compared with 65.2 per cent of the population as a whole. Among adult Travellers (those aged 15 years and over) only 3.4 per cent have completed upper secondary (Leaving Certificate or equivalent) education; 35.4 per cent of Travellers aged 55–64 reported a disability, versus 15.3 per cent for the general population. A 1987 report showed life expectancy for Traveller men was 9.9 years less than for settled men, and life expectancy for Traveller women was 11.9 years less than for settled women. This has not declined appreciably over the course of the Celtic Tiger. As a minority group, although protected under equal-status and incitement-to-hatred legislation, Travellers remain exposed to social exclusion and discrimination in access to services and the provision of accommodation. The number of Traveller families awaiting permanent accommodation at the end of 2004 was in excess of 3,500.

HOUSING

Drudy and Punch (2005) draw attention to the range of inequalities in the Irish housing system. They argue that this has produced a series of tax-incentivised winners and a large number of losers – people for whom the basic right to shelter is out of reach. The unregulated market and lack of price controls on land sites mean that a speculative market has put homes beyond the reach of many. There has been a failure to develop the rental market as a real alternative or long-term viable option. Public housing has been allowed to run down and has increasingly become the poor relation of the Irish housing stock. It has been privatised through tenant purchase schemes for housing and through public–private regeneration partnerships. All of this has produced clear winners and losers, as can be seen in Table 5.6.

With 89 per cent home ownership, provision of housing in Ireland has always been heavily reliant on the private sector. The experience of housing construction since 2000 has meant that housing provision, accelerated by tax incentives, has been led by property speculators who were free to act as they wanted in a largely unplanned and badly monitored market. The net result is poorly located and poorly built houses in an expensive housing market. While public discussion of the Irish property 'crisis' has focused on the implications of property developers' inability to pay back speculative bank loans, the establishment of the National Asset Management Agency (NAMA) to manage the bad debts of property developers, and the bank bailout (see Chapter 4), there is a much deeper story about the real losers in the story of Irish housing. The acceleration in the property crisis has also had a major impact on average households and in particular on poorer households. Social housing waiting lists have grown, social housing has become more marginalised, and new groups become vulnerable to homelessness. The private rented sector has become larger and is poorly regulated; old stock is in bad repair and new stock poorly built. Access to home ownership is now coupled to massive private debt, negative equity and increased threat of mortgage default and repossession. The poor location and badly planned infrastructure has also resulted in social dislocation for families and communities as families relocated to commuter rings outside Dublin and other urban centres (Kitchin et al. 2010).

Table 5.6   Winners and losers in the Irish housing system

Winners	Losers
Speculators and investors	Property-less
Developers and landowners	Homeless
Financiers (e.g. banks, building societies)	Low income/Unemployed
Estate agents	Ethnic minorities
Solicitors	People with disabilities
Landlords	Others in housing need
Home owners	Tenants
Government finances	First-time buyers
Newspaper property supplements	

Source: Drudy and Punch (2005: 11)

Those on social housing waiting lists fared badly over the Celtic Tiger. Despite an abundance of housing, the number of households on local authority waiting lists rose from 27,227 in 1996 to 56,249 in 2008, while Walsh estimates that in 2011 some 130,000 households are in need of housing (Walsh 2011). Despite a housing construction boom, the actual stock of local authority-owned housing units rose by 20,000 over the period of the Celtic Tiger (from 98,394 in 1996 to 118,396 in 2008). Housing costs have contributed to the growing need for state accommodation. Of those on the housing list, some 75 per cent earn less than €15,000 a year and cannot afford to meet the costs of their existing accommodation. Medical needs and overcrowding or involuntary sharing make up the other main grounds to qualify for state social housing. This suggests that those waiting are suffering. They live in poverty and/or unsuitable accommodation; this has an immediate impact on life quality. Even those with secure social housing have lost out badly in the political economy of the Celtic Tiger and its subsequent collapse. The reality of disadvantaged urban and rural communities and the crisis and marginalisation of social housing are perhaps best illustrated by the collapse of five social housing regeneration projects planned by Dublin City Council (Bissett 2008). Residents of these complexes have been left living in horrendous conditions. In May 2010, residents of Dolphin House, a housing development with 425 apartments owned and managed by Dublin City Council, challenged the Department of the Environment to a public hearing to vindicate their right to adequate housing as defined under the UN Covenant of Economic, Social and Cultural Rights. McGreevy and Holland (2011: 3) report that a survey by the Rialto Rights in Action group found that 45 per cent of adult residents and 42 per cent of child residents had respiratory problems; 84 per cent reported sewage coming up through sinks and baths and 64 per cent reported mould in their homes. Dr Maurice Manning, president of the Irish Human Rights Commission, concluded that residents' human rights were clearly being breached. This housing development had been part

---

Box 5.5   Michael

Michael is homeless in Dublin. After the break-up of his 20-year relationship in London, he experienced a spell of unemployment and the loss of both parents. Michael returned to Dublin, where he has been homeless for 12 years: 'People haven't a clue what is going to happen to them, Celtic Tiger my backside. They did nothing for us. It is dangerous to sleep on the streets, you can get kicked by young scumbags coming out of night clubs or you can get robbed by some of our own homeless people. You have to be careful. It is better not to sleep, just to sit there. A Garda kicked me one day I was sitting on Grafton Street' (Combat Poverty Agency 2007: 46). Since 2007, Michael's weekly social welfare has been reduced significantly, social housing waiting lists have grown and he must pay a greater proportion of his income to fund private rental housing.

of a public-private partnership (PPP) regeneration programme that was a victim to collapsing house prices.

Those with no housing at all are the greatest losers of the Celtic Tiger and its collapse. The tri-annual Assessment of Housing by the Department of the Environment (2008) estimated the homeless population to be 2,468 in 2002, 2,399 in 2005 and 1,394 in 2008, a reduction of 41.9 per cent over that period. However, these official figures are disputed. The Homeless Agency estimates that there are over 5,000 people homeless in Ireland. Their Counted-In survey estimates that 2,015 of these are in Dublin. Marked increases in street homelessness and destitution since 2008 have been recorded by homeless agencies (Simon Community 2010). There is also a shift in the composition of the homeless, with migrants and youth now comprising the significant substrata of the homeless population.

Over-indebtedness

Entry to the European Monetary Union and consequent lower interest rates, coupled with competition in a lightly regulated mortgage market, meant that borrowers could access discounted rates and new financial products. This opened up the mortgage market. Lending criteria moved away from the traditional multiplier of three times salary to, in some cases, double-digit multipliers of salary. Between 2000 and 2008 alone, more than 760,700 mortgages were issued in Ireland. Housing debt doubled in the five years to 2009. Massive increases in mortgage borrowing means personal debt rose faster than in most other countries in the eurozone. Personal debt was the equivalent of 58 per cent of disposable income in 1996, but by 2007 this had reached 175 per cent of disposable income, among the highest in the world (Walsh 2011). By 2009 more than 28,000 families were more than three months in arrears on their mortgage payments. While a Statutory Code of Conduct on mortgage arrears is temporarily holding off repossessions in the main housing market, there are growing numbers of repossessions in the sub-prime mortgage market. In January 2011, more than 40,000 borrowers are in arrears of three months or more and another estimated 40,000 homeowners at risk of arrears. The pace of increase in arrears are captured in a report by Price Waterhouse Cooper (2010) which estimates that residential mortgages have grown from €26.71 million in September 2009 to €40.472 million in September 2010. Some 80 per cent of the 200,000–350,000 households estimated to be in negative equity are thought to be first-time buyers. Liable for the difference between the resale value of the property and the outstanding mortgage, these people are restricted in their life options. Walsh (2011) reports significant effects on people's physical and mental health due to stress, worry and inability to plan for or control their futures. This impacts on family relationships and results in depression, increased risk of suicide and marriage separation.

Russell, Maître and Donnelly (2011) analyse 2008 data on over-indebtedness in Irish households, isolating as key indicators of over-indebtedness persistent arrears, payment burden, and illiquidity or inability to raise resources or access credit. The analysis shows a strong connection between low income, poverty and over-indebted households, which suggests that income inadequacy rather than high levels of personal consumption is a key factor in over-indebtedness. CSO (2010a: 21) SILC data show that in 2009 more than one-third (34.2 per cent) of households with a gross weekly household income of between €401.68 and €662.02 (second income quintile) had arrears on at least one of the four items (rent or mortgage arrears, utility bill arrears, hire purchase or other loan arrears and other bill arrears, for example, education or health). This compares to 15 per cent one year earlier. Of households with a weekly gross income in excess of €1,567.20 (highest income quintile), 17 per cent had arrears on at least one of the four items included. This compares to less than 2 per cent one year earlier.

SPATIAL INEQUALITIES

Location. Location. Location. It matters where you live in Ireland. The 1958 Irish economic development programme resulted in a greatly improved economic situation and a subsequent dramatic expansion in private house construction and the rapid development of Dublin City and other city suburbs. Lack of expertise, political corruption and inadequate governance contributed to ineffective Irish urban development and the growth of metropolitan spatial socio-economic inequalities. Redmond et al. (2007: 28) describe how 'social polarisation became highly interconnected with spatial segregation'. Inner-city and large suburban local-authority housing estates are characterised by high levels of unemployment, early school leaving and educational disadvantage, inadequate housing, low quality environment, health inequality and drug and alcohol addiction, and low levels of bridging and linking social capital (Kelly and Teljeur 2004). The impact of the crisis will hit most severely those areas most dependent on public services. Cuts in public transport, health and social services, special needs education, and sporting and voluntary services disproportionately hit working-class areas with fewer power resources to defend themselves.

According to O'Mahony (2008:1) the Celtic Tiger opened up space for a criminal monopoly based around a violent drug trade and an entrenched drug gang culture. He argues that 'violence has become more concentrated, more intense and more visible at the anarchic margins and amongst those with non-conformist lifestyles – the substance abusers, the criminals, the homeless and the teenage gang-members who resort to increasingly violent lifestyles'. Large sections of the population, already vulnerable, have fallen over the edge (Kinsella and Kinsella 2011). This is reflected in big increases in the numbers of people availing of food packages and soup kitchens run by the Capuchin Fathers and other religious orders, and a growing demand on the supplementary welfare allowance (a system of discretionary payments for urgent needs). Increasing numbers of households are being disconnected for non-payment of utility and housing bills, and there are growing reports of households resorting to credit and ultimately to debt to maintain basic livelihoods (Russell et al. 2011).

Much of this deprivation relates to personal lifestyle experiences and private in-house deprivation (heating, furniture and house visits). This suggests that the experience of recession is borne with most stress within the household. This is correlated with significant increases in suicide numbers over the course of the recession, rising from 424 in 2009 to 527 in 2010, together with 195 deaths recorded as inconclusive but with having 'intent' (CSO 2010e). While suicide has spread across all age groups and genders, it is still most pronounced in young men and closely associated with the despair and fatalism of those faced with experiences such as unemployment. Kinsella and Kinsella (2011: 93–8) are particularly concerned for the 25–44 age group, who are in the life-formation stages of the life cycle and are therefore less mobile. They warn that unemployment within a labour market such as now exists in Ireland has 'multiple adverse physical and mental health effects including depression, health complaints and impaired psycho-social functioning'. High clusters of unemployment mean that these adverse effects can also be suffered at a community level, with high levels of unemployment creating a vicious cycle of dependency, poverty and ill health.

CONCLUSION: POWER AND INEQUALITY

There has been a recent international and national focus on the issue of vulnerability (IMF 2003; UN 2003; World Bank 2000; Kirby 2006, 2010; Office for Social Inclusion 2009). Whelan and Maître (2010) understand vulnerability as a heightened probability of being exposed to a range of risks or shocks. Vulnerability refers to exclusion across many dimensions of disadvantage and results in severe negative consequences for quality of life, well-being and future life chances. Three indicators capture this heightened level of risk: the most important of these is basic deprivation, followed by economic stress and then income poverty. Old risks, such as employment status, social class and housing tenure, combine with post-industrialist risks, including changing family structures (separation, divorce and lone parenthood) and illness or disability, to cause this vulnerability (ibid.: 514). The people whose lives are documented in this chapter are the vulnerable; they were vulnerable before the crisis and they will still be vulnerable when this recession is over. No doubt the lives of the poor, hard during the period of the Celtic Tiger, are even harder now (Loftus 2010). In mapping the contemporary Irish class structure in a more pictorial fashion, this chapter highlights the fact that intersectionality, the overlap of class and inequality or discrimination, is a reality for many in Ireland. Gender, race, class and (dis) ability demarcate the reality of a society that is still class-ridden (Baker 2003). Attitudes towards people who experience class and other forms of discrimination can influence many aspects of their lives, including their self-esteem, how they are treated by the wider society, and public policy and service provision. Chapter 2 outlined the political elite of Ireland and Chapter 3 identified some of the bureaucratic agents with power to determine distributional outcomes in Ireland. It should come as little surprise that the losers identified in this chapter were not among those identified as power brokers in Chapters 2 and 3. Clearly, significant groups were neither recognised, heard nor represented in Ireland's democratic system. Their voices and experiences were reflected in the case studies and give evidence of the strong correlation between poverty, alienation, fatalism, powerlessness and political disenfranchisement.

6
The Winners

'There are always winners and losers' in times of economic change (Ruane 2007: vi). There certainly have been high-profile losses in the banking and construction industries and among developers. However, Slattery (2010b:1) describes some who 'lost' in the recent crisis as 'drowning in champagne'; despite their losses they still maintain a lifestyle of wealth and privilege. This chapter focuses on completing the task of mapping the Irish class structure by examining those usually neglected in the analyses of the social sciences – those who captured the bulk of the resources generated by the Irish boom. Chapter 5 highlighted the fact that patterns of winners and losers are not inevitable, but are the outcomes of political decisions relating to policies in education, housing and taxation, as well as industrial, competition and regulatory policies. This chapter begins by examining different data sources to estimate how much wealth there is and how many people are wealthy. The second section identifies formal and informal links both amongst the wealthy themselves (through, for example, directorships) and in their involvement with social networks of senior politicians. The third examines corruption. The fourth section examines three case studies of political decisions that benefited foreign and indigenous elites. These include reforms of financial regulations, corporate and capital taxes, as well as housing and education policies. We show how such decisions directly enriched a small globalised Irish elite and a larger domestic elite, and consider their wider negative impact for the development of Irish society. The concluding section reflects on the continuing political power of economic elites.

HOW MUCH WEALTH AND HOW MANY WEALTHY?

It is in outcomes that the winners become apparent. Statistics about wealth are hard to come by in Ireland. There is a long history of putting money into foreign bank accounts, of establishing bogus non-resident accounts and of using holding companies to evade tax (O'Toole 2009). Furthermore, the recent banking crisis has exposed the degree of financial corruption in Ireland's golden circle of wealth (Maguire 2010; Smith 2010). This almost certainly means that estimates of Irish wealth-holding underestimate the concentration of wealth inside and outside Ireland. ICTU's analysis of executive pay, pension contributions and bonuses is revealing. In 2007 pay and bonuses had grown to 3 or 4 times what they had been in 2000, and the majority of top company CEOs were earning more than €1 million a year. Publicly available data in company annual reports show that among the banking elite, Sean Fitzpatrick (Anglo Irish Bank), Michael Fingleton (Irish Nationwide Building Society) and Brian Goggin (Bank of Ireland) each earned over €2 million. Tony O'Reilly at Independent Media earned €2.2 million in 2007 (even though as a tax exile he could only work in Ireland 183 days per year). High earnings were not related to performance. Philip Lynch of the company 'One 51' was paid a €1.4 million bonus in 2009 despite his company making a €1.1 million loss that same year. The 2009 pay of CEOs was 14 times higher than Principal Officer-level pay in the public sector and 136 times the level of income at which people are estimated to be at risk of poverty (ICTU 2010: 22).

TASC (2010a) likewise highlights 'excessive remuneration' for the CEOs of both state-owned and private companies. On average, their pay rose by over 40 per cent between 2005 and 2007, while combined inflation for these two years ran at just over 9 per cent. The average pay of CEOs in the largest 21 companies was €1.1 million in 2007 and actually *rose* to €1.6 million in 2009 (a post-crisis 46 per cent increase). TASC (2009) showed high earnings concentrated in the top 0.5 per cent of the population. When analysed in terms of occupation, this group primarily comprises those in managerial or professional occupations with an annual income of €600,000 or more. This can be contrasted with the top five per cent of households, who live on incomes exceeding €134,000, 58 per cent of households living on less than €40,000 and 26 per cent living on less than €20,000. As seen in the previous chapter there is a striking 'education premium': the median gross income of those with no formal education, or primary education only, was €13,489, while those with a university degree had a median income of €45,707. Irish tax data on high-income individuals, while incomplete, still helps us to build a picture of Irish earnings. The returns by the Revenue Commissioners (2010) for 2008 showed that there were 38 people with an income between €1 million and €1.5 million, 11 with an income between €1.5 million and €2 million, and 23 people who received more than €2 million. Almost 6,000 citizens are tax exiles and pay no income tax, at least 440 of whom were the 'super-rich'.

What about Irish wealth? A 2007 Bank of Ireland wealth report remains the most recently published account of Irish wealth and shows that 5 per cent of the population owned two-thirds of Irish wealth. The gross wealth of the top 1 per cent was an even €100 billion. When residential property is excluded, 1 per cent of the population owned 34 per cent of Irish wealth. CSO data (2010d) show that the total value of Irish residents' holdings of foreign securities at the end of December 2009 amounted to €1,251 billion, an increase of €86 billion on the revised 2008 level of €1,165 billion; it found that the bulk of the increase was in equity assets (largely the result of a recovery in global equity markets). While Irish wealth reduced over the crisis, there is evidence that it is recovering. It has also moved; there has been a significant international transfer of Irish wealth and investment to locations outside Ireland. Taft (2009) shows that Irish investors owned €1.3 trillion worth of assets abroad; Ireland can be compared in this respect with France, where €2 trillion worth of international assets is owned by French nationals. The US Treasury in 2009 estimated that €42 billion or $50 billion dollars in US treasury bonds is owned by Irish 'residents'. Taft (2009: 30) estimates that in 12 months between 2008 and 2009 the equivalent of $35 billion fled Ireland, seeking greater security in the United States. The Finance Act (2010) sought to tap into this wealth by introducing an Irish domicile levy of €200,000 for Irish individuals with Irish assets of €5 million or more and whose worldwide income is greater than €1 million.

Income distribution became more unequal between 1987 and 2005, with the gap between those at the top and those at the bottom widening. While Chapter 5 showed that the 2008 and 2009 Gini coefficients suggest a recent drop in inequality, other evidence suggests that the incomes of the poor are decreasing, while the incomes of the very rich are again increasing. The *World Wealth Report* (Merill Lynch and Capgemini 2010) advises that, despite recession and crisis, the wealth of High Net Worth Individuals (HNWIs) has increased over the last two years. HNWIs have net assets (excluding domestic residences and luxury goods) of $1 million or more. Ó Broin's (2010) analysis of the report shows that 18,100 people had net assets of $1 million in Ireland in 2009 (an increase of 10 per cent over 2008). There were also 181 more Irish 'ultra-HNWIs' (owning $30 million or more of investable wealth). We can compare this to UK data, which show that the number of UK

HNWIs increased by 23.8 per cent in the same period, from 361,000 in 2008 to 448,000 in 2009. The Alliance Global Wealth Report (Steck et al. 2010) shows that Ireland is still relatively wealthy (clustered with Canada, France and Australia) and is still regarded as a high wealth country (2010: 78). The Irish global share of financial assets (0.37 per cent) amounts to €307 billion, and these assets had a 7.1 per cent year-on-year growth from 2008 to 2009. This represents financial assets per capita of €68,060, compared to GDP per capita of €35,182; with this wealth, in 2010 Ireland ranks ninth-wealthiest out of 31 OECD countries and fifth wealthiest of the EU 15. It is important to note that some of this wealth is heavily leveraged. Steck et al. (2010) also show that Irish household debt as a proportion of GDP has risen substantially. Ireland saw the steepest rise in the EU, with household debt doubling to 127 per cent of GDP within the eight-year period 2001 to 2008.

Webb's (2011) list of Ireland's 300 wealthiest individuals is remarkable in many ways. It is highly gendered, with fewer than 10 women among the 300 individuals who each own more than €19 million. It shows collective wealth of €57 billion, an increase of €6.7 billion from 2010, and a growing number of billionaires (11, an increase from 9 in 2010 and 6 in 2007). It shows a range of sources of wealth, including music, culture and sport; but most wealth is financial, investment or industry-related, with technology, telecoms and media businesses, commodities like gas, oil, gold, copper and food, and global construction and retail all listed as sources of wealth. Only two individuals are cited as inheriting their wealth, while one woman sourced her wealth through a lottery win. Webb (2011: 2) celebrates this culture of entrepreneurship, arguing that this Irish wealth is largely self-made. The next two sections question whether this is the case, drawing attention to the overlap between business and politics and the degree to which the wealthy benefited from, and continue to benefit from, a series of tax and economic policy decisions.

MEMBERS OF THE ELITE AND GOLDEN CIRCLES

Ireland is described by Lewis (2011: 1) as 'cosy capitalism at its worst'. Crony capitalism has become a byword to describe the networking of political, economic and social elites and a political culture of corruption. As described in Chapters 2 and 3, the political culture has been dominated over the last decades by short-term sectional gain in which electoral considerations with regard to winning and maintaining power were given the dominant political priority for Fianna Fáil. Leahy (2009) describes that this 'manic short-termism' involved cultivating sectoral communities of interest in finance, business, and the construction and property industries, which were given what they wanted as long as they supported Fianna Fáil's quest for power. Ross (2009) highlights the deference in this political culture towards those who are perceived to have wealth and capital, and how FF appeared to have the objective of creating and maintaining an Irish 'aristocracy' of citizens who would have no obligation to pay taxes. Chapter 4 discussed the extent of regulatory capture, whereby government departments and the state's regulatory agencies effectively came to serve those very interests they sought to regulate (Barry 2009). This led to a significant policy reliance on non-intrusive forms of regulation, self-regulation and light-touch regulation, as well as many tax breaks and subsidies for relatively unproductive economic activity, which might well have happened without such fiscal incentivisation. In the name of competitiveness, the state had permitted its own economic and policy-making capacity to be eroded, and had ceded power to an economic elite and vested interests (Regling and Watson 2010; Honahan 2010; Wright 2010; Nyberg 2011). This section explores this elite, and the formal and informal economic, social and political links, both amongst themselves (through directorships) and with senior politicians. To do this, it draws on TASC's (2010a) analysis *Mapping the Golden Circle*, and Allen's (2007) analysis of corporate Ireland, as well as 2009 publications about Irish elites by O'Toole, Leahy, Ross and Cooper. While Chapter 5 gave pen pictures of the poor in Irish society there is no need to provide pen pictures of the rich. Many are household names, enjoying a high profile in Irish social, sporting, media and cultural life, regularly featuring in Irish social columns and glossy magazines, and participating in public and policy debate. This class network, while not itself directly involved in politics to any great extent, overlaps with politics through appointments to state boards, political party funding and media ownership and comment. The following examples suffice to show the larger pattern. The first three refer to informal overlaps of power as part of political culture; the second three refer to more structured or institutionalised practices of power, which are embedded in state practice and policy through state boards, or which enable power overlap on the boards of private companies. The penultimate example refers to banking, while the final example genders this discussion of the Irish elite.

Some of the more informal social overlap between business and political power is captured by Cooper (2009: 72–5), who identifies a 'circle of friends', with media, property, legal and political actors brought together by key intermediaries. In one example of how crony capitalism works in practice, he observed how P.J. Mara worked as a pivotal mediator between political and business networks. Mara had served as the taoiseach Charles Haughey's adviser in FF. From 1992 he engaged in corporate work, providing a networking 'space' to elites in a series of house parties or soirées at which business and political elites met informally. As Cooper (2009:71) explains, 'Mara brought together his contacts and his clients, introduced people to each other and then left them to get on with doing business: that is what his parties were about.' Cooper recalls how some of the characters present at such house parties ended up in the Flood Tribunal of Inquiry into Certain Matters in the Planning Process, which in 2002 eventually found the former senior Fianna Fáil politician and minister, Ray Burke, guilty of a number of corruption offences (Flood 2002). The tribunal found that Burke, as Minister of Communications, 'had sought to advance private interests ... and not to serve the public interests' (ibid.: 76). Mara himself was found to have failed to cooperate with the same tribunal in relation to information about his offshore accounts. He went on to be appointed as Fianna Fáil Director of Elections in the 2007 general election. Cooper draws particular attention to the relationship between the media and the political world, and especially Independent Media Network CEO Tony O'Reilly's relationship with political leaders. Mara also acted as an intermediary in contacts between Bertie Ahern as taoiseach and O'Reilly, one of the richest and most powerful men in Irish business. Once again, informal social events were important, with politicians and business people mingling at soirées in O'Reilly's Castlemartin mansion. As Cooper put it (2009:5), 'Ahern's greatest support in this time of political need, between late 2006 and 2008, came from O'Reilly's flagship domestic title, the *Sunday Independent*.' Cooper (2009:5) argues that this support can be explained by the degree to which O'Reilly was grateful to Ahern for 'many decision that were of enormous financial benefit to the business man'. These friends overlap again in a more overt way in the Fianna Fáil tent at the annual end-of-July Ballybrit horse races in Galway, where the party had a fundraiser and facilitated access to key ministers; 500 people paid up to €400 each to rub shoulders with the political elite and each other, and Fianna Fáil netted as much as €170,000 from the annual event. As Cooper explains, it was not all about fundraising, and 'access was tightly controlled', with journalists being denied entry (2009: 82). Even local party members complained about the overtones of elitism. Former taoiseach Brian Cowen reacted to public criticism and closed the Galway tent when he became party leader in May 2008. However, good friends will always find time and space to meet; during an infamous round of golf at Druids Glen Golf Course in June 2008, Cowen continued the political tradition of FF, networking with private banking interests, economic consultants and central bank directors – most notoriously in the person of the disgraced former chairman of Anglo Irish Bank, Sean Fitzpatrick. Clifford (2011) observes that this culture of cosy cartels and crony capitalism was so embedded in Ireland that the elite never even thought to conceal it; he warns how 'Ireland is a small country where everybody knows everybody else. Yet the failure to observe even sensible precautions in avoiding the dangers of crony capitalism is still a major feature of the corporate landscape'.

The elites also overlap more formally. TASC (2010a) examined board membership of 40 Irish private companies and state-owned bodies, including household names such as Bord Gáis, the Central Bank, Allied Irish Bank, Smurfit, Anglo Irish Bank, Ryanair and Aer Lingus. The total number of directors involved in managing these companies was 572. In the period 2005–07, a network of 39 people held positions in 33 of the 40 top private companies and state-owned bodies. Between them, these 39 – referred to as the 'Director Network' in TASC's report – held a total of 93 directorships. *Mapping the Golden Circle* identifies how overextension of corporate governance led to the risk of 'groupthink', namely making decisions that ignore alternative evidence as a result of a group's desire to reach consensus. The Dublin Docklands Development Authority (DDDA) is a clear example of the overlap between business, land, property and Fianna Fáil. Cooper (2010) describes the state-run DDDA as collaborating with Anglo Irish Bank by using its statutory authority, complete with ministerial approval, to waive regular planning permission requirements in respect of the old Irish Glass Bottle site in Dublin. Anglo was the major lender to the proposed development on the site. As Cooper notes 'there was an overlap between the DDDA and Anglo Irish Bank boards at the time of the crucial decisions', as two directors sat on both boards. The result of these decisions now forms part of the debt burden. Allen (2007: 168) shows significant overlap between elites and governance. His review of membership of the board of the Health Services Executive (HSE) illustrates clear overlaps with medical, financial and business interests, with members being appointed, not on the basis of health expertise, but because they would support a health service delivery 'with a strong managerial and performance ethos' (Allen 2007:168). The HSE, when first established, was chaired on an interim basis by Kevin Kelly (president of the Irish Banking Federation and a former AIB director). The board was dominated by business rather than health interests. Allen (2007:171) outlines how the first chairman, Liam Downey, was a former CEO of a medical technology company and a board member of the Irish Business and Employers' Confederation (IBEC). Board members included Joe Macri (managing director of Microsoft Ireland), Eugene McCague (partner in legal firm Arthur Cox), Donal de Buitlear (general manager with AIB), Professor John Murray (President of the Marketing Institute) and Professor Niamh Brennan (academic and director of the Institute of Directors' Centre for Corporate Governance at University College Dublin). (ibid.:171). Evans and Coen (2003) review the influence of elites on agri-environmental policy. They identify an expert elite within the food safety policy arena in the Food Safety Authority of Ireland. This elite is enabled by a lack of transparency, democratic control or scrutiny by technical scientific experts. Chari and McMahon's (2003) case study of the privatisation of state industries found economic actors in strong alliances with government departments, especially the Department of Finance, and in privileged positions to influence the formulation of the sales policies for Irish Sugar, Irish Steel and Telecom Éireann, all of them state companies at the time.

The banking elite deserve special mention. Irish banks have significant ownership of Irish insurance companies, stockbrokers, auditors and financial law companies and have huge influence and direct control over small businesses. The media's consistent use of banking economists and the politicians' increasing use of economic consultancy firms for policy advice mean that the banking sector has a disproportionate input into national economic discourse and policy. Lyons (2009) points to how one financial law firm, Arthur Cox, dominated events in the bank bailout, with personnel from the law firm acting as advisers to taoiseach Brian Cowen, minister of finance Brian Lenihan, and Anglo Irish Bank and Bank of Ireland's lawyers, and then being appointed as legal advisers to the National Asset Management Agency. Ross (2009) warns about the dangers in a small country of powerful banking oligarchs or big banks which overlap too much with business, regulatory agencies and politics. His description of Anglo Irish Bank as 'a building society on crack' highlights graphically the degree to which the banking sector was unregulated and allowed to get totally out of control. His argument was subsequently confirmed in Wright (2010) and Nyberg (2011). Ross highlights how deeply this dysfunction was embedded, by reviewing the historical continuity of banking failures or corruption in a string of scandals in banking and insurance over the 1980s and 1990s. His finding that no bank was ever fined and no banker ever jailed for any of these still holds true.

Finally a striking feature in the narrative of winners in the Celtic Tiger is the absence of women. Whether in politics, as employers, in media or in corporate business, women rarely feature in the picture. Only one member of the directors' network identified by TASC was a woman, and women feature little in the story of the Irish banking collapse or subsequent bailout. Even when we analyse the gender of those recording the story of the collapse of the Celtic Tiger, women rarely feature as authors. There is considerable support for the view that the almost exclusively male, and often macho and testosterone-fuelled world of banking, business and politics contributed to the nature of risk taking, the aggressive and competitive culture of business and the ultimate nature of the crisis (Smith 2009; McCarthy 2010). The European Commission (2010) argues that having more women in senior positions in the public and private sector is crucial to economic recovery and stability, and to a culture of better and more sustainable decision making. Likewise Collins (2009: 2) argues that measures to support equality should be a key part of our economic infrastructure; greater equality adds to international competitiveness and can assist economic renewal. Table 6.1 shows how Ireland fares compared to the EU average and to best practice in Finland. There are glass ceilings or hidden barriers for women attempting to enter both formal and informal political spaces. There is no statutory requirement for gender parity on state national or local partnership boards; a voluntary 40 per cent gender quota on boards or committees is largely ignored. The unequal participation by women in formal political and state institutions is also reflected in the public sphere, in media contributions and in political discourse (McCarthy 2010; N. Ryan 2010). In the final irony, women have become more visible in the story as elite men, to avoid bankruptcy and the consequences of company liquidation proceedings, transferred company assets, houses and cars into their spouses' names.

Table 6.1   Women in senior decision-making positions (European Union, Ireland, Finland)

	EU average	Ireland	Finland
Parliament	24	15	40
Cabinet	27	13	55
Senior Bureaucrats	26	19	26
Supreme Court	32	22	26
Central Bank	18	15	31
Largest quoted companies	12	8	26

Source: http://ec.europa.eu/social/main.jsp?catId=778&langId=en

CORRUPTION

A White Paper on Crime (Department of Justice 2010) acknowledges the presence in Ireland of bribery, corruption and regulatory crime. Maguire (2010: 187) defines white-collar crime as 'abuse of power by persons who are situated in high places where they are provided with the opportunity for that abuse'. The absence of prosecutions for white-collar crime in no way reflects an absence of such crime. Arguing that there is now a 'steady tide of regulations heading towards increasing criminalisation of improper conduct in business' (ibid.: 188), Maguire says the now very obvious impact that improper conduct in business and banking has on the public interest brings a new impetus for stronger regulation, enforcement and sanctions in relation to white-collar crime. Smith (2010: 196) offers Transparency Ireland's definition of corruption, 'the misuse of entrusted power for private gain', and using evidence from various tribunals, strongly identifies corruption in Ireland with FF's longevity in power. Highlighting that three FF taoisigh in a row appeared at different times before the tribunals (Charles Haughey, Albert Reynolds and Bertie Ahern), she identifies the close relationship between politicians and business as being a feature of FF since the 1950s (see also Chapter 2). The 'Beef', McCracken, Mahon and Moriarty tribunals revealed the extraordinary extent of political favouritism, conflict of interest and corruption, as well as intricate networks of secret payments to politicians and public officials during the 1970s and 1980s (Smith 2010: 195).

G. Murphy (2006) argues that accusations of high levels of Irish corruption are contestable and offers the GRECO international report, ranking Ireland as 15th least corrupt out of 85 countries, as proof that Irish corruption is not as significant as is perceived.

Transparency International (2010) concurs that Ireland has made substantial progress in strengthening legal and institutional safeguards against corruption, with Irish 'petty corruption' now perceived to be amongst the lowest measured anywhere in the world and little evidence of contemporary political 'grand corruption' typical of the 1980s and 1990s. The report does, however, draw attention to high levels of 'legal corruption', in which 'no laws may be broken but personal relationships, patronage, political favours, and political donations are believed to influence political decisions and policy to a considerable degree and there is a lack of transparency in political funding and lobbying' (ibid.: 9). The Standards in Public Office Commission (2010) argued that the need to identify sources of income is a key aspect of making party funding transparent. The policy of thresholds below which donations need not be disclosed encourages parties and donors to accept and make donations below the threshold values; figures published in June 2009 show that political parties disclosed annual donations worth a mere €96,523 for 2008. There is a strong argument for 100 per cent state funding of political parties.

This brings us back to political culture. Byrne (2009:1) argues for a moral rather than a legal definition of corruption and understands corruption 'as undue influence over public policies, institutions, laws and regulations by vested private interests at the expense of the public interest'. She argues that cultural as well as legal change is necessary, as corrupt actions may often be within the letter of the law but outside ethical norms, and that corruption is most serious when the policy system is subconsciously biased towards policies that benefit economic elites. Irish elites are sustained by a political ideology that believes inequality to be inevitable and necessary, and by wider Irish attitudes of deference to power and privilege. This ideology was perhaps best captured by the then minster for justice, equality and law reform, Michael McDowell, who commented to the *Irish Catholic* newspaper in 2004 that 'a dynamic liberal economy like ours demands flexibility and inequality in some respects to function. It is this inequality which provides incentives' (cited in Crowley 2010: 88). Crowley notes the irony of the minister for equality so stoutly defending the value of inequality; but this value was deeply embedded in Irish political culture. Deference to authority was also deeply embedded in Irish culture. The *Report of the Commission to Inquire into Child Abuse* (Ryan 2010) showed how the absolute authority of the Catholic Church led to the assumption that it was above reproach or criticism. It seems that public attitudes towards big business showed similar deference. The Morris tribunal report on Garda corruption in Donegal continues this trend (Morris Tribunal 2008). The 2011 publication of the final report of the Moriarty Tribunal exposed an abuse of power that shocked even seasoned observers and that showed that this culture of politics went beyond Fianna Fáil to political actors in Fine Gael. Reflecting on the Moriarty Tribunal, McManus observes:

> An environment in which business and political leaders simply do not believe that ethical behaviour pays off, helps explain why the same names keep cropping up in Irish business scandals. You can travel a line from the granddaddy of them all – the so-called Telecom scandal of 1988 – through the beef tribunal to the Ansbacher affair to the Moriarty tribunal and on to Anglo Irish Bank ... The crossover in dramatis personae is astounding ... But the numbers making two or three appearances is truly remarkable. The pattern is evident not just among the leading players; it's also the lawyers, accountants and other advisers who provide supporting cast. (McManus 2011: 17)

HOW POLICY PROMOTED WEALTH ACCUMULATION

There is clear tension between private interests and the public interest. Many Irish winners won at the expense of those who lost out most (described in Chapter 5). Political decisions to reform corporate and capital taxes and to deregulate standards directly enriched a small globalised Irish elite. Some of the examples above illustrate how an unaccountable elite was allowed to shift national development priorities towards their own interests and away from Ireland's developmental needs. This section analyses the most profitable sectors of the Irish economy and the links between them, and examines the impact these sectors have had on the development of Irish society. It uses three case studies of policy to show how this happens. The first examines multinational companies (MNCs), which are enabled to repatriate much of their profits. The second examines how the domestic elite were enabled through tax reliefs to make money out of construction. The third examines how industrial and education policy also contributed to the development of the professional and managerial classes in software and related industries, and shows how state policy enabling private access to education acts to determine winners.

Foreign elite: Bankers and financiers

Ireland was once branded by the *New York Times* as the 'Wild West of European Finance'. Since the founding of the International Financial Services Centre (IFSC) in Dublin, Ireland has encouraged a speculative financial industry, through a combination of light-touch regulation and low corporate taxes. The 1958 transition to an open export-led economy was accompanied by a gradual shift in the Irish corporate taxation system.* The low tax rate and Ireland's relaxed transfer pricing rules have also encouraged the use of Ireland in international tax planning. The Double Irish Arrangement is a tax-avoidance strategy that US-based multinational corporations use to lower their income tax liability, by shifting income from a higher-tax country to a lower-tax country (facilitated by the absence in Irish tax law of effective transfer pricing rules). Murray (2008:9) offers the following example: in late 2005, 'the *Wall Street Journal* reported that Microsoft had saved $500 million on its US tax bill by transferring intellectual property rights to Irish-based corporate units'. Drucker (2010) refers to Google's practice of using Irish transfer pricing or income shifting to reduce its overseas tax rate to 2.4 per cent. The low corporate tax rate in Ireland contributed to inward investment and the Celtic Tiger boom; but it also represented a loss of potential revenue, leading to under investment in public services as well as an overemphasis on property-sourced taxes, which in turn contributed to the fiscal deficit. The degree to which foreign business benefits from Irish policy is staggering (Gallagher, Doyle and O'Leary 2002: 77). Gottheil (2003:731) argues that profit rates as a percentage of the sales of US multinationals operating in Ireland 'were scarcely short of awesome'. US pharmaceutical companies operating in Ireland had profit rates approaching 50 per cent, rates that Murray (2008) calls 'incredible', and a product of transfer pricing. This can be compared to 5 per cent profit rates for Irish companies operating in Ireland and for US companies in the United States. The facilitation of the foreign elite was not restricted to the macro-level of low corporation tax and IDA grants. GAMA,

---

* Various innovations included tax holidays for exporting firms and tax relief in respect of royalties and other income from licences patented in Ireland. A new corporation tax combined the capital gains, income and corporation taxes that firms had previously had to pay, and in 1981 a special tax rate of 10 per cent was introduced for companies involved in manufacturing, those in the International Financial Services Centre and those in the Shannon Free Zone. In December 1997, the then finance minister, Charlie McCreevy, introduced a 12.5 per cent rate of corporation tax from 1 January 2003.

a Turkish-owned construction company, successfully lobbied Mary Harney as minister for enterprise and employment to legislate a Pay-Related Social Insurance Exemption Scheme for foreign-registered construction workers. Dell and Intel also successfully lobbied on relaxing union-recognition policy, and pharmaceutical companies lobbied for the relaxation of environmental regulations. Murray (2008) observes that as US corporate investment became increasingly important, Irish unions in the private sector came to experience the same 'slow strangulation' that was being visited on their US counterparts. The impact of industrial policy was therefore not only to sacrifice potential tax income and to prioritise investment in foreign rather than indigenous industry; it was also to have a far wider impact on policy outcomes. To what degree, then, has foreign investment benefited Ireland? Promoters of a low corporate tax rate point to FDI growing to the extent that it represented 49.2 per cent of GDP in 2000 (World Bank 2000: Table 1.6), creating some spillover into various sectors of the indigenous economy, but not the type of linkages which would develop a strong export-led indigenous sector.

> Although only 16 per cent of local plants are foreign-owned, they produce 65 per cent of gross output and engage 47 per cent of manufacturing employment. About 40 per cent of foreign plants are US-owned, with 16 per cent British and 14 per cent German-owned. Foreign plants are much more likely to import their raw and semi-processed material inputs than indigenous plants. Irish plants export on average about 36 per cent of output while foreign plants export 89 per cent, rising to 95 per cent for US-owned plants. Thus the domestic market is of little significance to the foreign plants. (Barry, Bradley and O'Malley 1999: 50–1)

It was the absence of a strong indigenous manufacturing or services export sector that led to the unbalanced post-2002 Irish economy, dominated by construction and property industries. Low or light-touch regulation of these industries also contributed to Ireland's malaise. A recent decision highlights the overlap between national and international banking, national political elites and business interests, and the way in which lack of regulation contributed directly to the banking crisis and the subsequent bailout. According to Barrington (2011), despite concerns and resistance from the financial regulator, the Irish state responded to pressure from bankers, led by then Anglo Irish Bank chairman Sean

Fitzpatrick, to deregulate existing controls on raising investment bonds. Fitzpatrick lobbied the Irish government to allow Anglo to raise covered (guaranteed) funds backed by commercial rather than residential mortgages. The financial regulator resisted this move, arguing that commercial loans were too risky to be used as security against covered bonds. The then taoiseach, Brian Cowen, ignored the regulator and introduced the legislation in 2007, allowing Anglo to issue billions in covered bonds backed by commercial mortgages. In September 2008, Cowen then bailed out Anglo Irish Bank by transferring responsibility for honouring these very bonds to the Irish taxpayer.* Breslin, a senior civil servant in the financial regulator's office, was quoted as 'being under siege' from representation from the banks about implementing the Assets Covered Securities Act. The chief lobbyist in this was Pat Farrell, chief executive of the Irish Banking Federation (who had previously held the post of general secretary of Fianna Fáil). Barrington (2011) shows that he was aided in lobbying by Sean Dorgan, CEO of the Industrial Development Agency, and by international banks, including the German bank Depfa (a tenant of the IFSC). A central plank of the lobbyists' argument was that deregulation was essential to competitiveness, and that Ireland had to keep pace with other international deregulation trends. This process of policy making is informative and highlights not only the power of this class of bankers and their international allies, but also the overlap between the banking industry and political elites and the industry's access to key policy and economic agents.

Indigenous elite: Developers, landlords and software

The Irish class structure reflects a transfer of wealth, and the emergence of a new property class of landlords, construction magnates and property-related professionals. McDonald and Sheridan (2009) observe how many of the winners from Ireland's property boom do not appear a likely elite. There is ample evidence, however, from tribunals of inquiry and other sources, that this class benefited from a reduction in capital gains tax from 40 per cent to 20 per cent in the 2002 budget by the minister for finance, Charlie McCreevy, as well as from various tax incentive schemes

---

*   The German Bankgesellschaft Berlin collapsed having engaged in aggressive real estate lending at the height of a property boom which collapsed in 2001. The Berlin Länder state government subsequently guaranteed €21 billion of this bank's potential liabilities, a model of state bailout that inspired Fitzpatrick.

that enabled developers to avoid taxation and grow capital for new investments. As Kitchin (2011) observes, the start of the present cycle of property-led wealth accumulation can be traced back to the 1980s and the introduction of Section 23, a tax relief scheme for construction in designated areas, focusing on urban renewal. In 1998, the Upper Shannon Renewal Scheme extended Section 23 tax relief to five counties, effectively making it a tax relief for developers. It is little surprise that the excess of housing described in Chapter 5 can largely be found in counties covered under this scheme, where the building boom was encouraged by tax benefits and was unrelated to general or specific local demand. Kitchin et al. (2010: 25) refer to

> the effects of Upper Shannon Rural Renewal Scheme, inaugurated in June 1998, with Longford, Leitrim, Cavan, Sligo and Roscommon all being major beneficiaries of this tax incentive programme. In total, these five counties increased their housing stock by 45,053 (49.8 per cent) between 2002 and 2009, from 90,491 to 135,544 dwellings, with 1 in 3 houses built in this period.

The mismatch fed directly into the property collapse and the legacy of a large number of poorly planned and unfinished housing estates across the country. The same report estimates that up to 300,000 vacant housing units exist across Ireland. However, it was not just residential property that developers were incentivised to build. Fianna Fáil introduced tax breaks for building or refurbishing non-profit nursing homes in 2001 and, in 2002, extended the tax concessions to for-profit nursing homes and hospitals (O'Connor 2009: 23). O'Connor describes how nursing homes came to supersede golf courses as the investment of choice: by 2004 there were 427 private nursing homes with over 16,000 beds. In this way, the care of older people began to overlap with the business of real-estate management.

The tourism industry offers an interesting case study of how state policy benefited certain groups against the public interest. Investment in the hotel sector only grew after 1987, when the Business Expansion Scheme (BES) introduced tax incentives for tourism facilities, including accommodation. By 1990 accommodation accounted for 40 per cent of the scheme, and between 1996 and 2006 the number of rooms doubled from 26,000 to 52,000. O'Brien (2010) charts how, since 1997, over 30,000 additional rooms and 480 new hotels have been built, representing an investment of €4 billion, and increasing room stock by 98.7 per cent over the previous 10 years. Tax incentives, in the form of accelerated capital allowances introduced in the Finance Act 1994, allowed investors to claim 15 per cent of the capital cost of a hotel for each of the first six years of operation, and the remaining 10 per cent in year seven, against tax liability. These incentives were 'terminated' in the 2003 budget, but transitional arrangements for hotels allowed the continuation of a 100-per-cent write-off over seven years. Lobbying by the Irish Hotels Federation led to further extensions of the transitional arrangements in Finance Acts in 2004 and 2005, despite falling hotel occupancy rates. However, growth rose more rapidly than overseas demand, which remained weak, so that investment in hotels was motivated, not by sound business sense or anticipated demand, but through the availability of capital allowances for tax purposes. Tax allowances clearly distorted the market and directed investment away from other more productive activity. A. O'Brien (2011) notes that private-sector organisations had captured public agencies, and that these agencies in turn had no capacity to discipline the private sector towards an agenda of delivering a tourism product rather than just hotel development. Crucially, she argues that the state agencies' political 'masters' were primarily interested in local-level or constituency-based tourism 'development'; they were not concerned with the broader national tourism development strategy. Drawing on the Bacon Report (Bacon 2009: 39–40), O'Brien details the vested interests that gained from the property-related hotel-building incentives: these included developers, planners, local authorities, hotel operators, tourism development agencies and banks, as well as a traditional broker class of politicians; the activities of all these interests in turn enriched estate agents, auctioneers, solicitors, valuers – all property-related professionals.

Developers were a new subset of the traditional Irish 'property class'. A new class is also developing, the class of property-related professionals who will benefit from state policy to manage the property crisis. What to do with the excess property built during the boom is now a major policy challenge. There is also a parallel challenge of addressing social housing need. New winners will benefit from a controversial assessment by the Department of the Environment that leasing excess housing stock from private developers under a Social Housing Leasing Initiative (SHLI) would cost the state less than purchasing some of these excess properties

(Walsh 2011). This idea has been criticised by the Comptroller and Auditor General (2010: 311), who argued that a cost-benefit analysis would show no cost difference to the state between leasing and purchasing properties. In choosing to lease rather than purchase these houses, policy works to bail out developers and to transfer national wealth from the state to the private sector, rather than acting as a mechanism for rebuilding the national social housing stock. This is consistent with three previous social housing policy decisions (the Social and Affordable Act 2000, a Rent Supplement scheme and the Rental Accommodation Scheme). All of these made the market the supplier of social housing options and ensured that private developers would benefit from the provision of social housing (Walsh 2011). Social housing policy does less to develop housing than to develop a new class of property and construction industry individuals.

Earlier parts of this chapter have outlined the emergence of a developer, landlord and financial services elite. What of the Irish industrial elite? The early years of the Celtic Tiger saw what Ó Riain (2004) called a new class of software and information technology professionals. These entered into an alliance with state science and technology agencies, which had previously been overlooked as a result of the IDA's dominance in Irish industrial policy. There emerged from this space an indigenous software industry with strong export performance in key sectors like educational software and credit card security. Ó Riain (2000: 175) identifies a local network of indigenous firms that have become increasingly integrated into international business and technology flows and have been highly successful in international markets. Despite the presence of this class, Irish-owned companies accounted for only €1 billion of the €16 billion generated by the software sector in 2009. One clear outcome, however, was a new class structure which emerged from the growing number of professionally qualified software and information technology experts. Many either emigrated or became internationally mobile and overlapped with international elites, some now emerging as a new wealthy class in the annual Irish 'rich lists'.

Ó Riain (2000: 175) argues that 'the state, through its heavy investment in education had created a new class basis for an indigenous technology promotion and business expansion agenda'. Murray (2008) also links the remarkable growth of Irish software companies to extensive state investment in education. Chapter 5 reviewed how the unemployment crisis has had a sharp class impact, with the more educated classes to some degree cushioned and recovering more quickly than manual and low skilled classes (Forfás 2010; Ó Riain 2009). While educational mobility is changing, there are still dominant trends and entry locks to many self-regulated professions, such as law, medicine and finance. Many of the winners in Irish social and economic life benefit most from state investment in education. Maxwell and Dorrity (2010) find little change in social class differentials in participation rates in higher education – which is no surprise, as education inequality is already deeply embedded at primary level, and Irish investment in pre-school education is the lowest in the OECD. Removal of university fees in 1996, viewed as a move towards promoting greater access for those from lower socio-economic backgrounds, has in fact given rise to investment in second-level education for middle-class families. Maxwell and Dorrity (2010:3) argue that,

> given the competitive contexts in which educational goods are distributed and the feasibility of using economic capital to buy educationally relevant social and cultural capital, it is evident that those who are best resourced economically are best placed to succeed educationally.

The abolition of fees enabled more affluent families to use the savings from third-level fees to finance second-level private education or tuition, reinforcing the access to higher education of those from higher socio-economic backgrounds.

Increasing attempts to privatise public services, including education, will further exacerbate the degree to which citizens will have to buy education, with even state schools having to supplement their income from private sources (Lynch 2006). Private fee-paying schools remain funded by the Department of Education and Science to the tune of around €100 million per annum and operate discriminatory selective procedures. McMenamin (2008) points out that these exclude minority ethnic students or those with special educational needs by setting the level of fees so high as to put them beyond the reach of all but a minority, so that only the most affluent in society can afford to attend. This translates into a pattern in which such schools dominate league tables for feeder schools into Irish third-level education. The double-funding mechanism of state funding and tuition fees allows for better facilities, wider curricular choice, smaller classes and greater extra-curricular provision. Nor do cutbacks have the same impact on these schools as on public schools, with the latter's greater reliance on schoolbook grants, special needs assistants or other initiatives for the disadvantaged. Above all, private schools serve to introduce their students to elite circles of connections that consolidate status and power. In particular, as O'Toole (2009) argues, certain professions remain closed. Those entering professional faculties such as law, medicine and dentistry are still disproportionately drawn from middle- and upper-class backgrounds. As Lynch (2006: 2) argues 'universities have been embedded with professional interests in different countries, servicing those interests well from a functional perspective, but often doing little to challenge the evident social closure practices within powerful professional groups'.

CONCLUSION: ELITES AND POWER

Elites are small minorities of people who play an exceptionally influential part in political and social affairs. Economic and political elites play a particular role in small states, where there is more social convergence, educational overlap and attitudinal consensus. This is consistent with Nyberg's comment that a

> widespread lack of critical discussion within many banks and authorities indicates a tendency to 'groupthink'; serious consideration of alternatives appears to be modest or absent. A tendency to favour silo organisation and submissiveness to superiors strengthened this effect, particularly among the public authorities. (Nyberg 2011: 8)

There is now a clear indigenous elite class, and this overlaps considerably with an international elite. Other dominant elites include foreign capitalists, the scientific and technology knowledge experts, and some policy experts, who constitute a policy monopoly. Evident in the story of the Irish crisis is the lack of accountability of these elites and a series of conflicts of interest in decision making (Williams 2011). Barry (2009:10), consistently with Nyberg (2011), argues that the scale of the crisis shows the degree to which warning voices have been ignored; he puts this down to the cartelisation of policy advice, which insulates the system from a greater variety of ideas in the provision of policy advice, with 'greater opportunity for good ideas to challenge bad ones'. A second republic would have to have institutional and regulatory capacity to manage such conflicts of interest, and it would need to foster a political culture and value system that promotes the common good over narrow sectional interests. Wealth reports show that these elites are still winning. They are richer than before the crisis and they continue to operate golden circles and try to use their still considerable status to influence policy responses to the crisis. McCaughren (2011) reports on how 20 high-profile people from Ireland's business and economic elite have come together in a group called Ireland First to contribute a 'blueprint for recovery'. Unchastened by any roles they might have played in the crisis, they still maintain elite policy-influencing circles, champion their role in leading economic recovery and have significant access to media and circles of power. McManus (2011: 17) notes with irony 'the extent to which tribunal stars past and present populated the ranks of the Ireland First group' and questions how they can 'suggest to the citizens of a country they have profited from for 20-odd years how it should now sort itself out'. As long as elites are unaccountable to the public they are likely to promote minority interests. They threaten democracy to the extent that their activities are not open to public scrutiny; such a lack of transparency delegitimises politics. Transparency Ireland (2010) pulls no punches when it argues that a tradition of self-regulation and a crisis-led approach to fighting corruption is still evident within Ireland's public service, professions, civil society and business. There are still few data or statistics on wealth. No banker has ever been jailed or fined and no one has yet been convicted of any crime associated with the 2008 banking crisis. Various measures can be taken to reach the standards required of a republic, including comprehensive whistle-blower safeguards in the public and private sector, full and free access to official information, more scrutiny of appointments to the boards of public bodies, and an end to the delegation of key policy to quangos not subject to full parliamentary scrutiny. A republic also requires regulation of political lobbying and further powers for the Standards in Public Office Commission. Given the global nature of the Irish economy it is also necessary to safeguard against transnational corruption and to ratify the United Nations Convention against Corruption and the Council of Europe Civil Law Convention on Corruption. As Chapter 9 discusses, many of these political reforms are detailed in the 2011 Programme for Government. It is to be hoped that they are implemented in a thorough and comprehensive fashion. It is also necessary, however, to enhance the fight against white-collar crime and to regulate the activities of the rich.

Part III

International Context

This part sets Ireland's recent experiences in the context of globalisation and the international political economy of contemporary capitalism. Chapter 7 examines the European Union context, identifying the ways in which it has moulded the Irish political economy and how it may influence its future development. Chapter 8 reviews the lessons that can be learnt from the strengths and weaknesses in the political economy of other states comparable to Ireland, both ones that have experienced a severe bust and others that have managed to avoid this fate.

7
The European Union

Since Ireland joined the then European Economic Community (EEC) on 1 January 1973, membership has had a profound influence on the country's development. This chapter analyses the impact that EU membership has had on Irish political culture, on policy making, on the emergence of the Irish model, and on civil society. Central to the analysis is the contention that the EU subsidised Irish social investment, enhancing through the conditions attached to the funding the planning and policy-making capacity of Ireland's public administration, while at the same time permitting the Irish state to avoid the hard choices of how to raise revenue for key investments in national development. In this general way, the EU was an essential element in shaping the conditions for the emergence of the low-tax Irish model.

The chapter begins by surveying the various phases of Ireland's membership since 1973. It then turns to the contribution of the EU to the Celtic Tiger boom, with a particular focus on the role played by membership of the euro. Based on the analyses of the first two sections, the third section draws conclusions about the key ways in which Europe has influenced policy formation in the Irish state. It highlights some of the characteristics of dominant Irish attitudes towards the Union, most particularly a 'begging-bowl' mentality in the way both the state and Irish society have looked upon the EU, and the paradox that it has only acted weakly as a source of more progressive policy ideas for the political and bureaucratic elite. The chapter then turns to the EU itself as a political project which, following shifts in power elites at national and EU level, has been reshaped from a predominantly social-democratic to a more neoliberal model. This is the context for examining the prospect that Europe may contribute to the development in Ireland of political institutions and a political economy model more adequate to the challenges now facing the country.

IRELAND IN THE EUROPEAN COMMUNITY

It is widely agreed throughout Irish society that membership of the EU has been a very strong positive influence on opening up and liberalising what was still a strongly traditional and Catholic society when Ireland joined in 1973. The impact that membership has had on Ireland can be analysed in three key periods. The first, the 1970s to the mid 1980s, saw Ireland adjusting to membership; this contributed towards a significant modernisation of Irish political culture and policy administration. In particular Laffan and O'Donnell (1998) and Laffan and O'Mahony (2008) point to a more evaluative policy culture imposed but also nurtured through EU funding guidelines. Ó Cinnéide (2005) points to the influence of the EU in anti-poverty policy and the development of partnership approaches to local development. Barry (2008) points to the impact of EU equality directives on Irish legislation for gender equality in the workplace and on the social welfare system. Undoubtedly a major impact in this first period came through the Common Agricultural Policy (CAP). While much attention has been devoted to the impact of structural funds on preparing the ground for the Celtic Tiger in the late 1980s and early 1990s, it needs to be remembered that it is agriculture that has received the great bulk of EU transfers to Ireland since 1973. It is estimated that agricultural receipts constituted 70.3 per cent of the €53 billion of total EU receipts received by Ireland between 1973 and 2004 (Laffan and O'Mahony 2008: 161). Yet, while these CAP funds helped to improve living standards in rural Ireland, they failed to prevent the huge decline in agriculture as an economic activity. Partly this was because the bulk of funds go to a small number of large farmers and agribusiness companies. Department of Agriculture figures in 2009 reveal that 550 farmers had received more than €100,000 each the previous year. This indicates, therefore, the concentration of agricultural activity into a smaller number of larger farms, while the majority of farmers are forced to resort to off-farm employment to earn a living. Furthermore, payments increasingly came to be decoupled from production and linked to environmental protection. There was a certain disappointment, therefore, that the first period of Ireland's membership of the EU had not more substantially improved the country's economic fortunes; but there was clear support for its effects in giving an impulse to social liberalisation and modernisation.

The second period, from the mid 1980s to the late 1990s, was characterised by the development of the Economic and Monetary Union (EMU), the Irish decision in 1979 to delink its currency from the pound sterling (to which it had been kept at parity since independence) and float the Irish punt, and then the Irish decision to adopt economic and monetary convergence criteria and eventually to join the euro in 1999. Adoption of the Maastricht criteria in 1992, which involved a low budget deficit, low inflation and low interest rates, imposed stricter criteria on national budgetary and monetary policy, and these disciplines acted as an incentive to join the common currency. In this period, access to EU structural funds was seen as a key part of national development and a key trigger for escaping the recession of the late 1980s and early 1990s. This was also the period which saw new procedures to improve policy making being introduced within Irish government departments, such as evaluation units and auditing methods, and the establishment of a range of regulatory agencies. While much of the developments in this period concerned monetary, budgetary and social policies, public opinion tended to accept these with little debate or dissent; paradoxically, it was on security policy that most public concern tended to be focused, owing to the fear that EU policy was undermining Irish neutrality and its independent foreign policy. However, public support in Ireland for the Union remained high, rising from the early 1980s, with Ireland remaining consistently amongst the most supportive of all member states.

The third period runs from the late 1990s to the present and was initially marked by the social democratic 'social policy agenda' of Jacques Delors. However, the most dramatic changes over this period relate to a growing wave of opposition in Ireland to aspects of the Union (this must be distinguished from attitudes hostile to Irish membership per se) and the defeat of two referendums on EU treaty changes, the first Nice referendum in 2001 and the first Lisbon referendum in 2008. Coming amid the Irish economic boom, these were widely perceived abroad as the Irish selfishly turning their backs on Europe; however, in reality they reflected more a complacency among Irish political and economic elites about the solidity of support for every aspect of EU policy and the success of small lobby groups in sowing doubts across a range of issues, among which there was no consistency (tax harmonisation, liberalisation of abortion, erosion of workers' rights, diminishing neutrality and the curtailment of an independent foreign policy, and the undermining of social protections). Both defeats shocked elites and galvanised them into ensuring that reruns of the referendums would be passed; on both occasions they succeeded (Nice II in 2002 and Lisbon II in 2009). However, they have served to draw attention to the fact that, while overall Irish opinion as measured by regular Eurobarometer surveys remains very positive about the EU, a certain softening of the strength of support is evident; so that, for example, on specific issues like support for EU enlargement, the Irish are not so positive. This is also evident in the decline in the percentage of voters who voted yes in referendums on EU treaty changes (see Table 7.1). Another development of note over this period is the promotion of a three-legged strategy of competitiveness, job growth and social inclusion, known as the Lisbon Agenda. This prompted a new policy or governance process known as the 'Open Method of Coordination' (OMC) (O'Donnell and Thomas, 1998; EAPN 2010) whereby national states enter into a process of coordination of strategic action plans, with long-term common objectives and short-term actions agreed at European Council level. These are monitored by way of common indicators, joint EU evaluation, public accountability and the exchange of good practice. More a coordination of process than of policy, OMC is an increasingly dominant policy style across five policy areas, including social inclusion, pensions and employment-related social security issues; its impact on Irish policy making is examined below.

Table 7.1   Voting patterns in referendums on the European Union, 1972–2009

Entry	EEC entry	EEA	Maastricht	Amsterdam	Nice I	Nice II	Lisbon 1	Lisbon II
Year	1972	1987	1992	1998	2001	2002	2008	2009
Turnout	70.88	44.09	57.30	56.2	34.8	48.5	53.1	59.00
YES	83.10	69.92	69.10	61.7	46.1	62.9	46.6	67.13
NO	16.90	30.08	30.90	38.3	53.9	37.1	53.4	32.97

Source: Adapted from Laffan and O'Mahony (2008:108)

One major policy issue on which Irish voters have consistently voiced concern about European membership relates to foreign policy. Ireland joined the United Nations in 1955, and the first decade of its membership was seen as the 'golden years' of Irish foreign policy, when the country was willing to take stances that ran counter to the positions of major western powers such as the United States, Britain and France. Ireland's first application to join the EEC in 1961 is perceived to have tempered the Irish stand on such issues as the Algerian struggle for independence, for fear of alienating the support of key EEC member states. But the decolonisation of Africa in the early 1960s was also changing greatly the composition of the UN General Assembly, so that Ireland's stance on such issues as decolonisation or apartheid in South Africa was now eclipsed by the activism of the newly independent countries of Africa. Since joining the EEC, Ireland's foreign policy has become increasingly aligned with that of the EU, though it continues to maintain a strongly independent stand on certain issues, such as the plight of the people of Palestine; it is perceived by Israel to be the most anti-Israeli state in the EU. Ireland's most distinguished living diplomat, a former secretary general of the Department of Foreign Affairs and a former president of the Security Council, Noel Dorr, has written as follows of the effect on Ireland's foreign policy of involvement in the EU Common Foreign and Security Policy:

> One effect of this is that there is less opportunity to state a distinctive Irish position on many issues. Ireland's input comes instead during internal EU co-ordination meetings held to arrive at a common position. To balance this limitation however, there is the positive point that Ireland, small as it is, is seen as important by other countries in the UN because of the influence it may exert when the common EU position is being established. This perception of Ireland as a country of some influence and importance is further enhanced by the fact that, at intervals, like each other EU member state, it takes on the role of Presidency of the Union, and thus the responsibility for stating the common EU position. (Dorr 2002: 125)

Attention has also been drawn to the positive effect of EU membership on expanding the horizons of Irish diplomats. As Tonra has written: 'Their involvement in global issues today is both substantively wider and deeper than at any time in the history of Irish diplomacy' (Tonra 2002: 43). Not only have Irish officials been faced with taking a position on issues and on world trouble spots that previously they could more or less ignore, but much more of their time is now spent servicing a range of EU bodies, such as the EU foreign policy working groups, the CFSP Secretariat, a range of political, security and military committees and, when occupying the European presidency (1975, 1979, 1984, 1990, 1996, 2004), chairing all meetings around the world at which the diplomats of EU member states gather to discuss European business. This has stretched Ireland's small diplomatic service (of around 1,000 diplomats) and imposed huge burdens on its members during the course of each presidency.

However, membership of the EU has not been the only reason for what is seen by some critics as the moderation of the activist and values-based foreign policy that characterised the early years of UN membership. As Ireland has become more industrialised through attracting multinational companies to establish subsidiaries, so too has state policy become more attuned to the needs of these companies. For example, there has been an active civil society lobby criticising the Irish government's willingness to allow US military flights carrying troops to and from service in Iraq to land at Shannon airport, claiming that it infringes Irish neutrality and might make Ireland a target of Islamist terrorist attacks. In defending the continuance of this policy, politicians have referred to the need not to alienate the many US companies operating in the state. Ireland has also been in the forefront in defending the EU's CAP, reflecting the strong political influence of the agricultural lobby in domestic politics, even though this is seen by some to contradict the commitment towards some of the poorest developing countries that is the cornerstone of Ireland's overseas development policy.

When it comes to foreign policy, it is the impact of the EU on Ireland's traditional policy of neutrality that has generated most domestic debate. Even if much of the rationale for the state's initial neutrality (and the reason offered for Ireland's decision not to join NATO when it was established) was that Britain still occupied part of the national territory, the tradition of neutrality has taken very strong root among the Irish public, though its precise definition and content have been a source of constant debate. The state has never devoted serious resources to its military forces and throughout the cold war effectively shielded itself behind western defence arrangements, without being formally a part of them. Involvement in EU peacekeeping operations has given members of the Irish defence forces extensive overseas experience and has built a capacity for peacekeeping in volatile hotspots that is enviable for a small state. However, the new security situation following the end of the cold war proved very challenging for Ireland, and the 1990s were dominated by domestic debates about whether the state should participate in moves towards military and security coordination within the EU. For vocal sectors of civil society, these raised fears that Ireland would be on the slippery slope towards some kind of European army and that participation in groups such as the Western European Union (WEU) or the Partnership for Peace (PfP) required involvement with NATO. These concerns generated fears among the public and were among the reasons that led to a majority of voters rejecting the Nice and Lisbon referendums in 2001 and 2008 respectively. However, the adoption by the Irish government of the 'triple lock', namely the procedure by which any Irish involvement in European overseas operations requires the approval of the Cabinet and of the Dáil, as well as UN Security Council authorisation, and the decision to join the Nordic Battle Group, with Sweden, Norway, Finland and Estonia, appears to have resolved the debate on Irish security for the time being (Laffan and O'Mahony 2008:180–96).

THE EUROPEAN UNION AND THE CELTIC TIGER

What is striking in examining the Irish boom in the context of the EU is the extent to which Ireland, between 1994 and the mid 2000s, dramatically shifted its relative position from being one of the poorest countries (along with Greece, Portugal and Spain) to becoming one of the richest. When Ireland joined the EEC, it had a GDP per capita which was 53 per cent of the average in the community; by 2008, its per capita GDP was 140 per cent of the EU average, surpassed only by that of Luxembourg. While the subsequent collapse of the Irish economy and the impact of severe austerity measures to address the fiscal deficit and the costs of salvaging the banks will in time reduce its relative position, there is no denying the transformation in Ireland's relative fortunes within the EU. The major question to be asked is to what extent EU membership is responsible for this transformation.

In addressing this question a distinction needs to be made between two aspects, what we can call the contextual and the substantive. The contextual impact refers to the fact that membership of the EU provided the reason why so many US multinationals were attracted to establish a presence in Ireland, namely access to the European market. It is most unlikely that Ireland would have been as successful as it was in attracting such high levels of FDI without this access to a much larger and prosperous market, though of course the competitive edge that this gave Ireland has subsequently been eroded, as lower-cost economies in central and eastern Europe join the EU. The impact was most evident in transforming Ireland's trade performance. Not only did trade come to represent a far larger share of Ireland's GDP, so that by 2002 exports and imports constituted 176 per cent of GDP (Sweeney 2003: 210), but both the composition of what was traded and its destinations also changed fundamentally. When Ireland joined the EEC most of its exports were of agricultural goods, whereas by the early 2000s its trade profile was that of a modern high-tech manufacturing and services economy: pharmaceuticals and chemicals accounted for around 30 per cent of exports, computer services and business services around 15 per cent each, electronics 5 per cent and food and beverages 5 per cent. Furthermore, Ireland had diversified its markets away from its traditional dependence on Britain, with over half of all exports going to EU states other than Britain; though indigenous Irish firms still remained significantly dependent on Britain.

The substantive impact refers to EU investments in Ireland, particularly the high levels of structural and cohesion funds that were instrumental in creating the conditions for attracting such a large amount of foreign investment. These emerged from the argument put forward by the poorer member states during the negotiation of the Single European Act in the mid 1980s: that closer economic integration required investment by the wealthier states in upgrading the infrastructure and human resources in the poorer states to allow them to avail themselves of the opportunities opened by market liberalisation. As a result, there was a doubling both of structural funds and of cohesion funds in the late 1980s and early 1990s, from which Ireland benefited disproportionately due to its successful diplomatic lobbying. Overall receipts from the structural funds are estimated to have been equivalent to 2.6 per cent of GNP over the decade 1989–99 and to have increased the level of Ireland's GNP by two percentage points (Laffan and O'Mahony 2008: 43). O'Donnell goes further, estimating that Ireland's net receipts from the EU averaged over 5 per cent of GNP throughout the 1990s, with a peak of 7.6 per cent in 1991 (O'Donnell 2000: 185). These funds are regarded as having been used very effectively, through being invested in human resources, in upgrading the country's infrastructure and in aids to the private sector. Among these were improvements to the country's physical infrastructure; but investment also went into raising competi-tiveness and productivity and to improving the skills base of the workforce (MacSharry and White 2000: 179–81). Furthermore, as the OECD pointed out, the structural funds 'raised the quality of public investment outlays by forcing the introduction of longer-term project planning, so that short-term budgetary pressures have not led to stopping an undertaking with the extra cost of subsequently re-starting it' (OECD, 1999: 44).

This focuses attention on the impact of EU regulations on policy makers and policy making in Ireland. While this is more difficult to quantify, a number of consequences have been identified. The creation and regulation of a European single market, with the intensification of pressures towards liberalisation, including the removal of barriers to trade, introduced rules and regulations encouraging competition that have had a major impact on the Irish economy. This is evident in the ending of legal monopolies in the telecommunications, energy, waste and transport sectors, and the development of the Competition Authority and a number of other national regulatory authorities. O'Brennan argues that the liberalisation of the services sector was forced by Brussels on reluctant Irish policy makers, who were dragging their heels in this regard. The benefits in areas like air travel were immediately evident, with very significant decreases in air fares and big increases in passenger numbers. As he writes:

> Thus although Irish governments retained complete autonomy over much of the economy it can be demonstrated that in some crucial areas EU membership provided Dublin with the instruments necessary to provide a more competitive and pluralistic impulse within previously bounded and state-dominated markets. (O'Brennan 2010: 385)

In tracing what he calls the 'reinvention of Ireland' (1999: 32), O'Donnell has made a set of wider claims for the impact of the EU, writing that 'European integration and governance have been centrally important in the economic transformation', particularly through 'the alignment of state strategy with the action of economic and social interests' (2000: 162). From the traumatic experience of the 1980s emerged 'a new perspective on Ireland's position in European integration and a globalising economy' which resulted in the successes of the Celtic Tiger (ibid.: 177). He identifies European influences on the emergence of social partnership, such as the need to adhere to the disciplines of the European Monetary System and the lessons learnt by many Irish business and trade union leaders from the consensus-based approaches to economic governance in many European countries. He sees the combination of social partnership with the European internal market programme as being particularly benign, as the latter 'produced a steady pressure to make public utilities and services more efficient, consumer-oriented and independent of overt or covert state subsidy or protection' (ibid.: 183). As a result, 'Ireland's approach to market regulation, and the relationship between market, state and society, has been significantly reshaped by membership of the EU'; he sees this as 'a major change in Irish public administration and policy' (ibid.: 184). He credits EU structural funds with acting as 'a stimulus to policy innovation and experimentation' (ibid.: 187) by reintroducing developmental thinking and procedures to the Irish public service, by creating a culture of monitoring and evaluation, and by helping decentralise policymaking. While such impacts on policy making can be traced, the collapse of the Irish economy in 2008 and the failure of policy makers to recognise the emerging problems and address them indicate that the transformations claimed by O'Donnell were less widespread or enduring than he implies.

The other major impact of EU membership relates to Ireland's decision to join the euro when it was created in 1999. This gave monetary stability at the height of the Celtic Tiger boom which, with the depreciation of the euro against both the pound sterling and the US dollar in the years following its creation, added to Ireland's export competitiveness. However, membership of the euro also helped fuel the property bubble that eventually brought the Irish economy to its collapse. In their report for the minister for finance already referred to in Chapter 4, international financial experts Regling and Watson pose the question: 'Was it a coincidence that Ireland's economic fundamentals began to deteriorate when Ireland joined the euro area?' (Regling and Watson 2010: 24). They argue that certain aspects of EMU membership

> certainly reinforced vulnerabilities in the economy. Short-term interest rates fell by two thirds from the early and mid-1990s to the period 2002–07. Long-term interest rates halved and real interest rates were negative from 1999 to 2005 after having been strongly positive. (Ibid.: 24)

This situation contributed to the credit boom in Ireland, since low interest rates encouraged borrowing and the removal of exchange rate risk facilitated the banks in accessing foreign funding, ensuring that the flow of credit could continue. In this situation, official policies and banking practices faced key challenges, with 'scope to mitigate the risks of a boom–bust cycle through prudent fiscal and supervisory policies, as well as strong bank governance – thus raising the chances of a "soft landing" for the property market and for society at large' (ibid.: 5). However, the authors conclude that policy instruments such as fiscal policy, bank regulation and income policy 'were not used to offset the well-known expansionary effects of EMU membership on the macroeconomic environment or even fueled the fire, in particular tax policies' (ibid.: 24–5). This lays the blame on the failure of Irish policy makers to appreciate the particular requirements of policy making in a currency union, rather than on membership of that union in itself. For Regling and Watson add that being a member of a large monetary union 'helped Ireland to survive better the global financial crisis', since without it funding problems for the banking sector would have become bigger, firms and households would have borrowed more in foreign currency and so would have been exposed to greater risks (as happened in Iceland), and coordination problems for national central banks would have been significant. They add that 'none of the interlocutors in Ireland and abroad, with whom the authors of this report talked, questioned that EMU membership for Ireland has been, on balance, highly beneficial' (ibid.: 25). However, it needs to be asserted that Ireland's crisis was facilitated by membership of the euro. If Ireland had kept its own currency the crisis could not have happened, for two reasons: the first is that the lack of access Irish banks would have had to the levels of liquidity that allowed them to lend so extravagantly would have meant that such an inflated housing bubble would not have been possible, nor could the banks have taken on such high levels of indebtedness; the second is that, based on historical precedent, interest rates would have been set at a higher level by the Central Bank of Ireland, thus curbing the extravagance in property development.

It can be concluded therefore that membership of the EU and the euro certainly played a role in creating the conditions for the boom of the Celtic Tiger, creating virtuous circles in three particular dimensions of Ireland's macroeconomic situation: firstly its access to the European market, which was a major attraction for US multinationals to establish themselves in Ireland; secondly, the very significant levels of investment in Ireland's infrastructure and human resources that allowed the country to avail itself of such high levels of foreign investment; and thirdly, the exchange rate stability offered by membership of the euro, which began to become operative from the mid 1990s onwards. Claims about the impact of EU policy-making procedures and culture on Irish policy makers remain rather more speculative; there is much evidence to show that they did have a certain impact, but this tends to be overstated by some observers; from the vantage point of today it is clear that, whatever changes took place in the culture of Irish policy making, they were not deep or extensive enough to avoid the major failures by policy makers in not taking steps to address the growing vulnerabilities in the housing and banking sectors. On the other hand, it needs to be borne in mind that none of these factors was sufficient in itself to transform the Irish economy; this was due much more to the success of policy makers in attracting such high levels of foreign investment in high-tech sectors. It was these that acted as the engine of the Irish boom. It is perhaps fair to conclude that the EU was a necessary but not a sufficient condition for the Celtic Tiger.

AMBIGUOUS IMPACTS

Most analyses of Ireland's membership of the EU and the impact of that membership on the country's development tend to limit themselves to identifying the positive and negative features, as has been done in the previous two sections. Yet, a time of major crisis in Ireland's political economy requires a deeper probing of why the failures so evident in the Irish political and administrative system identified in earlier chapters of this book can have persisted, even as the EU is claimed to have had such a positive impact. The purpose of this section, therefore, is to probe more deeply some of the ambiguities evident in how the EU has impacted on Ireland and in how Ireland has viewed its membership.

A key feature of how Ireland has benefited from the EU that is rarely recognised is that it has in effect provided the country with significant resources to invest in social and infrastructural development, resources that would otherwise have had to be found by the Irish state itself. While at one level this can be seen as a major benefit, the effects of this on the state's longer-term options has been identified by some analysts as allowing it to avoid some hard decisions. As Adshead and Robinson put it, in Ireland 'the role of traditional developmental state was displaced on to the European Union, which channelled investment into infrastructural projects without the need for the Irish state to curtail consumption to finance developments to underpin general economic growth'. As a result, 'international economic liberalisation enabled the Irish state to "free ride" on the benefit of globalisation (in the form of access to global financial markets and to foreign direct investment)' (Adshead and Robinson 2009: 18). The former chief economist of the Central

Bank of Ireland, Michael Casey, identifies the consequences of this ability of the Irish state to 'free ride':

> In fact, our economic history is to some degree a story of soft options. There were lavish agricultural price subsidies for years after we joined the EEC; then there were structural funds, followed by generous cohesion funds from the EU. In the late 1970s and early 1980s we relied to an extremely high degree on 'expansionary' budgets and relentless increases in foreign borrowing ... Then we came to depend on FDI, including the jobs and tax revenues created by the International Financial Services Centre. There were also two periods when our exporters made easy gains from devaluations of the currency. But no one in government could see the artificial nature of all of these soft options. There was a belief that we could dine out on free lunches in perpetuity. There was no attempt to devise an alternative industrial model, a plan B. (Casey 2009)

Central to the 'soft options' made by the Irish state was the attempt to square the circle of the need on the one hand for significant investment in upgrading infrastructure and social services to catch up with more-developed European countries while, on the other, maintaining a low-tax economy. This is what EU investment allowed the Irish state to achieve; the collapse has shown up dramatically just how short-sighted and unsustainable it was. Boyle, in his study of the state's labour market agency, FÁS (An Foras Áiseanna Saothair) identifies a similar logic to the state's actions. FÁS was unusual among such European agencies because of the breadth of its responsibilities. Through establishing its own channels of communication with Brussels and through convincing Irish officials that it could spend EU funds effectively, it succeeded in winning a third of the total funds the state received in the first Delors round of EU structural funds (1989–93) and a quarter in the second round (1994–99). Boyle identifies as follows the basic reason for this high level of support from state officials: '[T]he Irish state quickly learned that it could address myriad problems cheaply and effectively by using FÁS. Other government departments and agencies became increasingly bypassed and FÁS became an all-purpose solution to various problems' (Boyle 2005: 71). What is most telling about Boyle's account, however, is his description of the agency as the 'Swiss Army knife of the Irish state', because 'it performs myriad functions, none of them well' (ibid.: 113). Furthermore, since

Boyle wrote his account, FÁS has been embroiled in a very public controversy about its lavish spending on foreign travel and the general wastefulness of its expenditure, to such an extent that a decision was made by the outgoing government at the end of 2010 to close the agency down. The example of FÁS indicates that EU funds had the effect of perpetuating long-standing habits of Irish state officials and senior politicians to seek relatively easy solutions, rather than to engage more profoundly with problems and develop longer-term strategies to resolve them – the 'soft option' as Casey calls it. All this is consistent with the populist political culture that is such a hallmark of the Fianna Fáil party and, partly through FF's dominance of the Irish state, of that state itself. Therefore, the positive assessment of the EU's contribution to Ireland's development needs to be severely tempered by the recognition that it served to perpetuate rather than transform a fundamental weakness of the Irish state.

The collapse of the Celtic Tiger also raises questions about the extent to which EU membership has served to transform Irish economic decision making and social policy. Laffan and O'Mahony claim that 'deep effects' of EU-style policy processes are evident in 'multi-annual programming, cross-sectoral policy-making, goal setting and evaluation' (Laffan and O'Mahony 2008: 149). The Open Method of Coordination (OMC) introduced in the Lisbon Treaty in 2009 has also impacted to a degree on Irish economic governance. However, its potential to have a positive impact depends on the capacity of the domestic policy community to use the OMC indicators as political tools to lobby for improved domestic performance. Evidence shows that the Irish policy community remains relatively insular, strategically using European and international discourse to selectively amplify domestic policy agendas. In a case study of social security, M.P. Murphy (2006) seeks to isolate the influence of international policy actors in the area of social security policy. She finds that while the OECD and the EU were influencing employment policy, the EU social inclusion policy and the World Bank pensions policy, none influences policy discourse as powerfully as might be expected in such a globalised state. Rather, these ideas are diluted as they become processed through domestic political institutions and a populist political culture that is immune to 'radical' policy prescriptions. The Irish state tends selectively to filter its engagement with international social security discourse, ensuring always that Irish policymakers are in control. As Smith puts it: 'I think maybe we are inclined to invoke

Europe… when actually the lines of policy are what we would do anyway' (Smith 2005: 183). This indicates that involvement in EU processes may serve to obscure just how much continuity there is in the ways policy is made at domestic level, distracting from the urgent need for reform.

What of Social Europe and the next stage of the OMC? Ó Cinnéide (2010:18) reflects that an important aspect of the EU is its 'recognition of the existence of poverty in the midst of plenty' and that this aspect of EU policy has in fact been significantly influenced by Ireland. EU policy on social inclusion has subsequently influenced policy in Ireland. Yet, despite progress in many areas, Europe has underperformed in the broader fight against poverty, exclusion and inequality (EAPN 2010: 8). Will the new Lisbon 2020 and its goals of poverty reduction, high employment and literacy make any difference in Ireland? Social Justice Ireland (2011) argues that Lisbon 2020 is underpinned by a false analysis and the same narrow economic understanding of human development as Lisbon 2010. It adds that not only are the targets relatively meaningless and inadequate given the scale of the problem to be addressed, but they will be overshadowed by the policy agenda and conditions in the EU/ECB/IMF Memorandum of Understanding, which will take political precedence over any anti-poverty or equality targets (see below). Johnston (2010) advises that while the EU OMC can offer tools and processes with which to work, it is not implementation instruments but a country's model of development and political priorities which ultimately determine whether the overall objective of poverty reduction can be met. She argues that the biggest threat to social inclusion and to what can be achieved through an OMC is the larger macro-political economy approach of the Europe Union which is further discussed below.

The ambiguities highlighted here draw attention to a feature of Irish attitudes towards the European project that has been widely commented upon domestically over the years since Ireland's entry. This is what is often referred to as a 'begging bowl' mentality, evident among politicians and policy makers as well as among the wider public. By this is meant that Irish views have tended to be dominated by what Ireland could gain from Europe, often with little understanding of what the European project was trying to achieve or little interest in contributing to the bigger debates about such issues as intergovernmentalism versus federalism. As Laffan and O'Mahony report, 'Ireland was said to be suffering from a "sponger syndrome", in viewing the EC/EU as a source of additional exchequer funding for a poor member state, Irish politicians and officials possessed a "begging-bowl mentality"' (Laffan and O'Mahony 2008: 31). Irish voters' defeat of the first Lisbon referendum in 2008 was widely viewed in Europe as an indication of the fact that the only interest the Irish had in the EU was to get money and, having grown rich with the Celtic Tiger boom, they now felt they could turn their backs on it. However inaccurate these views were in the light of the complex and contradictory reasons for the 'No' vote at the time, they did capture some deeper attitudes that were widespread. Interestingly, the more recent experience of having had to rely on a financial rescue package from the EU and the European Central Bank has fuelled a strong criticism of the EU even among very pro-European political elites, owing to what are perceived as the draconian conditions attached to the loan and the refusal of Europe to shoulder some of the burden. On closer examination, therefore, the largely positive evaluation of the EU's impact on Ireland needs to be tempered by a recognition that it has also permitted a postponement of badly needed reforms to the state's decision-making processes, political system and political culture.

CONCLUSION: IRELAND IN EUROPE – TOWARDS A NEW MODEL?

To what extent, therefore, is Europe going to help or hinder the emergence of a new republic that lays the foundations for a new political economy model, as argued for in this book? An answer to this question must first of all focus on the neoliberalisation of the European project itself, which has moved away from its much vaunted 'social market' model to become much more friendly towards the needs of global corporations. The original Schuman Plan that led to the foundation of the European Coal and Steel Community, the forerunner of the European Union, was 'inspired by the notion of coordination and cooperation rather than market-mediated competition' (Hermann 2007: 10); and even when the objective of a free-trade area came to the fore, with the establishment of the EEC in 1957, it was combined with the right of national authorities to intervene to stabilise the national economy. Commentators see the relaunch of the Single European Market project in 1984 as 'the decisive moment turning the European integration process towards neoliberalism' (ibid.: 11); however, in its early phase this project involved a debate between those who supported a completely free-market or neoliberal project and those who saw it as aiming to create European champions to compete on the global market, thereby requiring more state protection and interference than would be compatible with neoliberalism. A key proponent of a more neoliberal Europe at the time was the relaunched European Round Table of Industrialists (ERT) representing Europe's most powerful corporations. Over the course of the 1990s the project moved decisively towards greater deregulation and the liberalisation of trade policies; not only did these become predominant within the EU but the Union also required them of other countries with which it was negotiating free-trade agreements. This dynamic also tended to undermine standards in the fields of labour and social policies. As Hay et al. have written, 'the *positive integration* or *upward harmonisation* envisaged by the likes of Delors himself was always likely to yield to *negative integration or downward harmonisation* to something approximating a lowest-common-denominator level ... In this sense, economic integration itself implies a certain neoliberalisation and a residualisation of social models' (quoted in Hermann 2007: 13; italics in original). The steady advance of neoliberalisation can be seen in such developments as a European competition policy, which resulted in the liberalisation of public services in areas such as transportation, telecommunications, electricity, postal services and gas. These created the conditions for strong private-sector companies to emerge in these areas and then to become major global players; but they also had the effect of eroding protections to security of employment and working conditions. Economic and Monetary Union (EMU) is another area in which the neoliberalisation of the Union has advanced substantially and which is now clear to see in the conditions of Ireland's rescue package, as is discussed below. In conclusion, these developments can be summed up as follows:

> Major policy issues such as the Single Market Strategy, European competition policy, Economic and Monetary Integration and even the European Employment Strategy have enhanced 'free' trade and 'free' capital mobility, monetary restraint and budgetary austerity, the flexibilisation of labour markets and the erosion of employment security. In some areas, including monetary and fiscal policies, Euro-zone member states have gone further in following the neoliberal agenda than even the neoliberal front-runners, the US and UK. Contrary to the rhetoric of the European Social Model it was precisely the integration process that allowed policy makers, backed by leading sections of European capital, to circumvent and erode the social rights that were achieved in the

postwar decades and that represented the essence of the various
European social models. (Hermann 2007: 25)

The impact of these developments on Ireland has already been
discussed. However, they have largely been viewed in a positive
light – as shaking up entrenched state monopolies, as imposing
new disciplines on policy makers and as offering monetary stability.
While critics have raised issues about the imposition of neoliberal
policies during EU referendum campaigns, there is little evidence
that these have had a lasting impact on the attitudes of the majority
towards Europe. Indeed, during the Celtic Tiger boom, these
liberalising measures were seen as a major contribution to the Irish
success. However, the events of autumn 2010, when the European
Commission, urged by the European Central Bank, effectively forced
Ireland into a rescue package that has evoked a widespread anger
and sense of unfairness, had suddenly exposed the concerns that
have come to dominate the European project. A revealing exchange
that took place in the European Parliament on 19 January 2011
illustrates well the difference of opinion that exists. The Socialist
MEP for Dublin, Joe Higgins, attacked the rescue package, calling it
a mechanism to turn Irish taxpayers into vassals of European banks,
and he questioned the morality of transferring to taxpayers the
responsibility for the banks' bad debts. The package was, he said,
no more than a tool for cushioning banks from the consequences of
reckless speculation. Clearly angry, the Commission president, José
Manuel Barroso, replied that 'the problems of Ireland were created
by the irresponsible financial behaviour of some Irish institutions and
by the lack of supervision in the Irish market' (Beesley 2011: 1). What
made this exchange particularly interesting was the letter written
soon afterwards by former taoiseach and former EU ambassador
to Washington, John Bruton, to the Commission president, telling
him that his criticisms of Irish institutions were fully justified, but
that he was telling only one part of the story, as British, German,
Belgian, American and French banks, as well as the banks of other
EU countries, 'lent irresponsibly to the Irish banks in the hope
that they too could profit from the Irish construction bubble', and
that they 'must take some share of responsibility for the mistakes
that were made'. Furthermore, referring to the responsibility of
the European Commission for supervising the Irish economy, he
wrote: 'You ought to have acknowledged that responsibility of your
own institution, which the Commission shares with ECOFIN'. He
added that the ECB kept interest rates low, 'pursuing interest rate

policies that were unsuitable for Ireland' (Bruton 2011). This letter, from a strongly pro-European senior Irish politician, accurately reflects the widespread view in Ireland that the country has been unfairly treated by both the Commission and the ECB. Indeed, it appears from the evidence of members of the Irish government who negotiated the rescue package that an attempt was made by the Irish negotiators to get the European institutions to share some of the burden of adjustment with Irish taxpayers, but that this was not accepted. Instead, the complete burden of dealing with the banking crisis has been placed on the shoulders of the Irish state, a burden that is widely believed to be severely undermining the prospects of emerging from the crisis. The burden being imposed on Irish taxpayers to ensure that European banks get repaid for their risky investments at the cost of a lengthy period of severe austerity for Irish citizens shows the extent to which the EU now functions as a mechanism for protecting the economic interests of large companies rather than the social interests of citizens.

One of the great paradoxes of the situation in which Ireland now finds itself is that it has consistently supported a model of light-touch regulation and of relatively weak social provision, and was a pioneer in fashioning a low-tax model. In particular, it was the first to adopt a very low rate of corporation tax, afterwards copied by some of the new members from central and eastern Europe, and has staunchly resisted any moves by the EU to harmonise tax rates. As a champion of a neoliberal EU, therefore, it is now among the countries that are most severely suffering the consequences of prioritising corporate profits and balanced budgets over social need and national development. However, Ireland is also the country that is to a large extent responsible for plunging the European integration project into a major crisis and exposing the weaknesses of the common currency. For, as the lender of last resort within the eurozone, it is the ECB that has found itself haemorrhaging funds to support the Irish banks. It was the Bank's growing awareness that Ireland, a country with about 1 per cent of the EU's GDP, had ended up with more than 20 per cent of the ECB's lending by late 2010 that prompted a dramatic and sudden change in policy. Murphy argues that this emerged from the ECB's desire for a new mechanism to relieve it of some of the burden of its function as lender of last resort to the Irish banking system. He writes: 'As a result the Irish crisis, which has been initially a fiscal/funding crisis as highlighted by the bond markets, shifted to a full-scale crisis about the liquidity and solvency of the Irish banking system' (A. Murphy 2010: 3). It was the ECB's decision to discontinue lending to Irish banks, and to seek a new arrangement from the European Commission and the IMF to provide an alternative bailout strategy, that in November 2010 forced the Irish government to negotiate an €85 billion package of financial assistance, made up of €10 billion for recapitalisation of the banks, a €25 billion bank contingency fund and a €50 billion sum to support the state's borrowing requirements for the next three years. And, as pressure mounted in Ireland in early 2011 to renegotiate the package to gain more favourable terms, it was seen in Dublin that of the three partners in the deal – the EU, the ECB and the IMF – it was the two European members that were proving the least flexible.

Yet if Europe is being seen as saving its own skin at Ireland's expense, leaders such as the German chancellor Angela Merkel and French president Nicolas Sarkozy realise that the crisis requires a deeper reform of Europe's institutions to address the weaknesses that have been shown up in the single currency. Apart from enlarging the scale and scope of the present European Financial Stability Fund and making it permanent, both are seeking to deepen European policy coordination, to ensure that this type of crisis does not occur again. It is this coordination which will most impact on the Irish model. From an Irish point of view, the most prominent issue they are targeting is Ireland's low rate of corporation tax. French and German politicians and officials have long resented Ireland's ability to avail itself of generous European grants, while at the same time, due to its low corporation tax, undercutting the ability of other countries to compete for foreign investment. This is seen as one element of Ireland's low-tax model, and European leaders have made it clear since the outset of the crisis that Ireland has to increase its levels of taxation to European levels. However, Germany in particular would like to see more extensive coordination of taxation and fiscal policy, with tough rules for debts and deficits, and even common labour laws and retirement age across the EU. This is seen as the price to be paid for a permanent rescue package for countries in difficulties, which, in the Irish case, might result in an easing of the onerous conditions of its package. In the longer run, however, such a coordination of policy will impose more of a common model throughout the EU and, if standards are harmonised to the level of Germany, will ensure more adequate levels of exchequer financing and the inability to resort to the sort of bubble-based financing that landed Ireland in the mess it is in. Furthermore, Merkel realises that bondholders must be asked to shoulder part of the burden of adjustment; the difficulty arises in deciding how this can be done in a highly liberalised financial system, in which bondholders can use their financial transactions to punish countries which seek to impose burdens on them. To achieve this objective will require greater transnational regulation of financial markets, thus curbing some of the worst excesses of liberalisation over recent decades. None of these actions on their own will ensure that a more equitable and sustainable model of development will emerge in Ireland; but they will create the conditions for more adequate levels of taxation to underpin a more capable state with a greater ability to make the social and economic transformations that are necessary. Whether this ever happens will require new political leadership and institutions at a domestic level. These challenges are addressed in Chapters 9 and 10.

8
Reykjavik and Beyond

'What is the difference between Ireland and Iceland,' went the joke at the height of the Irish crisis. 'One letter and six months,' was the response. Though the banking crisis in both countries emerged at around the same time, in September 2008, it took somewhat longer for the severity of the Irish crisis to manifest itself, hence the reference to six months. Writing in the *New York Times* in November 2010, Nobel economics prize-winner Paul Krugman referred to this joke and added that

> at this point Iceland seems, if anything, to be doing better than its near-namesake. Its economic slump was no deeper than Ireland's, its job losses were less severe and it seems better positioned for recovery. In fact, investors now appear to consider Iceland's debt safer than Ireland's.

Wondering how this was possible, Krugman pointed to a number of differences between Iceland and Ireland: Iceland let foreign lenders to its banks pay the price of their poor judgement, whereas Ireland made its taxpayers carry the burden through its bank guarantee; Iceland helped avoid a financial panic, in part by imposing temporary capital controls; and, by devaluing its currency, the krona, Icelandic exports became more competitive. He ended his article by pointing out that, after three years of austerity, confidence in Ireland keeps draining away (Krugman 2010).

The comparison with Iceland reminds us that, even in this deeply interconnected globalised world, the sorts of decision made by national governments matter greatly and make a huge difference to outcomes achieved. We have therefore a lot to learn from comparing the decisions made by Irish governments in dealing with the current crisis with those in other comparable countries. This will help to identify the strengths and weaknesses of the Irish case, allowing more robust lessons to be drawn, which can inform the proposals for a second republic to be discussed in Chapters 9 and 10. Since Ireland has been regarded as among the most globalised countries in the world, this chapter begins by considering how this may limit the room for manoeuvre of Irish governments, and then goes on to consider another dimension of Ireland's situation that has been rarely given attention, namely its size. Do small states face particular challenges, and if so, how should they respond? Following these two opening sections, the chapter then examines a number of regions and countries. The third section looks at Latin America, a region plagued with severe financial and economic crises over its history. How has the present global crisis impacted on that region and how has Latin America managed to avoid the deep recession that affects North America and Europe? Following an overview of the region, a number of countries are singled out for more detailed examination. Two of these are small countries and therefore comparable to Ireland: Costa Rica and Uruguay. The third is Argentina, a country that experienced an extreme financial, economic and social collapse at the beginning of the 2000s but which has recovered very well since. The Argentine case has been referred to in Irish debates on whether debt default is desirable, as the government of Nestor Kirchner did effectively default on part of Argentina's debt and burn bondholders. This therefore merits examination. The fourth section compares Ireland and Iceland, focusing in particular on the claims made by Krugman that the actions of the Icelandic government have helped stimulate a more solid recovery. The following section looks at three other states to which Ireland has been compared in the present crisis: Finland, a small state that experienced a severe economic and banking crisis in the early 1990s; New Zealand, a small state which strongly neoliberalised its economy in the 1980s and which the OECD has presented as a model for Ireland; and Spain, an EU country that is facing a banking crisis which some analysts compare to that of Ireland. The final section draws conclusions.

IRELAND AND GLOBALISATION

Ireland's Celtic Tiger boom provided commentators with an ideal model to emphasise the benefits of globalisation. The concept of globalisation entered into academic and then public discourse around the time that Ireland's success also began to gain national and international attention. As the Irish boom was clearly linked to high levels of foreign investment, an expanding export sector, and the attraction of large numbers of migrant workers, it provided an excellent example to illustrate the benefits of globalisation. The influential globalisation index, published in the US *Foreign Policy* journal from 2001 to 2007, provided firm evidence that Ireland was one of the most globalised countries in the world; it occupied first place three years in a row (2002–04) and was always within the top six countries (see Kearney 2007, 2006, 2005, 2004, 2003, 2002, 2001). It is not surprising then that, in her book on the political economy of Ireland, Smith describes Ireland as 'perhaps *the* test case for globalisation' (Smith 2005: 2; emphasis in original), though she concludes that 'it is possible to understand Ireland's developmental trajectory without any reference to globalisation in analytical terms' (ibid.: 143), since the economy was an open liberal economy long before globalisation began to be employed. Far from being globalised, she argues that what was happening in the Irish case was a deeper integration into the US and particularly the EU economy; though why this did not merit being described as an aspect of the globalisation of the Irish economy is not clear from her book. What is most interesting about Smith's book is the evidence she assembles that many senior Irish policy makers welcomed globalisation and viewed it in an entirely positive light, failing to recognise any of its ambiguities or the challenges it posed to domestic policy makers (as has been mentioned in Chapter 4, these failures are highlighted in the report on the Irish banking crisis written by international financial experts Klaus Regling and Max Watson).

In seeking to benefit from globalisation, therefore, the Irish state played a decisive role in structuring the relationship between state and market. As Regling and Watson conclude (and as was outlined in Chapter 4), the state facilitated the freedoms given to the banking sector; it spurred the housing boom, and it put in place a light-touch regulatory system, seeking to encourage the market rather than restrain it. To this extent, the Irish case was sometimes seen as being an alternative to neoliberalism, because of the active role played by the state. However, this overlooks the fact that the state actively handed power to the market, abdicating to private market actors key responsibility for national development, with consequences that have been disastrous. All of this echoes themes that became common in the literature on the impact of globalisation, as experts argued that the pressures of international competitiveness, the mobility of capital worldwide, and intensified international trade were eroding the power of the state (Pierson 2004:100–2). Ruggie argues that the globalisation of financial markets and production chains challenged the premises on which the grand bargain between capital and labour rested, since that bargain presupposed a world in which the state could effectively mediate external impacts, through such tools as tariffs and exchange rates (Ruggie 2003: 94). In this situation, welfare states found themselves under pressure to reduce costs and erode the level and extent of protection they previously provided. Cerny describes the ways in which state actors, both politicians and bureaucrats, reacted to the pressures of the global market by 'promoting the competitive advantages of particular production and service sectors in a more open and integrated world economy' (Cerny 2000: 22). He saw a 'competition state' emerging out of the tensions between the demands of economic globalisation and the embedded state or society practices that had characterised the national welfare state. As a consequence, and through the public action of states, 'those rules that favour global market expansion have become more robust and enforceable' (such as intellectual property rights or World Trade Organisation trade dispute resolutions), while, at the same time, 'rules intended to promote equally valid social objectives, be they labour standards, human rights, environmental quality or poverty reduction, lag behind and in some instances actually have become weaker' (Ruggie 2003: 96–7).

Yet, while the pressures that globalisation was imposing on states were being identified, states were reacting in different ways, depending on the capacity of their political and administrative systems, their political cultures, the economic basis of state power, and of course the pressures from organised civil society. In the Irish case, as is now clear to many, the state abdicated to these pressures in ways that were evident to some before the collapse happened. Writing in the mid 2000s, O'Sullivan describes 'the lop-sided nature of globalisation in Ireland' (M. O'Sullivan 2006: 128) – lop-sided because it has not been harnessed to spread wealth to the parts of society that need it most. He identifies the major challenges facing Irish policy makers: the first is to derive growth from new sources and minimise the risks to the drivers of economic performance during the Celtic Tiger period; the second is 'to spread the benefits of growth in a more far-sighted manner' (ibid.: 98). He recognises that these tasks would require a greater role for the state, an increase in taxes to yield more resources for the state, and a reform of state institutions to make them more effective. He focuses on the challenge for policy makers who 'operate with a limited policy arsenal', but who have the opportunity to distinguish themselves through innovations in policy to develop 'a discernible Irish model of economic management' (ibid.: 99). However, it took the collapse to alert politicians, policy makers and the general public to the important need to use power in a more deliberate way to counteract many of the negative pressures of globalisation. It can be concluded, therefore, that Irish elites have adjusted to the pressures of a globalised world in a very uncritical and naive way. Accepting the opportunities of globalisation, they failed to appreciate the need to use state power in a way that strengthened national capacities and minimised the many vulnerabilities that derive from the extreme openness of an economy and society like that of Ireland. It can be concluded that, far from undermining state power, globalisation challenges political elites to a more sophisticated use of that power. In this, Ireland's elites failed catastrophically.

SMALL STATES: DEALING WITH VULNERABILITIES

In this context, it is useful to draw on the insights of political scientists who have been focusing on the issue of size, namely that small states face particular challenges in dealing with pressures that come from outside. Though it is a small state, the Republic of Ireland is not a micro-state, and size has rarely been employed as an analytical category through which to analyse it. Connaughton (2010) broke new ground in applying the small-states literature to the Irish case, concluding that while Ireland fits the small-state classification in terms of its geographical location in Europe, as 'an island behind an island', in terms of demographic, economic and social factors, its profile is more mixed. Its population of around 4.2 million makes it rather large in comparison to those states normally classified as 'small states' (Iceland, Malta, Andorra, Lichtenstein, San Marino); but Connaughton concludes that the structural openness of its economy and the significant role of trade in its economic structure and growth correspond well with the experiences of small states. She concludes, therefore, that characteristics that set small states apart from large ones, such as a strategy of greater international liberalisation, concertative policy-making institutions (known in Ireland as social partnership), the centralisation of policy making, personalism, fewer specialists, and a predisposition to informal policy coordination are all evident in the Irish case.

Another example of focusing on the issue of size is seen in the work of Katzenstein, who analysed the economic challenges facing a range of European small states (this time the Nordic states, Austria and Switzerland). He identifies a common feature of small states as being 'the perception of vulnerability, economic and otherwise.

Perceived vulnerability generated an ideology of social partnership that had acted like a glue for the corporatist politics of the small European states.' This, he adds, was the most important explanatory variable for the economic and social success of small states in his earlier book (Katzenstein 2006; first published 1985), but was largely missed by reviewers (Katzenstein 2003: 11). In her review of how the small-states literature applies to Ireland, Connaughton writes:

> The case of Ireland appears to comply with explanations that successful small states are likely to be more vulnerable to exogenous economic shocks and higher risks as their growth path is more unstable than that of larger states. The resilience to the impact of such shocks will greatly depend on a combination of endogenous resources and appropriate policies. (Connaughton 2010: 114)

For Katzenstein, the various forms of corporatist arrangement, what he calls 'the voluntary and informal cross-issue policy coordination' (Katzenstein 2003: 12), is what sets small states apart from large ones and allows them flexibly and successfully to respond to the demands of a fast-changing international environment.

Just before the Irish collapse, the Danish political scientist, Georg Sørensen, comparing the Irish and Danish models, drew attention to the fact that 'the Danish model has been developed and strengthened by having to cope with several major challenges, including two world wars and the economic crisis of the 1930s', whereas 'the successful Irish model has not faced a real critical challenge so far; it's been all smooth sailing in sunshine and tailwinds' (Sørensen 2010: 240). He was not hopeful that the Irish model would prove resilient when faced with difficulties. His prediction proved prescient: in December 2009 the general secretary of the Irish Congress of Trade Unions, David Begg, said that the government's withdrawal from talks earlier that month 'drove a stake through the heart of social partnership as a concept' (Carroll and Wall 2009). Katzenstein wrote that concertative structures 'encourage flexibility, collaboration, and the absorption of the political consequences of economic dislocations' and offer 'an institutional mechanism for mobilizing the consensus necessary to live with the costs of rapid economic change' (Katzenstein 2006: 200, 201). Yet, the fact that in the Irish case they broke down so quickly when put to their first real test raises questions about how well Irish policy makers have equipped themselves to manage the vulnerabilities that derive from being a small state that is very open to international pressures. An answer can be sought in the way the state has used its power within partnership. Firstly, as Hardiman highlights, the initiative within social partnership has always rested with government, which has never allowed it to limit its budgetary freedom. She finds that 'any prospect of a real trade-off between disposable income and improvement in social services is, for the most part, marginal to the negotiations' (Hardiman 2006: 359). Connolly draws similar conclusions. Finding that social objectives within social partnership have remained vague and aspirational, she writes:

> By 2003 it seemed clear that although social partnership contained strongly institutionalised ideas about both the form anti-poverty policy should take and its relationship to the state's other policy priorities, it was not a place where such policy was formulated and discussed. The over-arching policy ideas that informed social partnership also appeared to some to constitute a straightjacket on policy reform with any increased social welfare effort effectively defined as anti-competitive in this paradigm. (Connolly 2007: 32)

In other words, it can be concluded that a narrow business-friendly consensus was imposed by the state; this suited the employers' groups – deliberation was reduced to relatively minor issues of concessions on social spending and rights, but never allowed to revise, even in very modest ways, the dominant free-market development paradigm.

As a small state extremely open to the flows of globalisation, therefore, Ireland faced particular challenges in managing these in ways that maximised the benefits to Irish society, but that also built resilience in the face of the vulnerabilities that these benefits inevitably bring with them. It is paradoxical that the Irish state developed the sort of concertative mechanisms that Katzenstein found to characterise the successful Nordic states, Austria and Switzerland, but used these in a way that favoured one set of interests and that actually undermined state and social capacity. This derives in large part from the failure of policy makers and politicians to appreciate the challenges facing them in the much more globalised international environment that emerged from the early 1990s onwards. Certain features of small states may have exacerbated these problems, since the centralisation of policy making, personalism, the lack of specialists who might have understood better the risks involved, and a predisposition to informal policy coordination can all be seen to be features of the Irish state. These features tend to discourage sharp debate and disagreement within policy-making circles and favour the emergence of a consensus that is rarely challenged from within (see Chapter 3). And, in relating to interests and activists outside the state machinery, the bureaucrats ensured that dissenting voices were marginalised and went unheeded.

LATIN AMERICA: AVOIDING COLLAPSE

In examining how well other states have fared with these challenges, Latin America is a good place to begin. As a largely middle-income developing region, in which the state has in the past been used in a very deliberate way to build an industrial base and develop technological skills within the economy, there is a good basis for comparing countries in the region to Ireland. The strong liberalisation of the economies of Latin America since the early 1980s and their desire to benefit from the flows of globalisation through attracting foreign investment offer another basis for comparison (see Kirby 2003). Finally, the region has been subject to severe financial and economic crises over recent decades (in the early 1980s the crisis was a general one; since then individual countries have suffered major financial downturns, such as those in Mexico in 1994 and Argentina in 2001–02, the latter crisis also having a major effect on Uruguay). This section examines how the region as a whole has coped with the most recent global financial crisis, before looking at the particular cases of Argentina, as a state that has resorted to default as a response to its collapse, and Costa Rica and Uruguay, as small states that have weathered the global crisis relatively well.

A general comparison between Latin America and Ireland can begin by looking at the booms that both were experiencing before the financial crises hit. Between 2003 and 2007, Latin America experienced its fastest economic growth since the mid 1970s, resulting in a growth in formal employment, a fall in unemployment and a rapid decline in poverty. As in the case of Ireland, this was caused largely by very favourable external conditions, including access to international financing at historically low costs; many Latin American countries faced growing demand for their primary commodity exports, particularly from China, and some benefited from a high level of remittances from migrant workers. As in Ireland, the real crisis hit with the collapse of Lehman Brothers in the United States and the financial crisis this unleashed, which led to a severe recession in the developed world. Here the difference ends, however. For Latin America, the financial impacts were not as severe as in previous crises, largely due to the positive effects of domestic financial policies. As noted by Ocampo, these included 'strong prudential regulation ... promotion of domestic bond markets, limited dependence of most banking systems on external funding, and reduced dollarization in some countries' (Ocampo 2010: 21). In other words, the banking system in Latin America was better regulated and less vulnerable to external shocks than was that in Ireland. Added to that was a pragmatic use of exchange rate policy by central banks in the region, to absorb part of the initial shock and therefore minimise its impact. To help aid recovery, several countries used public-sector banks to inject credit into the economy, something proposed by the Labour Party in Ireland during the 2011 election campaign. This credit was used to stimulate construction, to invest in small and medium-sized industries, to support agriculture and to develop social policies (Bárcena 2010a: 17). This need for higher state spending resulted in an aggregated fiscal deficit in the region as a whole of –0.3 per cent of GDP in 2008 and –2.8 per cent in 2009, extremely modest compared to Irish deficits in these years. All of these policy instruments diverged from the orthodox policy framework supported by the IMF. From the second half of 2009, industrial production and exports began to recover, indicating the success of these policies. More important in aiding recovery, however, was demand for primary commodities, mainly from China; this helped many South American countries emerge from the crisis swiftly and return to growth. Growth dipped from 4.2 per cent in 2008 to –1.8 per cent in 2009 before recovering to 5.2 per cent in 2010. Overall, the recession between 2008 and 2010 reduced per capita GDP growth for the region as a whole to 0.6 per cent, a much stronger performance than that of the United States and most European countries over this period. However, this aggregate figure hides the fact that the downturn has been much more severe for Mexico and most Central American countries, which depend more on the US market; for most of South America, with the exception of Venezuela and Paraguay, per capita GDP growth averaged closer to 2 per cent over this period. The well-known US economist Nouriel Roubini summed up the prospects for Latin American recovery in December 2009: 'These countries have shown their own resilience. Their economic policies have been sound and they've been able to conduct countercyclical policies' (Roubini 2009).

It is important to move beyond the aggregated performance of the region as a whole to that of individual countries. For Ireland, the experience of Argentina holds important lessons, as it experienced a major financial and economic collapse in 2001–02. Yet it recovered more swiftly than seemed possible at the time and it has weathered the recent recession very well. Among the measures it adopted was a default on part of its debt to bondholders and paying off its debt to the IMF, effectively ending its relationship with the Fund. Similar measures to these were advocated by Sinn Féin and the United Left Alliance in the 2011 Irish election. It is important therefore to examine the means used by Argentina to recover, and whether defaulting on part of its debt contributed positively. After the economic collapse in late 2001, Argentina suspended payments on some $95 billion in foreign debt, the largest sovereign default in history. When Nestor Kirchner became president of Argentina in May 2003 he began negotiations with holders of Argentine bonds. These proved protracted and were only concluded in early 2005, when the government offered bondholders just 30 cents in each dollar for bonds they held if they agreed to swap their old bonds for new ones. Around three quarters of bondholders accepted this deal, saving Argentina $67.3 billion. Furthermore the new debt that it issued was on far more advantageous terms for the country, maturing in 26 years instead of 12, with an interest rate of around 6 per cent instead of 11 per cent, and much of it was denominated in Argentine pesos instead of US dollars, thus avoiding exchange rate risk. Through this means, the country's total foreign debt was reduced from $166.3 billion in 2001 to $107.8 billion in 2006. As a percentage of the country's GDP, this saw a reduction from 153.6 per cent in 2003 to 62 per cent in 2006. At the end of 2006, the Kirchner government went further and paid off all the $9.8 billion debt owed to the IMF – an immensely popular move, since the actions of the Fund in 2001 were widely held to have made the country's economic and financial difficulties far worse.

After a steep economic collapse, with GDP falling by 4.4 per cent in 2001 and a further 10.9 per cent in 2002, growth quickly returned and averaged around 8 per cent a year up to the end of the 2000s. Yet the important question for those in Ireland considering similar actions is whether burning the bondholders helped Argentina to return to growth or not. Examining the components of Argentina's success, Grugel and Riggirozzi point to the contribution made by the large devaluation of the peso in early 2002, adding that 'it was also aided by high international commodity prices for Argentina's principal exports, including soy and oil, the strong growth of world trade and a reduction in the volume of imports into the country'

(Grugel and Riggirozzi 2007: 100). Thus the savings on the debt were only part of the reason for the return to growth. Furthermore, these actions were not without their costs. Over $21 billion of bonds continue to be held by bondholders who refused the 2005 deal, and some of these have brought court cases against Argentina, while the country has faced a decade of isolation from international financial credit, making it impossible to raise investment for high-profile projects like a rapid rail link between the three largest urban centres. The non-payment of loans of $6.7 billion owed to the Paris Club of countries, principally Japan and Germany, has meant that these governments have banned their export-promotion agencies from providing subsidised credit for sales or investments in Argentina. In this situation, the country has had to rely on loans from the Venezuelan government, but interest on these is at a steep 15 per cent. Attempts to reach agreement with creditors has continued to cause serious political difficulties for the government of President Cristina Fernandez de Kirchner throughout her presidency from 2007–11. Perhaps the most important lesson from the policies followed by President Nestor Kirchner to pull Argentina out of recession relate not primarily to debt default but, as Grugel and Riggirozzi put it, to the charting of 'a new role for the state', breaking with neoliberalism and promoting 'an alternative project of political and economic governance' for national development (ibid.: 100, 106).

However, Argentina's size as one of the largest countries in the Americas limits the extent to which its actions could be followed by a small country like Ireland. More comparable is its neighbour, Uruguay, whose population of 3.4 million is closer to that of Ireland and which suffered severely from the Argentine crisis of 2001–02. The first left-wing government of Uruguay's history, the Frente Amplio (FA), elected in 2005, entered congressional and presidential elections in 2009 at the height of the international recession, thereby testing just how solid were the left's gains, and with the two traditional parties, the Colorados and the Blancos, sensing a possibility of victory. However, the FA had managed to steer the country through the crisis, maintaining economic growth which averaged 6.3 per cent over the period 2005–09 and an estimated 7.3 per cent in 2010, increasing investment and reducing the burden of debt from 110 per cent of GDP at the time of the 2001–02 crisis to 40 per cent in 2011. In 2008, the FA government had ended banks' self-regulation and created a new centralised supervisor of the whole financial sector, winning the praise of the IMF in late 2009 for the manner in which it regulated its banking system. Economic growth helped reduce unemployment and increase salaries, allowing an extension of social security coverage and anti-poverty programmes that succeeded in reducing poverty by almost a half. Among the government's most imaginative policies was the Plan Ceibal, under which every teacher and pupil in the country's public schools was given a free computer with internet access. Despite controversy surrounding the FA's presidential candidate, José Mujica, outgoing minister for agriculture and a former guerrilla leader, who in party primaries defeated the candidate of the FA leadership, outgoing minister of the economy and finance, Danilo Astori, the FA not only won the presidency (though voting had to go to a second round as no candidate got over 50 per cent of votes in the first round), but also won a majority in both houses of Congress, thus allowing them to dominate parliament until 2014 (Canzani 2010).

Costa Rica is the other small state in Latin America that is comparable to Ireland, having a population of 4.6 million and an enviable history of economic and social development up to the severe recession of the 1980s. While it was hit by the financial and economic crisis, with GDP growth falling from 7.8 per cent in 2007 to 2.6 per cent in 2008 and –0.7 per cent in 2009, this was entirely due to the effect of external factors on the country's exports and foreign investment flows. In addition, its important tourist industry was affected by a decline in the number of US holidaymakers. In response, the Costa Rican government implemented a stimulus package which increased employment in the public sector and helped to counteract the impact of job losses in the private sector: 31,345 jobs were lost in the latter but 29,144 were created in public employment (Rosales 2010: 12). More importantly, this helped to stimulate domestic demand, turning the economy around very quickly. After a decline of 3.5 per cent in annual production in the first half of 2009, by the second half it was showing signs of growth again, which continued to strengthen in 2010. Meanwhile, the banking sector remained strong and credit continued to flow. As the country recovered, attention was turned to addressing the growing fiscal deficit, which had reached 3.3 per cent of GDP at the height of the crisis. President Laura Chinchilla, of the social democratic PLN party, who took office in early 2010, is committed to raising taxes, but is reliant on the strongly free-market Libertarian Movement (ML) party in the Legislative Assembly, which opposes tax increases. Amid this standoff, and with Chinchilla committed to more spending on social programmes, the deficit is expected to widen to 5.3 per cent of GDP in 2011 and the debt burden increase to 50 per cent of GDP from 40 per cent in 2008. These figures, while requiring remedial action, would be the envy of any Irish finance minister. The lessons of these Latin American cases can be summed up in the words of the executive secretary of the UN Economic Commission for Latin America and the Caribbean, Alicia Bárcena:

> Governments didn't rush out, gripped by the panic, to save private banks and fiscal deficits have remained at levels reflecting great responsibility. Unlike previous crises, this time countries in the region were not part of the problem, but part of the solution, and have shown strong signs of fiscal responsibility, financial sobriety and concern for people. (Bárcena 2010b)

The contrast with the actions of the Irish government could not be greater.

IRELAND AND ICELAND: A REVEALING COMPARISON

Inevitably the cases of Ireland and Iceland have merited a lot of attention. Two small island states off the west of Europe, both experienced booms in the 2000s that were interpreted as revealing how successful each was in positioning itself to benefit from the new opportunities opened by globalisation. While traditionally wary of joining the EU, since it feared the constraints it would impose, particularly on its fisheries and agricultural policies, Iceland is part of the European Economic Area, through which, together with Norway and Liechtenstein, it has nearly tariff-free access to the European common market. It fully adopted the EU/EEA rules on financial liberalisation in the early 2000s, interpreting them in a very liberal fashion. Just as in Ireland, a centre–right coalition which ruled the country from 1995 to 2007 adopted a vigorous free-market model, privatising the financial sector and regulating it very lightly. Unlike Ireland, this government also dismantled the country's traditional consensus-building form of corporatism, or social partnership as it is known in Ireland. But the results were similar – GDP growth which reached an annual average of 6.3 per cent in the mid 2000s, a boom in construction which reached about 7 per cent of GDP (about half that of Ireland's at its height), a labour shortage which led to a large influx of immigrants and fuelled a steep increase in wages, and a boom in international investment (both inward and outward). Unlike Ireland, Iceland kept interest rates high to control inflation; this resulted in a large influx of foreign deposits boosting the value of the krona, which in turn made exports expensive and created a large trade deficit. Availing themselves of an overvalued currency, young Icelandic entrepreneurs moved abroad, particularly to Britain, buying up businesses. This was known in Iceland as the 'outvasion', and the entrepreneurial talent it showed was regularly praised by the country's political leaders.

And then came the crash. By March 2008 the krona was already depreciating significantly as markets lost faith in the state's ability to defend it. By September the banking system was collapsing and the state had to step in, firstly to take over two of the three largest banks, Glitnir and Landsbanki, in the hope that the third bank, Kaupthing might be able to weather the storm. When the British government invoked anti-terrorist legislation to take control of assets held by Icelandic banks in Britain, as a way of trying to ensure repayment of its citizens' deposits in Icelandic banks, the Icelandic state had also to take over Kaupthing. The fate of these Icesave online accounts, held by British and Dutch citizens and worth a total of €3.8 billion, was to drag on for years and precipitated a referendum in March 2010 when the president of Iceland refused to sign into law a government deal with Britain and the Netherlands to agree terms of repayment. This was rejected by 93 per cent of voters. A deal more favourable to Iceland was finally agreed in late 2010, though the president's refusal to sign it again prompted a referendum. Meanwhile, GDP declined by 6.8 per cent in 2009, the largest ever recorded in Iceland and inflation peaked at 18.6 per cent as a devalued krona made imports more expensive. Most onerous in the Icelandic case was the fact that, owing to a combination of high domestic interest rates and the overvaluation of the krona, many householders had borrowed in foreign currencies, and they have faced particularly severe stress. As a small island heavily dependent on imports, they also faced price rises, with an increase in food prices of up to 40 per cent between early 2009 and 2011. This has helped push the decline in domestic demand to 36.3 per cent by mid 2010, somewhat more than the low point reached by Ireland a few months later when the decline bottomed out at 27.2 per cent. Other effects were more similar to those experienced in Ireland: unemployment rose to 8.6 per cent in 2010, not as severe as in Ireland due largely to the greater scale that construction had taken on in the Irish case. Nominal property prices have decreased by around 15 per cent, but this is equivalent to a real price decrease of around 40 per cent, somewhat less than the Irish decline of over 50 per cent. The state's budget deficit turned

from a surplus of 5.4 per cent of GDP in 2007 to a record deficit
of 13.5 per cent in 2008, somewhat equivalent to the Irish deficit
in 2009. Government debt increased from 53 per cent of GDP in
2007 to almost 120 per cent in 2009 before declining to under 100
per cent at the end of 2010.

Yet, what really distinguishes Iceland from Ireland is the pace of
its recovery. Despite quite severe problems in accessing loans from
abroad in 2008, late in that year it concluded an agreement with the
IMF and it has also received additional loans from the Nordic states,
Poland and the Faroe Islands. The IMF has reported favourably on
Iceland's progress. The debt ratio is decreasing and the country is well
on its way to reducing its budget deficit; these are seen by the Fund
as significant achievements in such a short time. The IMF expects
GDP growth of 2 per cent in 2011 rising to 3 per cent in 2012, and
a decline in unemployment from 8.3 per cent in 2010 to 7.5 per
cent in 2011 and 5.8 per cent in 2012 (IMF 2011). Two issues merit
attention in comparing the ways Iceland and Ireland have dealt with
their very severe crises. Firstly, the Icelandic authorities took more
immediate and decisive action to reorganise the banking sector,
liquidating the old banks and establishing new banks that took over
domestic deposits and loans, leaving the bondholders with the old
banks. Over time, creditors of Glitnir and Kaupthing are expected
to get some 20 per cent recovery, while creditors of Landsbanki
can expect 5 per cent (Doyle 2009). In this way, an entirely new
banking system was set up overnight, favouring domestic creditors
over foreign ones. In Ireland, by contrast, it took far longer for
the state to face up to the extent of the crisis: after five attempts
to estimate the cost to the state of salvaging the banking sector, it
was only at the end of March 2011, with the announcement of the
results of very severe stress tests on the banks and an estimate of
€70 billion to bail them out, coupled with a decision to restructure
the Irish banking sector on two 'pillars', that there was hope that
a final line might be drawn under the banking crisis. Among the
differences here may be the fact that popular protest forced the
fall of the Icelandic coalition government formed in 2007 between
the conservative Independence Party and the social democrats; a
general election in April 2009 saw a social democratic and Green
party government take office. By contrast, it took almost two further
years before the Irish electorate got a chance, in late February 2011,
to vote out of office the government that had presided over the
crisis. This is one major factor in the greater confidence in Iceland

mentioned by Krugman and reported in this chapter's opening comments. The second issue that merits attention is the role of exports and the option of devaluation. Having its own currency, Iceland was able to devalue the krona, thus boosting exports, but at the enormous cost of fuelling inflation, and with 'a particularly large and protracted consumption contraction' (Ólafsson and Pétursson 2010: 25–6). Despite lacking the option of devaluation, however, the paradox in the Irish case is that exports are buoyant, though these are largely from the multinational sector and are proving ineffective in stimulating general economic recovery. However, as O'Brien has put it:

> Iceland suffered all the downside of having its own currency, but far less of the upside. Iceland's export performance has been nowhere near as strong as one would have expected following a 50 per cent devaluation, while Ireland's has been better than could even have been hoped for. (D. O'Brien 2011a: 6)

Ireland's membership of the euro therefore has protected it from the severity of the impact on living standards experienced by Icelanders. Despite this, the outlook for Iceland seems to be somewhat better than for Ireland. One can only conclude that the quality of governance matters.

OTHER CASES: FINLAND, NEW ZEALAND, SPAIN

Finally, three further cases are worth considering as they may hold some valuable lessons for Ireland. Finland, since it experienced a comparable financial and economic crisis in the early 1990s, but has recovered very successfully; New Zealand, a small island state of similar size to Ireland, which is presented by the OECD as a model for Ireland; and Spain, the severity of whose banking crisis is being compared to that of Ireland.

While larger territorially than Ireland, Finland is also a small and remote country. Gaining independence from Russia in 1917, like Ireland it experienced a civil war immediately after independence. It chose to be a neutral country after the First World War and its foreign policy and economic development have always been determined by its special relationship with the Soviet Union. Following the collapse of the USSR, Finland joined the European Union in 1995 and the EMU in 1998 (Caramani 2004). Kiander outlines a number of crises which caused fluctuations in Finland's economic development – unrest and civil war in 1917–18, the Great Depression in 1930–32, the Second World War of 1939–45 and war reparations and reconstruction after it, recession in the 1970s following the oil price rise (1975–78), and the crisis of the 1990s (1990–93). In between these crises, growth has been stable (Kiander 2010).

The 1990s crisis was triggered in part by market liberalisation, but also by the collapse of the Soviet Union, which was followed by a financial crisis and restructuring between 1991 and 1994. This shared several common features with the current crisis in Ireland: similar conditions helped create it, including financial deregulation, rapidly increased domestic liquidity, the fuelling of an investment boom, an asset price bubble, full employment and balanced government budgets. A sudden shock due to the loss of Soviet trade (which resulted in a 10 per cent contraction in exports between 1990 and 1991) and a downturn in the international economy undermined competitiveness, leading to falling private investment and consumption and ultimately to a stock market collapse. From 1990 to 1994 Finland experienced four years without economic growth and three years of falling output. There was decreasing real income, soaring unemployment and exploding public deficits (similarly to Ireland today, GDP fell by 13 per cent and house prices by 50 per cent, unemployment rose from 3 to 18 per cent and there was embedded long-term unemployment and poverty). Public debt increased from 12 per cent of GDP in 1990 to 60 per cent in 1995, and the cumulative credit losses of Finnish banks amounted to 15 per cent of GDP. As with Ireland, there were tax-payer-financed bailouts, nationalisation, state recapitalisation and bank restructuring. The government restructured and downsized the banking industry, merging the two largest commercial banks (KOP and SYP became Merita) and then merged that bank with a Swedish bank (Merita and Nordbanken became Nordea). One third of bank staff were laid off, while help for bank customers was not even discussed. Managers of failed banks were prosecuted, which resulted in some long trials but few convictions.

The budget deficit was addressed by cuts in public-sector expenditure and employment, cuts in social spending, and tax increases from 1991 to 1994. Abandoning fixed exchange-rate policy led the Finnish markka to depreciate by 40 per cent, and a shakeout of unproductive businesses led to dramatic improvements in competitiveness. A strategy of technology-driven growth and structural change was also put in place, so that today Finland achieves high rankings in competitiveness, technology, education and economic growth; in most comparisons it ranks among the top three in the world. Recent success has largely been embodied in the growth of the Nokia group in particular and of the indigenous ICT sector more generally. Fiscal consolidation and fulfilment of the EMU criteria in 1997 led to record surpluses in 2000 and 2007. This was maintained by tax cuts and the steady growth of expenditures, as pro-cyclical policy fuelled the recovery. Economic growth picked up from 2004, with average annual GDP growth of 4.7 per cent in 1994–2000 and 3.5 per cent in 2001–07. Unemployment fell from 18 per cent in 1994 to 10 per cent in 2000 and to 6 per cent in 2008, though it is still not down to pre-crisis levels. However, deep long-run gains have been made, mainly associated with investment in education. But Kiander notes that the Finnish crisis was solved by currency devaluation. For countries within the eurozone, deflation appears to be the only viable alternative, an adjustment process that is slow and painful.

New Zealand is in many respects an ideal comparator for Ireland. An ex-British colony, and still part of the commonwealth, rather than a republic, it is a small island state with a population of 4 million overshadowed by a larger island neighbour. Like Ireland, it adopted a Westminster parliamentary system, differing however in its original choice of a first-past-the-post electoral system. Two of New Zealand's recent experiences are relevant to this discussion. In the late 1980s it became a laboratory for an experiment in the transformation of the world's first welfare state into the world's first post-welfare state, adopting a radical 'new public management' (NPM) reform agenda; this was consistent with other neoliberal reforms, including the work activation of lone parents. In 1996 it engaged in significant electoral reform and moved to a mixed-member proportional electoral system. As Ireland faces a challenging period of public-sector reorganisation and cutbacks, labour market activation and political reform, what lessons can be gained from the New Zealand experience?

Under a fourth Labour government (1984–90), New Zealand made a name for itself as an international leader in NPM, which focused on a radical translation of private-sector management techniques into the public sector (Pollitt and Bouckaert 2004: 280). These included departmental chief executives on five-year, fixed-term, performance-related contracts, greater managerial authority and discretion, outsourcing or competitive contracting of public services to private-sector and non-government organisations, the full privatisation of many state-owned assets, and a large number of public-sector redundancies. While drawing many positive conclusions, Schick's (1996) review raised questions about whether the 'New Zealand model' of public-sector reform had been applied too zealously. There were high transaction costs of accountability arrangements in the now large number of small departments, there was too 'slavish' an acceptance of NPM principles, and there was evidence of downgrading and neglect of the wider organisational and policy capacity of departments and the skills sets of senior public-sector managers. The net result was shortcomings in organisational capacity and performance in many quarters in the public sector, and public concern that fiscal goals had overridden concern for social-service quality (Duncan and Chapman 2010). The 1999 Labour–Alliance coalition government took on the incremental task of restoring public trust in public services and rebuilding capacity in the state sector and significantly modified the original OECD 'New Zealand model'. The three-term centre-left government renationalised previously privatised enterprises, including Air New Zealand, the railways, and workers' compensation (jobseeker's benefit), reversed the trend to separate policy-advisory ministries from service delivery, changed the culture of contracting out services to a more streamlined and flexible focus on outcomes and, since 2000, has focused on re-strengthening central public-sector department services by enhancing outcome-focused coordination among agencies. While privatisation is still very much part of the political agenda, there is now more evaluation of policy outcomes rather than a fiscal preoccupation with inputs and fiscal controls. The lesson for Ireland is that an over-zealous application of NPM led to a loss of values and trust in public services, which had to be regained by focusing on standards of conduct, integrity and values. Labour market reforms had introduced compulsory work for lone parents, but this too was scaled back as the state realised that low-paid and low-quality employment could not lift people from poverty and added to the stress of those already living in poverty and having care responsibilities (Baker and Tippin 2004; O'Brien 2004).

Following decades of public despair with what was perceived as an unfair and unrepresentative electoral system which encouraged strong majority governments to take often abrupt and radical policy turns, a Royal Commission on the Electoral System recommended in 1986 a shift to a MMP electoral system*. While the political elite did not favour such reform, the people passed it overwhelmingly in a binding 1993 referendum. New Zealand has had a long process of managing a bicultural identity, and there are lessons to be learned here about how to establish a parliament that is more diverse and representative. In 2006, 39 women, 21 Maori, four Pacific Islanders, and two Asians were elected among New Zealand's 121 MPs. Political parties have adopted selection practices that consciously select diverse candidates, and the MMP electoral system includes provision for 7 Maori seats (continuing a general feature of the New Zealand system since the 1860s). There is mixed public confidence in MMP, and the current National-led Government will test the waters on this issue by holding a referendum on MMP in parallel with the election in late 2011.

One lesson for Ireland from New Zealand is about the importance of values in guiding public-sector reform and labour market policy. Over-zealous reform agendas can be hijacked by ideological agendas (often on the right, as in the case of NPM and labour market policy in New Zealand). Clear values and visions for the public service and the role of the state are necessary for a programme of renewal of public services in a second republic. The New Zealand experience shows that electoral reform takes time. It requires significant investment in opportunity for citizens to participate in dialogue about electoral reform and voter education; in addition, reforming the system does not end the debate. The relatively modest but meaningful outcomes from New Zealand's electoral reform highlight how political institutional reforms are complex and require supporting public consultation mechanisms and citizen education processes; the advances in equality and diversity are commendable and worthy of a second republic.

Unlike Finland and New Zealand, Spain offers few bases for comparison with Ireland, being far larger and having had a totally

---

* This was modelled on the German-style MMP system (sometimes known as the AMS or additional member system), in which each elector would get two votes, one for an electorate MP and one for a party. The size of Parliament would increase to 120 MPs: half would be elected in single-member constituencies (as before); the other half would be selected from party lists, so that in general each party's share of all 120 seats corresponded to its share of the overall vote. The calculated combination of these two votes allows broad proportionality of votes while ensuring a constituency link.

different historical development. However, of all the countries in severe crisis, Spain is perhaps most comparable to Ireland, since the origins of its crisis lie in a real-estate bubble. With housing accounting for some 10 per cent of the Spanish economy, by the height of the boom some 700,000 housing units were being built a year, and construction accounted for 13 per cent of jobs. By 2009 this had fallen to 200,000 a year, with a surplus of between 700,000 and one million new properties to be cleared, according to estimates. Again, just as in Ireland, the collapse of the housing sector has been the main reason for unemployment reaching 20 per cent and stubbornly sticking there throughout 2010 and into 2011. Unlike Ireland, however, the initial phase of the international financial crisis did not impact directly on Spanish banks, which were tightly regulated and had high capital provisions. But the collapse of the property bubble in late 2008 soon revealed a major problem, not in the principal banks, but rather in the provincial *cajas de ahorro* or savings banks, closely linked to provincial governments, which had a heavy exposure to the property market. Since they play a central role in the provision of credit to small and medium-sized businesses in Spain, the crisis in the *cajas* is having a severe impact on the economy as a whole. The initial response of the Socialist government was to provide support, in an effort to stimulate the economy and keep credit flowing. This has largely failed to boost growth; but it has had the effect of generating a large public deficit, which the government is now pledged to reduce through the implementation of cuts in expenditure and increased taxes. These measures have trimmed the budget deficit from 11.1 per cent of GDP in 2009, to 9.3 per cent in 2010, with a target of 6 per cent in 2011.

What has exacerbated the Spanish crisis, however, is the lack of international confidence in the measures being taken to deal with the depth of the banking crisis. The Spanish media estimate that the banks have yet to reveal the true extent of their exposure to the property market, which may be as high as €80 billion. International observers point to the fact that housing prices have only dropped by an average of 13 per cent from their height during the boom, and it is widely believed that they need to fall by between 30 and 40 per cent to allow the property market to recuperate. On the other hand, the Spanish government claims that the property price adjustment has already taken place. This lack of international confidence is what causes international markets to raise their interest rates on Spanish government bonds and to raise the fears of the European Union that Spain is going to have to apply for a rescue package that could prove too heavy a burden for the Union. The pressure to reassure the markets has increased the pressure on the Socialist government to deepen their austerity measures and to begin dismantling social protections in the name of eliminating rigidities in the labour market. Critics of this approach recommend instead that taxes be raised on those on highest incomes and on corporate profits, and that various tax breaks for corporations be tightened, ensuring that it is those who benefited most from the housing boom who will carry most of the burden of adjustment (Navarro 2010). Pointing to the impact that austerity has had in Ireland, deepening the recession rather than recuperating the economy, these critics fear the same may happen in Spain. As the European Commission urges more cutbacks to reduce the budget deficit, they see this as helping to save the French and German banks that had lent to fund the housing booms in Ireland and Spain. As Navarro writes:

> We can see therefore that neoliberal dogma is destroying the European Union ... Believing that reducing public deficits is the solution is to show the power of dogma over common sense. One doesn't have to add that the perpetuation and promotion of the dogma is because it serves well-defined interests – among them those of financial capital. And this dogma has come to be accepted by parties representing the popular classes such as social democratic parties which have converted themselves into social liberal parties, becoming part of the problem instead of part of the solution. (Navarro 2011)

CONCLUSION: LESSONS LEARNED

The various cases surveyed here point to a number of clear lessons. Firstly, and most importantly, the quality of governance matters; there is no inevitability about the course that a severe crisis takes. Secondly, it is paradoxical that the case which resembles the Irish one most closely is that of Spain rather than that of another small state. Indeed, the actions of governments in all the small states surveyed either helped to minimise the impact of the global crisis or, in the case of Iceland, decisively charted a route out of a most severe crisis, once civil society had forced an early election that resulted in a Green–left coalition taking office. Therefore, who is in power and how they use that power makes all the difference. While it would take a much more detailed examination of each case to identify precisely the measures that were successful, we know enough to draw a number of general lessons. The first concerns ideology: in all cases it was left-of-centre governments that implemented the successful policies; what distinguishes these is a belief in the importance of using the state to stimulate the economy and to regulate the private sector. The most severe crises in the 2000s – in Argentina, Iceland and Ireland – were all caused by right-of-centre governments that had liberalised their financial sectors and then failed to put robust regulatory authorities in place. In the first two cases, it took left-of-centre governments to strengthen the state and take decisive actions to deal with the crises they inherited. The case of Spain is also interesting in this regard. The Socialist government inherited a housing bubble that had been fuelled by the liberalisation of building regulations and land ownership by the previous right-of-centre PP (Partido Popular) government, and it did initially seek to stimulate the economy as a way out of the economic crisis; however, it is now being accused by its critics of following a neoliberal route and of effectively handing over the previously publicly owned *cajas de ahorro* to the private sector. In New Zealand also, it was a Labour government that introduced sweeping neoliberal reforms in the public service, but, once the lessons of these were learnt, that further modified these reforms, turning the clock back in some aspects. This reminds us that ideology does not necessarily provide clear solutions; the cases surveyed also show how it needs to be tempered by a creative pragmatism. This, then, draws attention to the design of adequate public policies and to ensuring the administrative capability of implementing them efficiently – crucial issues highlighted by the New Zealand case. As is clear from the Irish case, the right-of-centre governments that presided over the boom of the Celtic Tiger eroded the capacity of the state, not least through cutting taxes and spending its income in highly wasteful and inefficient ways. So a state needs capacity, as well as the checks and balances that can ensure that public monies are spent efficiently and in ways that help achieve the goals set by the state. While these general points do not permit any detailed conclusions about what political economy models can best guarantee the public good, they do point to the need for an efficient and capable state to try to ensure that the free market serves the good of society. These broad lessons will inform the proposals for a second republic in the final two chapters.

Part IV

Towards a Second Irish Republic

The purpose of this final part is to draw the lessons from the previous chapters and to show a way in which a new politics might emerge, with an agenda for a fundamental reshaping of the Irish political, economic and social system, to overcome the weaknesses identified in this book. Chapter 9 examines the contents of the reform agenda and provides answers to the 'what' questions: what sorts of reforms are required? It begins by discussing the principles and values needed to effect reform and then outlines three different options for political economy models, their implications for social policy, and the role of an active citizenry to underpin them. Chapter 10 turns to the question of how this ambitious agenda might be realised, identifying the spaces for change that are opening up in the present situation and arguing for how these could be used by social forces to realise their objectives. This chapter also engages with debates on the politics and political economy of Northern Ireland, asking whether prospects for radical change are converging in the two Irish states, thus creating the conditions for an all-Ireland polity to emerge.

9
Facing the Challenges

In July 2010, Emer and Ana, two 15-year-old Irish secondary school children, were visiting the town of Antibes in southern France. Passing a local secondary school they paused to read the words *Liberté*, *Égalité* and *Fraternité* painted in large letters over the school door. The girls wondered aloud what would be the equivalent Irish values and whether the Irish state expects schools to promote such values. Despite having just sat their Junior Certificate state examinations in history and civil and political studies, the girls were at a loss as to how to answer their own question. Nor could the adults in their company provide an answer. The values of the Irish state are far from clear to most Irish citizens. Little wonder that market values so easily began to permeate Irish life and culture.

The first task in building a second Irish republic relates therefore to finding a firm bedrock of values that can underpin it. For this reason, this chapter begins by discussing three sources of such values – in political and equality theories, and in a return to the essential meaning of republicanism. The following section surveys the active debates on political reform that are taking place in contemporary Ireland, especially in the wake of its banking and economic collapse, identifying the principal areas of agreement and the new government's political reform commitments, the issues on which there are differences, and the issues neglected by the debate. The conclusions of this discussion help, then, to inform what political reforms are required. The third section moves beyond political reforms to wider models of development, and groups these into three options or political economy models that can be extrapolated from the range of reforms being discussed, presenting them as the choices now facing Irish citizens for the second republic and highlighting the implications of whatever choice is made. The final section returns to the values outlined in the first section, focusing on the role of an active citizenry as a crucial dimension of what will help constitute the second Irish republic and form an essential part of its political economy model.

VALUES FOR A SECOND IRISH REPUBLIC

Since the purpose of this chapter is to map out what needs to be done to lay the foundations for a more sustainable and equitable political economy model for Ireland, it begins by arguing the need for a fundamental realignment of institutions, interests and ideology based on a set of progressive public values. The first challenge in the making of a second republic is to discuss the core values of that republic. Drawing on political theory, on equality theory, as well as on republican concepts of the public good, can help to map out these core values.

Various political theorists have focused on the importance of equality as the essential basis for a genuine democracy. Dahl (2005) outlined six core institutions for democracy: elected officials; free, fair and frequent elections; freedom of expression; alternative sources of information; associational autonomy; and inclusive citizenship. Despite the clear evidence that inequality is pervasive in capitalist societies, Dahl argues strongly that in designing a republic we have to assume that a commitment to equality is truly a moral commitment to intrinsic equality (2007). As he writes, 'governments are obliged to give equal consideration to the good and interests of every person bound by those decisions' (Dahl 2007: 65). By inclusive citizenship, Dahl understands that no group will ever get a fair share of resources unless fully engaged in a democratic system; hence limits to participation, such as economic inequality, illiteracy, lack of capacity to acquire the resources to participate, and unequal status, cannot be allowed to become real obstacles for a functioning democratic republic. There is a negative relationship between economic inequality and democratic political engagement (Skidmore 2009). Gallego (2007) stresses level of education as the most significant variable determining political participation. Income inequality powerfully depresses not only participation in elections, but also political interest and the frequency of political discussion. Chapters 5 and 6 illustrated Solt's (2008) argument that relative economic inequality concentrates power into the hands of the wealthy, giving them greater influence not only on what is decided, but also in shaping the political landscape and the content of political discussion. Freedom means being able to have control over one's own life, as well as having the ability to foster resilience in the face of shocks and change. Power inequality is thus associated with the concept of vulnerability, discussed in Chapter 5.

Clearly, no matter how well political institutions are designed, a condition of equality is a necessary prerequisite for a functioning republic. The focus on the importance of true equality of condition as the essential basis for a genuine democracy requires an examination of the contribution of equality theory to the essential values underpinning a second republic. Moving beyond a focus on issues of distribution alone, Baker et al. (2004) outline an equality framework that understands inequality across four interrelated dimensions. This attends to the social structures and institutional context that shape inequality, the consequent need to reform decision-making power and procedures, how work is distributed, and culture itself, all of which determine the underlying inequality in society. Their framework covers the following dimensions of inequality:

Economic Equality: Its goal is equality of resources. There can be no substantive equality of opportunity without equality of economic conditions. Liberal equal opportunities policies merely redistribute inequalities across different groups – they do not eliminate them.

Socio-cultural Equality: Its goal is quality of respect and recognition. It reflects the interests and needs of different status groups, such as cultural minorities, Travellers in Ireland, people with disabilities, older people, migrant workers, women and men, lone parents, and gay, lesbian and bisexual people.

Political Equality: Its goal is equality of power in public and private institutions. It focuses on sharing power in designing, planning and implementing programmes – what is sometimes called the politics of presence.

Affective Equality: Its goal is equality in the doing of care work. It espouses equal access to love and care in life, and equality of respect for loving, caring and solidarity as human activities.

The equality legislation of Ireland's first republic, enacted in the 1990s and resulting in the establishment of the Equality Authority, gave legal support to the recognition of equal status, but was based on a limited liberal notion of equality of opportunity. This individualist approach to equality neglected class or socio-economic inequalities and had little focus on resource, representational or affective equality. A challenge therefore for the institutions, laws and practices of the second Irish republic is to enable and achieve a true equality and inclusiveness – the intrinsic equality that Dahl identified and that enables the freedom of capacity that is at the heart of Pettit's

(2005) concept of republic. The key feature of Pettit's republic is the absence of domination: nobody should feel so vulnerable that they can be dominated by another, nor should the state be able to dominate, beyond ensuring the common good. Absence of domination requires a symmetry of power between equals, and that people have the power of contestation to challenge the actions of the state. It is these notions of freedom from domination, equality, participation and contestation that can inform the development of a second republic. Participation rests on a bedrock of equality. The institutions of a second republic need therefore to tackle political inequality, to reverse trends in social inequality, and to ensure educational equality as a necessary prerequisite for both social and political equality and participation. This will require empowering the least well-off to create a core of engaged, well-connected change agents in every local community who care about improving public services and building a robust public realm.

The importance of the public realm brings us to the essential meaning of republicanism. Honohan (2001b: 7) acknowledges that while there are many hues of republican thought most stem from a fundamental belief in the interdependency of human beings and that people have common as well as separate interests. Cullen (2008: 9) stresses that interdependence is the basis for citizens' responsibility to take an active part in developing policies that can deliver the common good. It is paradoxical that in the first Irish republic, the term 'republican' came to be equated with a nationalist view of reunification, while its essential meaning was not only forgotten, but contradicted in the way Fianna Fáil – 'the republican party' – governed the Republic. But instead of laying the foundations for a strong civil republicanism, Irish republicanism has tended to be obsessed by its constitutional form, while paying little attention to its social substance. For, if self-determination and equality are essential conditions for achieving a true republic, the essence of republicanism finds expression in the *res publica*, the public goods. A republic therefore requires a strong robust public space in which the public rules. In contradiction to this, our republic has over the past two decades systematically privatised our public spaces, handing more and more power to the market through the commodification of housing, of social security, of health care, and the creeping com- modification of education – all of which profoundly contradict the essence of republicanism. A republic must be committed to decom- modification, to ensuring that public authority directs and governs the private interest of market actors: the first Irish republic inverted that logic with ever greater determination. If equality and a robust public space are to be affirmed as the central values of an Irish republic, how can these be given practical reality in the practice, policies and institutions of a new republic?

Pettit outlines a number of legal rules as a way of limiting the tenure of those holding power; these include the classic democratic mechanism of periodic elections and term limits, so that there can be a regular alteration of those holding power. But Pettit goes further in underlining some demanding conditions intended to ensure that these widely used practices do indeed result in genuinely competitive electoral contests among equals. Among these are ensuring that the free play of ideas is not warped by campaign financing or media ownership; that there is a broad choice in who stands for election; that all electors have the capacity to question candidates and comment on their proposals; and that an active citizenry exists to invigilate and challenge any defects in the electoral process. It is clear that the last two requirements imply a genuine equality of condition among citizens, with everyone having a voice and their contributions getting equal treatment (Pettit 2005). In applying these principles to Ireland, O'Ferrall argues for a new public philosophy and for a civic republicanism 'to reconstitute, restructure and rethink our failed political and economic systems' (O'Ferrall 2010: 5), and for the principle that wealth should not dominate in determining anyone's capacity for citizenship. O'Ferrall argues that citizens need a sense of agency and empowerment similar to Sen's concept of 'development as freedom' (Sen 1999), which requires putting equality and well-being at the heart of national development.

Recession is an ideal smokescreen for ideologues pursuing an agenda that hijacks and downgrades equality issues in the national policy agenda as 'luxuries we cannot afford'. The truth, however, is that increasing equality is a prerequisite of economic recovery, as important as other investment strategies, such as those of a 'smart economy' or of green technologies, that seek to modernise the physical infrastructure. Ireland in the twenty-first century remains a patriarchal state in which gender inequality is caused by and embedded in the structures of economic, social and political systems that systematically benefit men more than women. A more equal society embeds time and support for care into social and economic policies and enables care and work to be shared more equally between men and women. An ethic of care, interdependence and solidarity needs to be fostered as a core national value (Lynch and Lyons 2008; Fischer 2011). Finally, the core values of a strong public realm, in which an effective state guarantees citizens freedom from the domination of the market, and which itself is held in check by a well-functioning democratic system and an activity citizenry, require the addition of a final value, namely sustainability. This focuses on achieving a sustainable balance between the functioning of the economy and society on the one hand, and the wider ecosystem on the other, since human flourishing in the twenty-first century and beyond will depend on such a sustainable balance. In some ways, the emphasis today on sustainability can be seen as extending to the sphere of the environment the principles of equality and of freedom from domination. What Cruddas and Rutherford wrote about Britain applies equally to the second Irish republic, which 'has to make the transition from casino capitalism to a low-carbon, more equitable and balanced form of economic development … The fundamental logic of this new economy must be ecological sustainability' (Cruddas and Rutherford 2010: 69). This principle will require a strong and effective state to ensure the transition from the present high-carbon and growth-obsessed economy.

AN EMERGING REFORM AGENDA

What kind of political institutions would enable the state to be held accountable to active citizens in a transparent way? What kind might enhance political equality? This book is not the first to argue for a second republic. In the mid 1980s, at the midpoint of the last major economic crisis in Ireland, there was a lively debate about constitutional reform and a new republic (Roden, De Buitleir and Ó Brolcháin 1986). A 1996 Oireachtas All-Party Committee on the Constitution reviewed key reform options; and a range of reports on the constitution have been published by the committee over the last 15 years. The 2008 political, economic and social crisis provoked a variety of responses arguing that political institutions were unfit for purpose and proposing a range of political reforms. A trio of international bankers and financial commentators (M. O'Sullivan 2006; D. O'Brien 2009; A. Sweeney 2009) were pioneers in this debate. Hardiman (2009) produced an insightful reflection on political reform priorities. O'Toole (2010) argued that the key public issue for the next five years 'will be what kind of republic we want, for whom and how'. The issue was debated in a number of public forums, such as the MacGill summer school (see Mulholland 2010), the *Irish Times* 'Renewing the Republic' series (2010), TASC's 'The Flourishing Society' series (Slí Eile 2010), and Claiming Our Future (2010). A number of high-profile blogs debated the various merits of reform options.* The Oireachtas Committee on the Constitution reported on electoral reform in 2010. All political parties produced political reform manifestos (these were ranked on politicalscorecard.ie). Media commentators made regular contributions to national debate, and various campaigns published opinions. Academic publications debated the pros and cons of political reform (MacCarthaigh 2005; Coakely and Gallagher 2010; McGrath and O'Malley 2008; Adshead and Tonge 2009; MacCarthaigh and Manning 2010; O'Malley 2010; Hardiman 2011).

The programme of the government that took office in March 2011, entitled *New Government for National Recovery 2011–2016* (Programme for Government 2011), is committed to addressing a wide range of political reform. How do these proposals measure up against the values of a republic? On parliamentary reform, there is commitment to a series of early referendums, including abolition of the Seanad and strengthening the powers of Oireachtas committees to carry out investigations. Consistent with the view that the government of a republic should serve the people, the programme is committed to reducing the number of TDs and reducing ministers' salaries, political expenses and political pensions. On accountability, Oireachtas committees will have full powers of investigation, the number of committees will be reduced, and key committees will be given constitutional standing. The reforms will make the Dáil more efficient and productive and bring more of the administrative infrastructure of the state under Dáil surveillance. The powers of the Ceann Comhairle (speaker of the Dáil) will be increased and Dáil processes improved, with the parliamentary questions system and the Oireachtas committee system extended to ensure that all state agencies are answerable, through them, to the Dáil. Financial scrutiny will be enhanced through an independent Fiscal Advisory Council (FAC) and comprehensive spending reviews of all public spending. The Oireachtas will have full scrutiny of EU draft proposals and will be committed to proper transposition of EU legislation. A 2011 constitutional convention will consider how the Irish Constitution should meet the challenges of the twenty-first century. While not specifying the full work of the convention, the Programme for

---

* politics.ie, politico.ie, 2nd-republic.ie. PoliticalReform.ie, with posts from Elaine Byrne, Eoin O'Malley, David Farrell, Jane Suiter and others, became a main site of debate over 2009–11.

Government states that it will establish a constitutional convention to review the Dáil electoral system and voting age, to reduce the term of office of the presidency of Ireland from seven to five years, to provide for a referendum on same-sex marriage, to amend a clause of the constitution valuing the work of women in the home, to encourage the greater participation of women in public life, and to remove from the constitution a clause on blasphemy. All are appropriate for a second republic for the twenty-first century, and if implemented would make a real difference to the quality of political and public life.

Other reforms promised will make elites accountable, and conflict of interest and policy processes more transparent. To rebalance power from elites to citizens, an independent electoral commission will oversee spending limits for all elections, lower limits on political donations to political parties and candidates, and ban corporate donations to political parties. To enhance transparency, the Official Secrets Act will be amended; and conflicts of interest will be addressed by means of a statutory register of lobbyists and the introduction of rules concerning the practice of lobbying. To effect a shift in power from the state to the citizen there will be legislation to reduce cabinet confidentiality, restore and extend the Freedom of Information Act, and protect whistle-blowers. To empower citizens, an investigations, oversight and petitions committee of the Oireachtas will link the Oireachtas and the Ombudsman, the Data Protection Commissioner and the Local Government Auditor. A citizens' petition system will also be introduced. The opportunity for citizens to engage actively in the political process is most practically realised at local level. The programme commits the government to moving functions currently being performed by local agencies back to local government and to making property-related revenues part of the income stream of local government. A democratically decided regional or city plan will replace the present top-down strategic planning guideline model; and councillors will acquire legal powers to seek reports from, and question in public, all providers of public services and relevant private-sector providers.

The Programme for Government performs well on accountability and more effective policy making and political leadership. These reflect the substance of debate about political reform and are necessary but not sufficient reforms for a new republic. There is less focus in the Programme for Government on equality, participation and separation of power. Slí Eile (2010) has argued that a constitutional convention is necessary to enable wide participation in debate about constitutional change, but warns against the danger of using it to take 'low lying fruit', avoiding the more difficult reforms. It is difficult to assess how other issues, including electoral reform and gender equality, will be processed under the proposed constitutional convention. Carney and Harris (2011) argue that without knowing more about the proposed convention it is difficult to judge its deliberative potential and, while few proposals for participative reforms reached the Programme for Government, some of the legislative reforms set out in the document do offer possibilities for enhanced deliberation. While there is a reference in the Programme for Government to democratic planning at local level and to a citizens' petition, the programme has few concrete proposals in relation to enabling participation and creating deliberative democratic forums, and there is relatively little discussion of diversity or of the need to make the political class more reflective of the population it serves. This suggests that while the government vision is ambitious in relation to accountable, transparent and efficient government, it is perhaps less ambitious in relation to a republican concept of an active citizenship or contestatory democracy. A number of reforms are now being discussed which have the potential to further enhance the democratic functioning of a second republic (Slí Eile 2010; De Buitlear, Ó Brolcháin and Roden 1998). From wide-ranging discussions on political reform, we identify broad themes unaddressed in the Programme for Government proposals: the question of values; the issue of separation of power between the executive and the legislature; how to achieve increased participation and local government reform; electoral reform; and finally, gender equality.

Values

We argued in Chapter 2 that the values of the Irish state have always been subservient, firstly to the power of the Catholic Church and, more recently, to the power of global capital. A strong bedrock of publicly shared values is a requirement for a second republic, and a renewed constitution should be a statement of values and fundamental rights. The 1996 Constitutional Review Group discussed the possibility of embedding principles such as equality and sustainability in the preamble to a redrafted constitution. While not so far proposed by the government, this might be part of the ambition for a constitutional convention. A republic requires the clear separation of church and state and the removal of constitutional provisions which confer special status or power on any one elite, gender, class or ethnic group. The review offers the opportunity to give a clear statement about the values of accountability, equality, care, sustainability, inclusion and participation that should anchor a twenty-first century republic. The constitution can guide social and economic policy, including the balance between the right to private property and the exercise of the common ownership of national resources for the common good. This might include limits on wealth or income and ownership of property, and a commitment that policy would strive towards a minimum and a maximum income. There is a clear need in a republic to have a bill of rights; in the Irish context this would have the added advantage of enabling incremental evolution towards the harmonisation of rights on the island (making the Republic's bill of rights consistent with that of Northern Ireland, as envisaged in the Good Friday Agreement). This would also enable full incorporation of rights as enshrined in wider EU and UN conventions. Lastly, the constitution can give substance to the notion of cherishing all the children equally, with a specific constitutional clause protecting children from discrimination and guaranteeing them the right to well-being and development.

Separation of powers

Chapter 2 also referred to the debate about separation of powers. Powers can be separated in a number of ways: between institutions of the state, or territorially at national or sub-national level. Like the United Kingdom, Ireland has a fused parliamentary system, in which members of the cabinet or executive are almost exclusively chosen from the legislative chamber, the Dáil. Some argue that this causes a structural weakness in the Irish cabinet, with ministers having a short-term interest in re-election and retaining a focus on their local representative roles as constituency TDs. The concern is that this may distract them from the wider and longer-term view needed for policy making: that the workload of ministers as elected representatives may overwhelm them in their executive and managerial functions. There is also the disadvantage of having a narrower pool of people to choose from when appointing a cabinet (O'Malley 2006). Some countries have a complete separation, whereby cabinet ministers can only be appointed from outside parliament (France); in others, ministers can be appointed either from the legislative assembly or from outside it (most Nordic countries). Various solutions to this structural weakness have been proposed. The most radical proposal, from Roden, De Buitlear and Ó Brolcháin (1986), is for a complete separation of the executive from the legislature along US lines, with a directly elected taoiseach nominating a cabinet of non-elected personnel. D. O'Brien (2011b) concurs that TDs should be prohibited from holding ministerial office. The Constitution Review Group (1996: 23) considered and rejected this approach, arguing that there is no demand for such a change. A compromise position is to give more flexibility in allowing the appointment of external ministers from outside the Dáil; however, as Cox observes, states whose rules allow the choice of appointing external ministers generally appoint from within the legislative assembly nonetheless (P. Cox 2010). Hardiman (2009) points to the immediate solution of making more effective use of the existing constitutional provision which allows up to two Seanad members to be appointed to the cabinet. This could most certainly be used to greater effect; and in the event of the abolition of the Seanad, there should be constitutional provision to allow a number of cabinet seats to be filled by external appointment.

Participation and local government reform

The role of the Irish second house, the Seanad, has also been the subject of much recent debate. Despite the All-Party Oireachtas Committee on the Constitution (1997) recommending retention of the Seanad, the new government appears committed to a referendum on abolishing the second house. At first glance this seems reasonable: Ireland is the only small non-federal state with a bicameral parliamentary system; other small states, including Denmark and New Zealand, have abolished their second chambers (Hardiman 2009). Apart from the general arguments about enabling checks and balances and a diversity of representation, there are two specific arguments for reforming rather than abolishing the Irish Seanad. Ireland has a relatively passive civil society (Mair 2010: Keane 2011). A more contestatory republic requires an active citizenship. Slí Eile (2010) argues that the constitution is a statement of the government's relationship with the citizen, that the original Seanad accommodated the role of the citizen in governance and that there is a case for reforming the Seanad to give effect to a creative participative forum for Irish civil society. Instead of the present Seanad, it is possible to envisage a space or public sphere that prioritises participation and the inclusion of all, including emigrants. This is not easily achieved. Young (2006: 249) asserts that inclusion and participation of all in social and political institutions requires special rights 'that attend to group differences in order to undermine oppression and disadvantage'. Participatory democratic structures, without acknowledging the need to support the specific participation of oppressed groups, tend simply to reproduce existing political inequalities. This requires practical public support for the self-organisation of groups experiencing inequality, and the reversal of the present trend to dismantle statutory and community supports for rebalancing participation and power.

The second argument for reforming the Seanad relates to the context of Irish unification and the long-term possibility of a federal structure for all-island governance. In the short term – and continuing the theme of participation and inclusion – a reformed Seanad could accommodate a north–south civic forum and also offer the opportunity to reform sub-national governance and local government. This raises the possibility for the Seanad to be reformed into a federal chamber to accommodate a devolved territorial separation of power and sub-national state representation. Reforms to enable citizen participation can often be most meaningful at the local level, and a reformed Seanad offers opportunity for revising the relationship between national and local governance. Ó Broin and Waters' (2007) mapping of local governance structures in Ireland draws attention to the various experiments in local governance over the last decade, none of which has amounted to meaningful local government reform. Devolution of functions and local revenue sources are essential for local government reform, as is democratic planning at local level, in processes that go beyond consultation and enable participation, deliberation and decision making.

Electoral reform

Electoral reform could also enhance citizen participation and the diversity of political representation. Neither of the government parties appears enthusiastic about significant electoral reform, but it is on the agenda of the constitutional convention. The most widely promoted and seriously considered option for electoral reform has been to change the single transferable vote form of proportional representation (PR-STV) to a mixed-member proportional system (MMP) along the lines of the German system, in which single-seat constituencies fill a substantial number of seats, with the remaining seats being allocated from party lists in proportion to their share of the national vote, the end result being proportional representation in the legislature as a whole. This is advocated by Laver (1998) and Fitzgerald, Hussey and O'Brien (Mulholland 2010) but resisted by Gallagher (1987) and Farrell (2008, 2010). The main argument for reform centres on breaking the perceived relationship between the Irish PR-STV electoral system and a brokerage or clientelistic political culture (Laver 1998). Farrell (2008), however, argues that this culture predates PR-STV and is likely to survive electoral reform. He considers the problem is better addressed by tackling it at source: stronger devolution to local government of key public services, and a stronger emphasis on citizens' rights in public service reform and education, might address the citizens' perceived need to revert to constituency clinics to realise basic rights.

The latest assessment of the electoral system was undertaken by the Joint Committee on the Constitution (2010). This assessed its performance against a range of criteria, including partisan proportionality, government stability, public support, intra-party competition, the balance of legislative and constituency work undertaken by TDs, and the representation of women and minority groups in the political system (ibid.: 13). Noting that a survey of Irish parliamentarians had found 57 per cent in favour of retaining PR-STV, the report concluded that there was no compelling case for reform. It recommended instead various improvements, including addressing the level of women's representation, improving the political engagement of young people, implementing a comprehensive, accurate and up-to-date electoral register, redrawing constituency boundaries, filling casual vacancies, changing the method of distributing surplus votes, improving ease of access to the ballot on election day, and enhancing the proportionality of seats won to votes cast. Based on the argument that any future electoral reform should be non-partisan in nature, it also recommends a citizens' assembly to examine the performance of PR-STV in Ireland and make whatever proposals for change it considers necessary (ibid.: 14). While some arguments for MMP are impressive, changing the Irish electoral system is not necessarily the greatest priority for reform. There is a danger that debate about electoral reform might overshadow and possibly distract from other pressing meaningful reforms – such as local government reform or education for citizenship – that would deliver more meaningful outcomes than electoral reform (Farrell [2010] found that electoral reforms do not always deliver the impact that reform advocates anticipate). There are many other ways of changing electoral rules to enhance participation and representation. Electoral rules to place time limits on representation can encourage turnover and can safeguard against a culture of complacency or a cosy consensus of elites; they are a feature of reforms undertaken in Latin America. A. Sweeney (2009) suggests limiting TDs to two Dáil terms. Options for enabling participation include multi-option referendums, citizens' recall and plebiscites (Baker and Sinnott 2000). Options that address equality of participation include lowering the voting age to 16, giving emigrants voting rights, and reforming voting rights for prisoners and people with mental health or physical obstacles to voting. However, the biggest impact on achieving equality in political representation and participation would be made by redressing education and income inequalities, so that citizens begin their political lives from equal starting points. Chapter 5 discussed the embedded nature of educational and economic disadvantage; tackling this is as urgent as any other political reform. Enhancing citizenship education in our schools is another way to achieve better outcomes from the electoral system.

Gender equality

Many public debates about electoral reform focus on the issue of clientelism and the constituency workloads of TDs, but fail adequately to address the issue of the diversity of the group which gets elected as TDs. The present electoral system may well be largely proportional in terms of translating votes into seats, but it is not proportional in reflecting the diversity of the population in the makeup of the Dáil. The 1996 Constitution Review Group (1996: 55–7) highlighted the unrepresentative nature of the Dáil and the Seanad. This is clearly the case for women; but it also applies to class, age, ethnicity and occupational background. The MMP system proposed by Laver (1998) has the immediate advantage of a significant number of seats being appointed through a party list system, which parties could use to ensure an appropriate and fair balance of representation. In New Zealand, MMP reform resulted in enhanced diversity and skills range within the national parliament (see Chapter 8). This however assumes that political parties would want to use national party lists in this way. Given that candidate selection strategies by parties in the 2011 general election ended up with 85 per cent of candidates being male and with women occupying only two out of 15 cabinet seats in the government that emerged, there is no case for believing that a list system would necessarily be used by Irish political parties to achieve greater political diversity or gender equality in politics. Regardless of the election system, it seems that gender equality in politics will not be achieved without some form of legislative intervention to require political parties to nominate a reasonable number of women candidates. Around the world, it can be seen that countries that have achieved progress in gender equality in politics have all used some form of affirmative policy. The rationale for such measures is that the problem is about the nature of political culture and not about women. Building in opportunity for women does not give unfair advantage, it compensates for existing obstacles to women's access to politics. Legislation is temporary; a 'sunset clause' ensures that the law lapses once the stated proportion of women is reached. Candidate quotas are considered the most moderate form of intervention, since they influence equality of opportunity rather than outcome. They simply widen the choice for voters; voters retain the final choice of the candidates presented to them. Such rules work best when enforced with sanctions, including financial penalties on political parties; but they also need to be accompanied by a package of other measures, to include civic education programmes, financial supports, facilitation of childcare and family responsibilities, a data bank, mentoring and training programmes, and support for women's networks (Bacik 2009). The government is committed to 2011 legislation that will tie public funding for political parties to a minimum target of at least 30 per cent female and 30 per cent male candidates in national elections. The challenge will be to ensure that the 30 per cent target translates into meaningful rather than tokenistic opportunities and that the necessary range of supports accompanies the legislative change. The legislative change would be all the stronger if it applied to local government elections and was implemented in time for the 2014 local elections.

WHAT MODEL DO IRISH CITIZENS WANT? POLITICAL ECONOMY OPTIONS

Reform of the political system has generated most debate, but is only one dimension of what will help constitute a second Irish republic. For, as we argued in Chapter 1, every society is structured not only by its political system but, much more profoundly, by its political economy model – namely, the ways in which state, market and society interrelate to one another and thereby largely determine the shape of that society: whose interests the economy predominantly serves, the strength or weakness of redistributive mechanisms, the nature of the public realm and the values underpinning it and, ultimately, the quality of life for the majority. Yet, as we stated there, 'critical junctures, arising as the dominant model enters into crisis, do not in any way determine what new model, if any, might emerge – this can only happen through political and social action'. This section therefore maps the options for different political economy models to structure the second Irish republic. The discussion will be informed by the values already discussed in this chapter, showing how strong or weak variants can present quite different options. The section begins therefore by highlighting some central principles, derived from the values already discussed, for guiding policy making in the second republic, and by proposing a new goal of human development as the objective of policy and considering ways in which this might be measured and monitored.

Economic and social policy in a second republic needs to be developed within an understanding of development that gives high priority to social well-being, cohesion and equality as fundamental goals. Ireland's model of development during the first republic, and most particularly over recent decades, has rested on values of individualism, income maximisation, and economic growth as ends in themselves rather than as means to social development. The domination of the policy-making process by a narrow political and economic elite has tended to reinforce these values and to isolate them from challenge. An alternative model will require values of social solidarity to take priority, economic growth to be seen as a means to sustainable and equitable social development, especially for the poorest and most vulnerable in our society, and decision-making processes to be broadened to include a much wider range of stakeholders (as seen in the participatory budgetary processes now common throughout Latin America). The alternative model needs to balance efficiency with a concern for equity.

Consideration of different political economy models draws attention to the partial nature of the reform debate since the collapse of 2008, with its focus predominantly on the defects of the political system, but with less public debate on the deeper defects of a model that prioritised the economic interests of elites over the social needs of the majority, particularly the most needy. O'Ferrall (2010: 5), writing on the theme of a civic republic, makes the case that civic humanism has often emerged out of crisis and disorder. Arguing that the sustainability of a successful economy depends on the moral framework of its political order, he promotes five key strategic issues: measuring what matters through indicators of national and local well-being; developing a sustainable economic model; putting in place a new education system that promotes human flourishing; creating a universal approach to public health; and strengthening civil society to permit an active citizenship. These are similar to the five 'decencies' (security, health, education, equality and citizenship) outlined by O'Toole (2010) in his own argument for a new republic. Pentony (2010) reflects a similar vision for a flourishing society. Others have mapped agendas for change from a variety of ideological perspectives (M. O'Sullivan 2006; Kirby and Murphy 2008a; Allen 2009; Ryan 2009; Slí Eile 2010; Smith 2009; A. Sweeney 2009; Casey 2010; Collins, Healy and Reynolds 2010; Kingston 2010; O'Brien 2010; O'Hanlon 2010; O'Neill 2010; *Village* 2010; Coffey 2011). Overall, however, proposals tend to focus on specific economic, social or political reforms rather than on the interaction of all three within particular political economy models. Therefore, while proposals are regularly made for better-resourced and more effective social policies (on social welfare, housing, health care, for example), these are often presented as discrete reforms, divorced from consideration of the wider economic model that might help deliver them and embed them in a sustainable way as features of Irish society. The purpose of this section is to draw attention to the contours of that political economy model and how it would influence an agenda of reform for key institutions of the state, including the civil service, the Industrial Development Agency and other agencies of industrial policy, the state's institutional infrastructure to foster a research culture, the education system and the labour training agency FÁS, and local government. While some of these reforms are mentioned in the 2011 Programme for Government, there is no overall framework or set of values to guide the government's reform agenda and no mention of a political economy model to structure the relationship between state and market. Rather, the programme is a compromise between the centre–right proposals of Fine Gael and the centre–left proposals of the Labour Party, and lacks coherence because of the absence of this framework.

Policy should be guided by a definition and measurement of sustainable human development. This is likely to be a complex definition, with numerous measurements, and requires that the values underpinning such an alternative definition are made clear. A very useful tool that has been largely neglected by Irish policy makers is the UN's Human Development Index (HDI), which was developed to offer a broader measure of human development than the mainstream measure of GDP growth. The HDI, published annually in the *Human Development Report* is, in essence, a composite measure comprising measures relating to education (years spent at school), health (life expectancy) and income (gross national income per capita). Since its first introduction in 1990, it has been steadily refined to include measures of political participation, sustainability (vulnerability to environmental impacts), civic and community well-being, and perceptions of well-being and happiness, among others. It has been complemented by a Gender Inequality Index, measuring the differential impacts of development on women and men (see UNDP 2010). The value of a measure like the HDI is that it guides the inevitable trade-offs that characterise all policy deliberations, ensuring that wider social objectives, such as gender empowerment, civic well-being, political participation and social sustainability, remain central objectives in their own right rather than as by-products of a policy that gives priority to economic growth as its principal objective, as has happened far too often under the first Irish republic. Furthermore, the annual measures of these many objectives make transparent to society the extent to which they are being achieved. This is not a new debate in the Irish context, and various policy initiatives, think tanks and policy publications have championed the idea of an alternative development model and alternative ways of measuring national progress (Feasta 2005; Social Justice Ireland 2009; NESDO 2009). The second Irish republic should follow the example of states around the world which draw up regular national human development reports, entrusting them to teams of prominent academics and activists to ensure that they capture in a rich way the challenges of development facing their societies (see the website hdr.undp. org for these reports and Stiglitz, Sen and Fitoussi 2009 for wider international discussion of this issue).

While these principles are the essential starting points for the political economy model of the second Irish republic, they lend themselves to different variants, as outlined below. These variants constitute the fundamental terrain of political struggle for the second republic; different sectors of Irish society will seek to structure the variant that they perceive as best serving their interests. In outlining the different variants, it needs to be borne in mind that a political economy model is centrally defined by the way in which the productive sphere and the distributive sphere, or what using shorthand we may call the economy and society, relate to one another. For this reason, the description of each variant pays central attention to this core relationship. The three variants may be described as the weak liberal model, the developmental social democratic model, and the ecological socialist model.

The weak liberal model: This model would be closest to the model that has structured development since the late 1950s, with a productive economy still heavily dependent on winning and maintaining high levels of foreign investment and with a much weaker focus on developing indigenous Irish industries and services. The strong battles fought by Irish political and economic elites to prevent any interference by EU authorities with Ireland's low rate of corporate tax underline just how dominant this model remains. It is liberal in that the state effectively abdicates to the private sector, particularly private global capital, the responsibility for developing Irish society; it therefore runs the risk of continuing to allow the interests of global capital to exercise a major influence over public policy and the allocation of public resources, as has happened over the recent decades of the first Irish republic. This is most evident in the immense influence of powerful lobby groups like the American Chamber of Commerce, which effectively foreclose any possibility even of having an open discussion about the desirability and social consequences of a low-tax model of development. Therefore, the challenge that this model has never seriously addressed over the course of the first Irish republic is how to ensure adequate resources to invest in social services and in developing robust state capacity – with the consequence that more and more the economy has served the interests of wealthy elites, both foreign and native, at the expense of the most needy in Irish society. The fact that Fine Gael labelled itself the 'low-tax party' during the 2011 election indicates that this remains the favoured model of the state's largest party. It is important to note that no features of the political reforms widely discussed in the wake of the 2008 banking and economic collapse, and summarised in the previous section, are incompatible with the continuance of such a weak liberal model. What they would provide would be a more accountable and responsible state to preside over this essentially private-sector model of economy and society. However, it would be more difficult for this model to achieve the strong principles of equality and a robust public realm discussed earlier in this chapter; without these Ireland will remain a republic in name but not in practice.

The developmental social democratic model: This model has been advocated principally by the Irish Congress of Trade Unions (ICTU), especially by its general secretary, David Begg, and also by TASC in its vision of a flourishing society (Pentony 2010). Such a model would require the strengthening of state capacity to develop a stronger economy through more active state involvement and direction (the strategic state investment bank proposed by the Labour Party during the 2011 election, and included in the Programme for Government, could be a key mechanism for this).

The challenge would be to develop strong Irish companies with the capacity to establish themselves successfully in certain niche sectors in the international marketplace. Following the example of Finland, as outlined in Chapter 8, this might be called the Nokia option, since Finnish success was based on the capacity to develop such a strong global brand. Such a model would wean the Irish economy off its excessive dependence on foreign investment, helping to embed in the indigenous economy the skills and technological innovation that so mark the foreign-owned sector. This model requires higher levels of taxation, both to build strong state capability, and also to fund high-quality universal social services and strong redistributive mechanisms to address the gross levels of inequality in Irish society. The NESC's *Developmental Welfare State* made some overtures towards this model, arguing that a more knowledge-based and innovative economy requires significantly improved social policies, and rejecting a 'low road' of passive social policy in favour of a 'high road' of active developmental policy (NESC 2005). This would require deep reform to Ireland's educational and training systems and to its welfare state. Specifically it requires stemming the intergenerational transmission of educational disadvantage, the 'brain waste' of child poverty, the neglect of people with disabilities, the under performance of ethnic minorities, and the discarding of older workers. However, NESC never developed the other part of the equation – the type of taxation system required to sustain this model. The political reforms outlined in the previous section could provide a political system more suited to the development of such a social democratic model, but such reforms alone would in no way ensure that such a model emerges. This would depend on convincing enough citizens of the merits of this option; in this regard, the higher vote for the Labour Party and for other parties of the left in the 2011 election offers some grounds for hoping that support for such an option may be growing; but the volatility of the electorate and the strength of public discourse in Ireland in favour of low taxes makes this far from certain. What such an option has in its favour is that it provides the means to implement effectively the core values of social equality and a strong public realm as the guiding values of the second Irish republic.

The ecological or ethical socialist model: This remains the model least likely by far to win majority support, since it would entail radical reforms to economy and society not yet seriously implemented anywhere in the world. What distinguishes this model from the previous two is its recognition of the unsustainability of economic growth as the principal means of achieving development, for two fundamental reasons. The first is that the continuous growth on which all capitalist models depend is fast reaching the limits of finite resources, particularly of oil. The second is that science is alerting us with ever greater urgency to the need to radically reduce greenhouse gas emissions into the atmosphere if the world is going to remain habitable for the human species. The central challenge that this model addresses is to put the transition to a steady-state economy at the heart of public policy, radically reforming the taxation system along the lines of shifting the burden of taxation from economic goods (such as incomes) to ecological bads (such as pollution), stimulating flourishing local economies to supply as much of their needs from their own resources as possible, developing strong systems of public transport and new forms of locally based health care. While the contours of what such an economy would look like are still vague (see Jackson 2009b) and their social outcomes very uncertain, the challenges of peak oil and climate change are going to force them on to the political agenda before too long. Two dimensions of this model are of particular interest. The first is that the end of economic growth as the imperative of public policy would focus attention on the quality of our social lives (central to which would be the achievement of far greater levels of social equality); this would become the primary means through which to achieve development – what Jackson calls 'prosperity without growth' (Jackson 2009b). The second dimension is that achieving a transition to a steady-state economy would require a strong state, but one held in check by very strong mechanisms of deliberative democracy. For this reason, a transformation of our democracy is a precondition of this model. While this model is espoused by various Irish campaigning groups (O'Hanlon 2010), the electoral collapse of the Green Party suggests that this change agenda will be absent from Irish parliamentary debate and policy action for some time to come.

The purpose of this section has been to draw attention to the contours of the political economy model needed to give expression to the values of a robust democracy, an equal society and a genuinely republican polity for the second Irish republic, while not neglecting the urgent challenge of sustainability that faces humankind. The section has also drawn attention to the fact that an active citizenry is essential if the option for a political economy model is not to be left to powerful elites, but is going to reflect the values and needs of the majority. To this the chapter now turns.

CONCLUSION: AN ACTIVE CITIZENRY

Chapter 2 has already outlined the taming of civil society in the Ireland of the Celtic Tiger – the severe restriction of its sphere of activity, the effective silencing of alternatives to the dominant neoliberal policy paradigm, and the development of a stiflingly narrow consensus that allowed elites to inflict severe damage on Irish society with few critical voices being raised. Establishing a second Irish republic that is shaped by values of democratic participation, by a robust social equality and by a commitment to a strong public realm will require that this legacy be replaced by an active and vigilant citizenry. This is necessary to ensure that those chosen by the electorate as its representatives within the institutions of Ireland's representative democracy do indeed genuinely represent the concerns, values, expectations and ideas of citizens within the spheres in which policies are fashioned and decisions are made on their implementation. However, much more is required of civil society if the second Irish republic is to meet expectations for the refashioning of economy and society. For civil society is the incubator of the ideas and projects that will give shape to a new economy and society. For this we need to develop in Ireland a strong civic republicanism.

The influential work of Iseult Honohan has developed the foundations for this project through examining the basis of our obligations to one another. She seeks to move away from basing these obligations on a shared identity, as was common in the first Irish republic, as she argues that 'the specific interdependence of citizens entails special ties between them distinct from those between co-nationals who share a common culture or identity' (Honohan 2001a: 51). She has a number of difficulties with identity. Firstly, grounding obligations on identity is suspect, as the latter can be negative or insignificant; 'it is not clear that identity *per se* gives rise to any obligations to others' (ibid.: 65). Secondly, she finds identity to be too exclusive and not to permit of the diversity that characterises modern societies. Thirdly, basing obligations on identity may limit the extent of one's obligations, excluding wider international obligations, such as those that find expression in international aid programmes or international solidarity movements, for example. Instead Honohan proposes a civic republicanism based on the analogy of the mutual obligations that characterise the interdependent relationships between colleagues. As she writes: 'The relations of colleagues resemble neither a close-knit community nor an association of strangers. Like citizens, they are based on involuntary interdependence ... and they are marked by degrees of equality, difference and relative distance' (ibid.: 55).

What makes these views of particular interest is that they were drawn on by the Taskforce on Active Citizenship to inform its concept of citizenship. As it argued:

> Civic republicanism acknowledges the mutual interdependence of all those who belong to a society or community while recognising the possibility of different identities within or across societies as well as overlapping and multiple identities. Hence, any number of different and possibly overlapping identities such as Irish, British, Celtic, Ulster, European, etc. can find expression in political or social institutions based on the principles of democracy and cooperation. (Taskforce on Active Citizenship 2007: 3)

This, then, provides the basis for a broadly shared and inclusive sense of citizenship based on a sense of shared responsibility for the quality of Irish society. Furthermore, as the reference to republicanism indicates, this inclusive citizenship derives from the secular project of building a national community through the aegis of the state, and this is always a work in progress. In this way, states and citizens mutually constitute one another, and each requires the other.

While the taskforce used this language, many of its recommendations veered more towards sustaining volunteering and a more communitarian interpretation of active citizenship (Gaynor 2009a; Cronin 2009; Geoghegan and Powell 2009). This is consistent with the first Irish republic, in which the state tended to control and emasculate an active citizenship while itself becoming ever more subservient to the market. This understanding of citizenship urgently needs to be replaced by a robust sense of civic republicanism which has the potential to provide the foundations for a new all-Ireland political culture and sense of belonging, replacing the twin nationalist and unionist political affiliations that have been the basis for the division of the island into two states. The paradox, however, is that this very active citizenry is what is necessary to lead and achieve such change in the first place. Chapter 10 addresses the challenge for society in moving to a second republic.

10
Achieving the Second Republic

The challenge of achieving the fundamental political, economic and social renewal that is encapsulated in the idea of a 'second republic' requires much more than outlining a series of necessary reforms; the far greater task is to implement them. Discussing the prospects for achieving a second republic in Ireland is the subject of this chapter. It opens by placing the calls for a second Irish republic in a wider context. The chapter then goes on to examine the prospects for a second republic: the second section looks at the political possibilities opened up by the 2011 general election and the third at the civil-society activity for political and social change that has emerged following the economic collapse of 2008. Both of these spaces are critically scrutinised and conclusions drawn about the prospects for change to emerge. The fourth section examines what has been happening in Northern Ireland, linking this to the prospects for change in the Republic. The chapter closes by returning to the discussion on models of capitalism in Chapter 1: drawing on a framework for understanding how a critical juncture can lead to a shift in paradigm through the interaction between ideas, interests and institutions, the prospects for such a shift in the Irish case are discussed.

TOWARDS A SECOND REPUBLIC

While Ireland must determine its own future, it is not alone in seeking to renew itself; indeed most countries go through periods of realigning social, economic and political institutions. This reminds us that there is nothing unusual about the process of fundamental renewal being widely proposed in Ireland at the beginning of the second decade of the twenty-first century. Müller and Myllyntaus (2007) review how small European countries coped with economic integration and disintegration during the twentieth century, how they adapted flexibly to drastically changing conditions outside their borders and found ways of maintaining their political autonomy even in the context of economic dependence. Understanding the integrated nature of state, society and economy is crucial to this task of realignment and renewal. Learning from other experiences is also crucial.

It is often the case that economic crisis provides the seeds for systemic change in political systems. In many instances renewing political institutions through constitutional changes has preceded economic recovery. Indeed it has been the prerequisite. The change from the Fourth to the Fifth Republic was an integral part of the French success that built up slowly over the subsequent 30 years. The most recent second republic resulted from the August 2010 constitutional referendum in Kenya, in which voters voted two to one for a series of legislative reforms amounting to a new constitution, laying the ground for a second republic to replace the post-colonial republic established when Kenya gained independence from Britain. The 49 legislative reforms include judicial reforms, the introduction of a land commission, strengthening prime ministerial powers and reducing presidential powers, a bill of rights and greater parliamentary accountability. These indicate the scale of the project of renewing or reconstructing the institutions of a republic and are consistent with the range of changes discussed in Chapter 9.

BALANCE OF POLITICAL FORCES

What of the 31st Dáil?

Is there any momentum for a second republic, based on values of equality and sustainability, from those parties which won power in the 31st Dáil following the 2011 general election? Certainly the rhetoric is alive and well. Fine Gael, the dominant party in government, uses the language of 'building a new republic', arguing that its 'new politics' plan is the most ambitious political reform package since the 1930s and that it would place the citizen firmly at the centre of government. Its vision of a new republic is of a 'smaller, more nimble government ... held to account ... trust is restored in our democratic institutions and the concerns of the citizen, rather than the elites, are placed firmly at the centre of government' (Fine Gael 2011). There is no mention of the values of equality and sustainability in this vision of a republic; and the requirement for small government suggests that FG sees a limited role for the state in achieving national development, leaving this instead to the private sector.

Michael D. Higgins, the Labour Party president, has consistently advocated a more active and participatory understanding of citizenship and the need to recover the promise of a real republic (Higgins 2007). Labour Party leader and Tánaiste (deputy prime minister) since March 2011, Eamon Gilmore, used the language of a 'second republic' when he spoke of building a republic that reflects the ideals and ambitions of its founders (Gilmore 2010). He argued in the 2009 and 2010 MacGill summer schools that Ireland had moved from an insular period of state building between 1921 and 1958 to a period since 1958 of embracing the external world and the European Union; and that it must now enter a third phase of a new republic embracing political change, creating a new and better Ireland and developing a framework and vision of the future captured by the original democratic programme of the first Dáil in 1919.

Is there evidence in the FG–Labour government of giving practical effect to such rhetoric about a second republic? As reviewed in Chapter 9, the 2011 Programme for Government commits the government to a constitutional convention to review and renew the Irish Constitution. It is not clear how ambitious the scale of any such reform will be. The difference between the parties in government is likely to be about the scale of the ambition for that republic to realise significant reform and substantive outcomes. The rhetoric about a new republic is also evident in the three main opposition parties. Both Fianna Fáil and Sinn Féin regard themselves as republican parties. However, they understand this quite differently, with FF seeing it as being consistent with a strongly neoliberal political economy model, while SF argues for a more developmental state-led model, at least in the values that inspire their current policies. The United Left Alliance, while less likely to use the language of republic, is committed to values of participation, equality and sustainability. Given the greater emphasis of left-wing parties on equality and sustainability, it seems plausible that a left-led government might be more expected to have the political will and commitment to build a second republic based firmly on these values.

What of the left parties in the 31st Dáil?

Various optimists dubbed the 2011 election the 'democratic revolution' or the 'pencil revolution'. However like the marks of a pencil, the results of the 2011 General Election may be easily erased. To be deemed a revolution there must be evidence of transformative change. To what degree has any realignment towards the left actually happened and to what degree is it likely to be permanent? Chapter 2 examined the general factors that militated against the development of a strong left Irish political party. The last five years and the context of crisis have seemed to offer hope for the prospects of such a political realignment. For some who held such hopes, a FG–Labour coalition is a disappointing result. For others who also hope for realignment, a FG–Labour coalition was always the most likely result in the 2011 election.

Clearly it would be foolish to make any guesstimate about what Irish politics might look like in five years' time. The most crucial determinant on the possibility of future politics is the scale of the potential crisis hovering over Ireland and whether Ireland survives the period without some form of default; the scale of any default and whether it is a managed restructuring or imposed may also be critical determinants. M. Kelly (2011: 13) writes about the possibility of national bankruptcy and argues that the destruction caused by any such scenario would not just be economic but also political, and could go as far as to wipe out both Fine Gael and the Labour Party on a scale similar to the defeat of Fianna Fáil in the 2011 election. Assuming some continuity, however, how might the political mix thrown up by the electorate in the 2011 election contribute towards the achievement of a second republic? A new republic based on equality and sustainability is unlikely to emerge either under the stewardship of a resurrected FF, nor if Fine Gael continues in power over a considerable period of time. It is much more likely to emerge from a strong left; this would most likely be led by the Labour Party. Some have optimistically argued that with almost 35 per cent or a combined 60 or so left-wing seats in the 31st Dáil (comprising Labour, SF, ULA and some left independents) 'the finishing line for a left government is close and, with greater cooperation, that finishing line is in sight … this needs to be part of a short-term continuum – a set of dominos falling; first Fianna Fáil, then Fine Gael' (Taft 2011). However Boyd-Barrett (2010: 13) reflects on the challenge of a divided Irish left, further hampered by its failure 'to communicate its message in a language that ordinary people can understand'. As Taft (2011) acknowledges, a government of the left requires a new level of cooperation within what has been a traditionally splintered and fractured Irish left (*Village* 2010: 4).

Whatever the politics of the next five years, it would be naive to underestimate the degree of the challenge required to arrive at a realignment of the Irish left. In exploring this possibility, Ó Broin identifies the difficulty of realigning the different political strategies of the three left parties, with Labour following an institutional tradition, the various bodies that comprise ULA following a mobilisation tradition, and Sinn Féin emerging into an institutional strategy from a long history as an adjunct to a republican movement committed to the use of physical force (Ó Broin 2011). Distinctions can also be made among these parties between those that are more reformist, with a government-oriented policy agenda, and those with more radical oppositional strategies. Differences in political analysis and different strategies and tactics would make it difficult to present a credible left alternative to the electorate and also to develop a common Programme for Government. Such challenges should not be underestimated; as the crisis deepens, real differences in the analyses of problems as well as tactical differences may well widen the gaps that separate the different left parties. How the left in opposition tactically relates to the left in government will also influence the capacity for realignment. While it is clearly the job of the opposition to oppose government, the left in opposition needs to focus on the real target of capital and its political allies and not be tempted to focus on its impatience with Labour. It is essential that the left takes leadership and approaches this oppositional role in a way that maintains the possibility of a left-led government in 2016. However, Labour will only be able to play a lead role in forming a left-wing government if they can, from within the current government, promote a left-wing analysis of the crisis and maintain themselves as a strong left-wing force in Irish politics. It is essential that they do so if there is to be any hope of a shift of paradigm in the future. It also remains to be seen how the Green Party develops following its disastrous performance in the 2009 local and European Parliament elections and the loss of all its TDs in 2011. It is likely to remain a key exponent of the politics of sustainability, and its presence as part of a left alliance would seem highly desirable given the importance that the issue of sustainability centrally informs public policy.

What of a left new party? McGraw (2008) pointed to the resilience of established Irish parties in managing change, but the scale of defeat of FF in 2011 opens up significant possibilities in the political landscape. De Burca (2010) argues that a citizens' assembly might animate a new political party with a focus on the fullest possible engagement of all stakeholders in society. A *Village* editorial in 2010 argued for a party of the radical left formed of those who have shown willingness to engage with and publicly comment on the need for radical change. While the 2011 election saw the emergence of groups such as Democracy Now, New Vision (an association of independent candidates) and Fís Nua (a registered political party), none had any impact, and it is not clear that any will survive as political forces. One significant development was the coming together of People Before Profit, the Socialist Party and the Tipperary Unemployed Workers' Action Group to form an electoral alliance called the United Left Alliance, which won five seats in 2011. However it is not clear whether the United Left Alliance, or other leading figures of the 'independent' left grouping in the new Dáil, will form a new party or parties.

CIVIL SOCIETY MOBILISES FOR CHANGE

Polanyi's concepts of 'double movement' and 'active society' understand the role of civil society as a transformative agent which acts to re-embed the economy to meet the needs of society (Burawoy 2003). Piven (2008) argues that substantive change comes by activating 'power from below'. Edwards (2004) draws from three traditions in civil society literature to develop an understanding of civil society as a tripartite relationship between associational activity, normative values or ideas of a good society, and a public sphere in which to deliberate and negotiate outcomes based on those values. Edwards' vision of civil society is of collective, creative and values-based action capable of being a counterweight to individualism, an antidote to cynicism and a balance to state and market. This is consistent with Powell's (2007) argument for a 'social left'. In the absence of trust in the state, trust in society and belief in society's capacity to lead change become even more important. There is growing awareness within the civil society sector that it has been captured by a populist form of democracy and needs to challenge itself and critically break this type of pervasive political culture (L. Cox 2010).

Connolly and Hourigan's (2006) assessment of the role of Irish social movements as transformative agents in Irish life is encouraging and shows capacity for real change in the context of a 'people's movement' to channel the demand for a new republic. Such a movement of people power is required to capitalise on the opportunities presented by the crisis, the centenaries of the 1916 rising and the independence struggle from 1919–22 that are now emerging on the Irish political horizon, and the opportunities presented by the constitutional convention being established by the Fine Gael–Labour government. Without significant demand from below, the level of ambition for change is unlikely to emerge from above. It is not clear that a substantial proportion of Irish people yet share such progressive values, and the task of such a movement would be to popularise such values in civic society, parties and institutions. How might such a movement emerge, and what impact is the new political context likely to have on the possibility of such a movement emerging?

Allen (2011) argues that two different political realities will impact on progressive civil society strategies: that of the government and that of the opposition. The strategies adopted by the FG–Labour government will have a significant impact on the way in which organisations mobilising for progressive change might operate. Strategies will be influenced by how supportive or disaffected people are with the parties in government and by the extent to which traditional lobbying makes progress on core demands. Whether or not the government seeks to re-establish and/or restructure social partnership arrangements will influence how the relationship between trade unions and government, and specifically between trade unions and the Labour Party, develops and, in turn, how relations between the trade union movement and other civil society actors develop. Government attitudes will also determine how the relationship between the community and voluntary sector and government develops, whether current antagonism and conflict will continue, or whether the government will find constructive new ways of engaging with the sector in responding to the current crisis. The strategies adopted by the opposition will also impact on the possibilities for civil society (Allen 2011). Left parties generally do not have a strong track record of cooperation with civil society organisations. Ó Broin (2011) argues that they often treat NGOs and civil society as little more than a recruiting ground. Nonetheless, they overlap with civil society, and how they choose to work and develop alliances will impact on civil society (and, of course, vice versa). Distinct political parties or electoral groups will each be seeking to develop movement capacity as 'an alternative voice' to the government and to mobilise support outside the Dáil. The various opposition parties and any new progressive parties are likely to take different strategies: Sinn Féin has a long engagement with urban community organisations and will seek to ensure that the party gives voice to their dissatisfaction; in this they will be vying for space with the United Left Alliance, which is likely to mobilise campaigns against cuts and water charges. The Greens need to rebuild with the environmental and 'sustainability' agenda. Civil society may be particularly confused if Fianna Fáil attempts to rebuild by re-establishing itself as a broad-based, catch-all movement using left-of-centre rhetoric and following its tradition of co-opting civil society into its own 'national movement'.

The biggest challenge for movement building, however, lies not with political parties but with Irish civil society. Irish civil society is broad ranging (Daly 2007). A very diverse range of different civil society groups pursue political reform agendas; some are neutral about or compatible with a neoliberal model; other progressive think tanks and trade unions pursue social democratic agendas; ecological movements and groups give reality to ecological values. Each of these can be seen as consistent with the three political-economy options for Ireland outlined in Chapter 9: the weak liberal model, the developmental social democratic model and the ecological socialist model. Civil society can also be viewed from the perspective of those groups explicitly promoting second republics. We now go on to map these spaces in Irish civil society, drawing lessons from Latin America, analysing the challenges for civil society, and arguing the need for progressive spaces in the public sphere and in mainstream as well as new media.

Neoliberal: Some movements, while calling for reform, are largely looking for reforms that are consistent with or reinforce a neoliberal model of development. Ireland First (an informal group of high-profile businesspeople and ex-politicians) launched 'A blueprint for Ireland's recovery' (Ireland First 2011) which, while looking to enhance accountability, specifically sought a process of reform to recapture competitiveness, without reference to equality or sustainability; if implemented, these reforms would be likely to result in greater inequality. Also, the 'Reforming the Republic' MacGill summer school and Dublin City Business Association focused on political reforms to renew competitiveness within the present model (Mulholland 2010; Coffey 2011).

Social democratic: The Ireland Institute for Historical and Cultural Studies actively seeks to promote republican ideas and thinking and to develop a republican critique of society. While a small number of political activists is inspired by traditional Marxist socialism, mostly by Trotskyist ideas, a larger number of projects for reform come from think tanks promoting equality, sustainability and wider republican values that can be loosely grouped together as being social democratic. TASC is an independent think tank dedicated to combating Ireland's high level of economic inequality and ensuring that public policy has equality at its core. Social

Justice Ireland is a membership-based organisation of individuals and groups who support basic values relating to poverty, inequality, social exclusion, sustainability and the environment. Community Platform, a coalition of 26 community and voluntary sector groups, has worked to develop broad alliances around progressive policy agendas such as those contained in *A Better Ireland is Possible* (Kirby and Murphy 2008b), and also on the issue of tax reform. Is Féidir Linn (2009), a network of individuals promoting development of an alternative Ireland, has produced 'Shaping Our Future' and contributed towards building alliances for a more equal sustainable Ireland. Trade unions play a key role in civil society and have been a traditional source of mobilisation for equality. Like unions across Europe, Irish unions have been challenged in their response to the current crisis. Some unions have revived an anti-capitalist logic and rhetoric while others are inclined to defend members' interests through dialogue, advocating partnership approaches to managing the crisis (Hyman 2011). Irish trade unions suffer low and declining membership, and two decades of social partnership have weakened their capacity to mobilise around alternatives. They are traditionally divided along pro- and anti-partnership lines, and these tensions continue to reflect divisions between public-sector unions in relation to the Croke Park Agreement on public-sector reform. Doherty (2011) argues that social partnership is unlikely to be revived; he notes the new trend for some trade unions to focus on strengthening their capacity to mobilise membership-based campaigns. This includes engaging in wider public discourse, forging civil-society alliances like The Poor Can't Pay, and involving themselves in movements like Claiming Our Future. This partially addresses what Daly (2007) notes has been a trend for the community and voluntary sector to organise separately from the trade union movement.

Ecological: Various environmental groups promote progressive demands for a sustainable future. Many are members of the Irish Environmental Network, a network of civil society groups focusing on environmental sustainability. Feasta (the Foundation for the Economics of Sustainability) promotes economic, cultural and environmental change required to achieve a truly sustainable society. Sustainable Futures Ireland, a group of environmental NGOs, engages with Claiming Our Future and a wider change agenda. Leonard (2010) draws attention to how issues of wider rural identity have shaped grassroots environmentalism in the Irish case. Ecological movements have often been local collective community responses to Ireland's dramatic transformation from a primarily agrarian and rural society to an industrialised economy in which the demands of rapid growth threaten communities, environment and heritage. A.B. Ryan (2010: 64) argues that ordinary people, acting together in initiatives for local food, transport and energy, can educate elected leaders and lawmakers and contribute to cultural change. Similar practical processes are occurring through the work of the NGO Cultivate, through food cooperatives, and through movements like the Cloughjordan Ecovillage and the Transition Towns movement. Other such places aimed at direct action to build alternatives include Seomra Spraoi, an autonomous social centre in Dublin city centre run by a non-hierarchical, anti-capitalist collective on a not-for-profit basis, which is a hub of positive resistance around alternative values.

Second republic: Within groups most associated with the concept of a second or renewed republic there is a range of understandings of what the concept means. Individual publications have been significant sources of ideas for groups concerned with change. For example, O'Toole (2010) focuses on a wide range of economic, social and political reforms, while Ryan (2009) offers the concept of 'enough' as a value and a guide for a more sustainable future. TASC (2010b: 18) shows that the recession has heightened awareness of income inequality, and there is now a majority demanding government action to reduce it. The 'Renewing the Republic' series in the *Irish Times* (2010) revealed a growing consensus in favour of fundamental political reform, but uncertainty about how to achieve it and an unsurprising lack of unanimity about which reforms should be prioritised. There does however appear to be growing agreement that citizens need to take ownership of the reform process, and lessons from deliberative democratic processes in Iceland were promoted in the *Irish Times* series by Farrell, MacConghail and Mulgan (*Village* 2010). Others, intentionally or otherwise, use different language to call for similar visions. TASC's call is for the Flourishing Society (Pentony 2010), an integrated set of economic, social and political reforms; Social Justice Ireland and Claiming Our Future likewise offer expansive reform agendas. The 'Reforming the Republic' MacGill summer school concentrated on the nature of institutional and administrative reforms, as did a contribution from the Dublin City Business Association, which sponsored 'a ten-point manifesto for a second republic' and emphasised that most reforms required neither referendums nor participatory processes (Coffey 2011).

A number of projects focus directly and exclusively on political reform and as such are 'neutral' regarding wider economic and social objectives. One project led by political scientists argues that the path to rebuilding a republic should start with a citizens' assembly (Byrne et al. 2010). In 2011, the Atlantic Philanthropies foundation has funded 'We the Citizen', a series of regional citizens' meetings on political reform, culminating in a national citizens' assembly. This offers an opportunity for mobilising citizens; however, there is no explicit agenda of equality or sustainability informing the design of this project. The Second Republic campaign is a broad-based movement, with members from many different political perspectives uniting around a shared desire to see a reformed Ireland. Central to this movement is the belief that reform should not be decided solely by politicians or expert groups. Instead, it sees itself as a lobby for a national convention to deliberate and decide on reforms and for a referendum on political reform.

While all of these ideas have a contribution to make to developing a robust civil-society movement for change, it is unclear who can provide the leadership to develop more powerful horizontal alliances and common agendas. What is the likelihood that the range of progressive forces described above will coalesce into a social and political movement capable of capturing the public mood for a second republic? Can these various models of change and traditions of organising rise above the inevitable tensions and contradictions amongst themselves? (Scandrett 2011). It is vital that any such movement reflects values of equality, inclusion and democracy and operates in a spirit of dialogue and listening. It is a significant challenge in building new solidarities between citizens to ensure that existing class, gender and status inequalities are not replicated and that groups are creative about mobilising and enabling participation in ways that embrace the greatest number of people. Intense cross-sectoral fragmentation remains a significant obstacle to movement building.

Taking just one example of new ways of organising and breaking down such fragmentation, Claiming Our Future began in 2010 when a number of groups committed to a more equal and sustainable Ireland (Is Féidir Linn, the Irish Congress of Trade Unions, environmental groups, the Community Platform, Social Justice Ireland and TASC) began a series of meetings to explore how best to cooperate and coordinate endeavours for a more equal, inclusive and sustainable Ireland. It now operates under a banner of 'a progressive movement for an equal, sustainable and thriving

Ireland' and embraces thousands of people from many backgrounds, organised into 25 local groups around a variety of events, activities and thematic working groups on issues such as income equality, health, models of development and political reform. There is appetite for cooperation between groups like Claiming Our Future, Second Republic and others, and a sense that the public is animated about the idea of reform.

How does the Irish experience compare with and what lessons can be learnt from the broad civil society movements that created the conditions for the emergence of new left governments in Latin America? Silva analyses in detail the experiences of building a social left in four Latin America countries: Argentina, Ecuador, Bolivia, and Venuezeula (Silva 2009). He sets himself the task of finding out what transformed protest by individual movements, frequently localised, into 'a nationwide concentration of diverse social actors demanding change on a wide variety of connected issues' (ibid.: 10). He finds that, though unions were the first to mobilise against neoliberal reforms, popular sectors soon took over the lead due to the weakening of the unions. Over several waves of popular mobilisation about concrete issues, they built forms of collective power from the late 1980s up to the 2000s, eventually creating the conditions and the constituency for the emergence of strong new left governments. Five key lessons can be learnt from this experience. Firstly, crisis was used as the opportunity to create and use political 'space'. Secondly, alliances were built with often quite marginal left-wing political leaders, thereby greatly strengthening their positions. Thirdly, broad-based alliances were built across and between different sectoral interests. Fourthly, transnational ideas and networks were utilised to create broad domestic agendas to sustain alliances. Finally, it was through promoting practical pragmatic reformist agendas that advances were made and, in time, significant changes were achieved. While patient coalition building takes time, Silva shows that it also produces results.

In attempting to apply these lessons to the Irish case and identify potential coalitions for such a movement, the differences in language, tone and agendas within the broad debate for a second republic present a challenge for alliance building. Only a sub-sector of Irish civil society has an objective of influencing macro-political change, and not all groups that wish to impact at this level are progressive or argue for an equal, sustainable or democratic Ireland. Others are relatively small, closed groups and are not oriented towards or interested in movement building. This intense sectoral fragmentation results in extensive duplication of effort and less than effective use of resources. Many groups struggle to sustain themselves. Civil society formation appears also to be subject to electoral cycles, with some groups explicitly forming for the period of the election and some succumbing to electoral burnout, ceasing to exist once the election is over. On the positive side, however, it is clear that a significant number of diverse groups with a range of creative skills and expertise is willing to put significant time and energy into working for a better Ireland, and that these groups are talking to each other. There is also a wide range of models of working, which often differ across generations, and increasing evidence of a social entrepreneurship which enables small groups to use internet and information technology. In this context of a flourishing but fragmented civil society, leadership is essential. Silva's second key lesson relates to the issue of alliance building between civil society and left-wing political leaders. Given the fragmented nature of Irish left parties, and with the largest party in government and a range of smaller parties in opposition, it will be challenging to recreate this overlap in the Irish context. There is also the challenge, noted earlier, that left parties do not have a historically cooperative relationship with civil society organisations (Ó Broin 2011). A February 2011 initiative of left-wing academics brought together a range of civil society and left political party activists to discuss the future of the Irish left and the political possibilities for left-wing parties to forge partnerships with civil society, but it is not clear how or whether such partnerships might develop. Finally, there is the challenge of promoting practical pragmatic reformist agendas that can make advances and contribute to change over time. Given the Irish focus on austerity it is likely that sectoral defensive campaigning will dominate the next half decade; however, campaigns on issues of broader economic justice, broadening the tax base, workers' rights and environmental issues are all possible and have the potential to contribute towards the emergence of the cross-sectoral movement for change that is so urgently needed in Ireland.

Silva also drew attention to using transnational ideas and networks to create broad domestic agendas and sustain alliances. Bearing in mind the relationship between power elites at national and EU levels and the role of the EU in shaping Irish political economy choices in the present crisis, it is also necessary to think about a reform agenda in the context of a movement for a renewed social democratic project for Europe and to consider how international processes like Agenda 21 can progress national ambitions for ecological sustainability.

A number of international and national interests are adopting similar themes about developing alternative models of economic development and social and political reform. The Spring Alliance, a coalition of EU-level NGOs, trade unions and environmental groups, has produced an alternative agenda for change. The Irish Environmental Network takes its inspiration from Agenda 21; other groups are inspired by the World Social Forum. The Foundation for European Progressive Studies (FEPS) has initiated the 'Next Left' project, gathering 40 journalists, politicians and academics from across Europe and publishing a range of books, articles, discussion papers, reviews and research publications, as well as organising a series of national meetings with member organisations to develop a vision of a progressive future, with a view to influencing political parties affiliated to the Party of European Socialists (PES) across the EU. As the EU takes on more competencies on wages and pensions policy (as part of the German insistence on the greater harmonisation of policy across the EU), the prospect is raised of unions growing stronger at EU level (Erne 2011). Canada has been a source of ideas about citizens' assemblies, and eastern Europe about civic forums (Harvey 2009). As with Latin America, Iceland has been a source of inspiration for a range of groups. The Ireland : Iceland Project, for example, is a collective experiment bringing Irish and Icelandic people together in a space where ideas can be incubated for inspirational collaborative projects.

Chapter 2 discussed the challenge of creating an open communicative discourse about values, without which more fundamental transformative change will not come about. This is consistent with Edwards' (2004) focus on the public sphere. Habermas (2006:103) speaks of the importance of a political public sphere concerned with the practice of the state and describes how this sphere has been weakened in the welfare state. The creation of a movement for change requires a communicative discourse, and this means a pivotal focus on the role of the media. Many groups share an analysis about the need to challenge hegemony and the importance of building progressive alliances to impact on the public realm. These groups are rightly critical of the role of the Irish media in framing politics and power (Cooper 2009; Leahy 2009; Feeney 2003). The Carnegie Trust (2007) points to issues of ownership of new and old forms of media and the need to have a media strategy at the heart of challenging inequality. The small mainstream media community oriented towards progressive change is crucial. New media 'movements' based on information technology are increasingly common and are a creative base for organising actions and resistance for many loose networks of activists, bloggers, media workers and academics. All of these initiatives help create communities of interest among users. However, as Bua (2009) argues, assuming that internet-based media may overcome the limitations of traditional media is over-optimistic. Dahlgren (2005: 161) warns that internet deliberation can result in a form of Balkanisation, with people interacting only with people with whom they already agree, in 'echo chambers' or 'cyber ghettos' (Dahlgren 2005: 161). Bua (2009) draws attention to how new media can mirror and perpetuate existing unequal patterns of participation; the relative absence of Irish women contributing to economic and political blogs bears out this point. The same challenge faces the significant number of emerging innovative social and cultural spaces which mix political debate with socialising. All of these are part of an emerging creative public space for political debate. There is an emerging public sphere; a wide range of social public arenas in which citizenship can be animated and a sense of collective demand can grow and develop. Once again, an explicit emphasis on inclusion is essential. EAPN (2010) stresses the particular challenge of including people experiencing poverty in new public spheres.

TOWARDS AN ALL-IRELAND REPUBLIC?

Many think of Ireland as an island and organise life as an island community. There always have been a large number of north–south or all-island civil society federations in areas such as sports, culture, the churches and social rights organisations. Amongst the new north–south bodies established under the Good Friday Agreement (GFA), the North–South Ministerial Council and the British–Irish Council have been sites for political and administrative cooperation on issues relating to staff development, fraud control, migration and information technology. This practical policy collaboration has the potential to result in greater policy interdependencies. What, then, are the prospects that the second Irish republic might be an all-Ireland state? While the GFA created a new Northern Ireland politics after 1998, its largely consociational mechanics to some degree cemented existing ethno-cultural divisions in the North, with even more peace walls dividing ethnic communities and the more sectarian parties gaining increased electoral power. In the ongoing debate about institutional reforms, those favouring maintenance of the consociational structures argue for reforming the assembly and executive, while those seeking greater transformation in political institutions argue that what is needed is a complete redesign of the political apparatus of the GFA. Political evolution is therefore complex. As Tonge (2005) argues, the logic of the institutional arrangements of the GFA does not significantly progress cross-border or confederal institutions. The north–south institutions (as outlined in Chapter 4) cannot in any way be described as federalist in nature, nor as a joint authority under which Northern Ireland would be ruled by Britain and the Republic. Tonge also raises the question of how anti-sectarian initiatives in the North can work when the province's existence as a separate political entity rests in the unwillingness of a significant number of its citizens to share political structures with the Republic (ibid.: 260). He argues that, unless placed in a federal or confederal context, any realignment of Northern political institutions will be largely irrelevant. The clear embedding of the North into British political structures does not seem propitious for Irish unification and, as Tonge puts it, bi-national aspects of the agreement are woefully thin (ibid.: 258).

What then are the options as seen by those who promote the idea of an all-Ireland state?

From different starting points, Humphries (2009) and E. Ó Broin (2009) both aspire to greater unification and see potential for this to occur across economic, social, political and cultural activity and policy. The potential for economic unification and an all-island economy has been heralded by government politicians from both jurisdictions. However, with the Northern economy firmly embedded in the British economy, and with different monetary systems, economic unification remains a huge challenge. The present crisis highlights two key yet contradictory trends. Aspects of the economic crisis in the Republic highlight the economic links between the two states on the island. For example, up to 20 per cent of property held by the National Asset Management Agency (NAMA) is located in Northern Ireland. The fact that NAMA's portfolio contains so much property in the North suggests that an all-island economy is a growing fact of life. At the same time, rising unemployment highlights the real cost to the London government of sustaining the weak economy of the North, where poverty levels are higher than in the Republic and benefit dependency impacts on more than a third of working-age adults.

The growth in Sinn Féin representation in the Dáil and that party's strong commitment to moving towards an all-Ireland state, as well as the opportunity presented by the centenary of 1916, may give the issue more visibility in the political life of the Republic, but it is unlikely in the foreseeable future to become a widely held priority objective. Neither is the context over the coming decade likely to be a promising one, as the centenary of the events of 1916 to 1922, which resulted in the partition of the island, has the potential for entrenching attitudes on both sides of the sectarian divide. Kilmurray identifies a series of issues: the potential for paramilitary resurgence; conflict about the categorisation of victims and survivors; the demonisation of ex-prisoners and ex-combatants; claims that a bill of rights would be a concession to republicanism; differing interpretations of the 1916–22 period in the commemorative events; and alarm in the unionist community at any strengthening of a narrative of reunification. She identifies as worrying the disengagement in working-class communities, to which the peace dividend has not trickled down in any meaningful way and where health and income disparities are wide. In this context, she asks, 'Where is the vision for a future society?' and where might the constitutional form of that society be devised and agreed? (Kilmurray 2010). Murphy describes the gradual transformation of relations north and south of the border: by 2010 the 'porous' nature of the border had brought about 'multifaceted and multisectoral' advantages, bringing economic, social, cultural and political benefits (M.C. Murphy 2010: 398–9). However she is realistic that there may be limits to such relations and cooperation and that what has been achieved to date is in the context of maintaining Northern Ireland as a constituent part of the United Kingdom (ibid.: 414). Development in Northern Ireland will also be further influenced by debate in the United Kingdom and the possibility of fuller devolution, which may even lead to the break-up of the United Kingdom as we know it.

Harvey (2010) characterises early 2010 in the context of the diminished violence and the routinisation of cross-border cooperation; but also of disappointment in the failure to complete the north–south forum and equivalence of rights in the GFA. He notes that with devolved government now being institutionalised, many now look to civil society as holding the best prospects for substantive progressive change. The GFA includes a north–south civic forum, though this has been delayed by the non-cooperation policy of the Democratic Unionist Party despite being reaffirmed in the St Andrews Agreement. A 2010 initiative by the Taoiseach's Department has led to a number of informal civic forum meetings between key civil society groups north and south, offering some hope for a renewed dialogue across civil society; but this is impeded by the lack of priority afforded it by civil society groups in the Republic and the involvement of only a limited number of civil society groups in the North. Despite this, it is possible to see a north–south civil forum advancing common cross-border issues, such as ambulances, bank charges, taxation of trans-border workers and philanthropy across the island. Harvey offers examples of good practice in north–south initiatives on mental health and environmental policy and practice (Harvey 2009). Many cross-border initiatives (Hanna's House, the Power Partnerships, the TASC/Democratic Dialogue Democracy Commission and the Practice and Participation of Rights) have followed transformative processes in their methods of working. Generally however among civil society groups in the Republic, there is little awareness or analysis of the potential of the GFA instruments for meeting some of their own aspirations for greater participation in decision making and rights. In the Republic, civil society-led collaboration with Northern Ireland is often considered as being of secondary importance to core activities and so is the first to be cut as funding becomes scarce. While the range of cross-border activity is impressive in its scale and scope (Pollack 2010, 2011), evolving to an all-Ireland state through civil society cross-border activity is highly unlikely. This has always been difficult to develop and, without EU funding to make it possible, the level of cooperation is likely to drop considerably.

The May 2011 Northern Ireland Assembly Elections were marked by a decrease in voter turnout, with the Democratic Unionist Party and Sinn Fein each increasing their number of seats, so reinforcing themselves as the dominant parties; the former won 38 seats and the latter 29 seats. The Ulster Unionist Party won 16 seats and the Social Democratic and Labour Party 14 seats, in both cases fewer than in the previous assembly. Alliance secured 8 seats and others took the remaining 3 seats. While this represents an opportunity to consolidate progress, the fragility of what had been achieved was pointed out by an *Irish Times* editorial (2011: 15). This celebrated the cessation of the work of the Independent Commission on Decommissioning, but noted the vulnerability of young men in deprived areas to being recruited by paramilitary and criminal gangs. As in the Republic, tackling educational inequality is the key to social cohesion. In the context of the economic, political and social divisions outlined here, and in the absence of any strong political will in either north or south to give priority to addressing the issue of an all-Ireland state, there seems little likelihood that the second Irish republic will in the near future overcome the divisions of the past. This is underscored by the degree to which debates that have been taking place in the Republic about reforming politics and renewing society are largely characterised by the absence of any all-island dimension (Adams 2010; Slí Eile 2010).

CONCLUSION: IRELAND AND MODELS OF CAPITALISM

This chapter has set itself the task of examining the actors which might carry the project of a second Irish republic. As is clear from this book, the first Irish republic is at a critical juncture, both in terms of its economic and financial crisis, and also in terms of the widespread recognition of the need for extensive political renewal. In Chapter 9, the broad options for change were identified as a weak liberal model, a developmental social democratic model or an ecological or ethical socialist model. Our survey of reform proposals in Chapter 9 and of the balance of political and civil society forces in this chapter allow us to assess what is currently at play in Ireland. There is a struggle between powerful proponents of the liberal model (who remain dominant in the political system, in civil society and particularly in private-sector economic interests), and weaker but by no means negligible forces seeking to coalesce around a project for a more regulated and socially just form of capitalism. More marginal groups espouse radical actions for environmental sustainability and social regeneration consistent with an ecological socialism or, indeed, a more traditional Marxist socialism, mostly inspired by Trotskyist ideas. Returning to the discussion on models of capitalism in Chapter 1, therefore, Ireland seems firmly within the parameters of the 'varieties of capitalism' debate. In drawing the strands of the book to a conclusion, however, the evidence set out can be usefully interpreted through the framework outlined by Hay (2004). He argues that at critical junctures of crisis the interaction of three discrete independent variables – 'ideas', 'interests', and 'institutions' – determine the pace and direction of transition from one paradigm to another.

For a society deeply divided for a century into two states as a consequence of colonialism, the significance of the shifting sands of political allegiance and of civil society activism should not be underestimated. For each of the two polities that emerged on the island was dominated by a narrow religio-cultural identity and ethos that succeeded in ensuring that strong movements for change, both political and socio-economic, failed to emerge. While political change was finally forced on the Northern state, partly through the myopia and stubbornness of its unionist ruling elite, Fianna Fáil in the Republic showed far greater ability to maintain its hegemony and deflect attention from the failings of an ever more dysfunctional political system. However, the power of a socio-economic elite (largely made up of property developers and, latterly, bankers) became far stronger in the Republic through its alliance with Fianna Fáil while, in the North, the social reforms of the post-war period and, finally, the collapse of the unionist ruling monolith in the early 1970s, had the result that economic power became more concentrated in the hands of the state. One of the consequences of the collapse of the Celtic Tiger south of the border was to expose not only the abject weaknesses of the political system but also, more importantly, the close links between Fianna Fáil and a ruling socio-economic elite which had grown fabulously wealthy, powerful and, in some quarters, corrupt (see Chapter 6). In Hay's terms, therefore, we can see a break-up of the close nexus between ideas, interests and institutions that has so successfully and for such a long time underpinned Irish capitalism and maintained a neoliberal hegemony. This highlights the extent of the critical juncture through which the country is currently passing.

While it may be initially disappointing that this book could not have identified greater prospects for a new paradigm to emerge, either a developmental social democratic model or an ecological socialist model, what it does show is that the realm of ideas has for the first time in a century become a lively battleground. In this way, the interests of a much wider section of the population now find expression, particularly through the exposing of the elite interests that were given continuous priority in the policy options of the Irish state when under Fianna Fáil dominance. But, apart from the fact that a wider range of critical ideas is now helping to educate Irish citizens about the way power has worked and the elite interests it has served, the depth of the banking crisis and the scale of the cutbacks being forced on Irish taxpayers to help bail out German and French banks are dramatically shifting the interests of wide sections of the population. People who had felt their interests well served by the dominant socio-economic model now face a grim future of economic insecurity, negative equity, and a lack of hope (as identified in Chapter 5). This inevitably opens up spaces within which more radical critiques may find acceptance, thereby opening the eyes of many to the elite interests which power has served to protect and promote at the expense of the majority. The conditions are therefore ripe for a major shift in the ideas and interests that have shaped and dominated Irish society – conditions that are unlikely to change in the foreseeable future, since the Irish financial crisis shows no signs of abating.

This shifts the potential to the realm of institutions. For critical junctures may require a shift in ideas and interests to underpin them, but it is through fashioning new institutions that the power relations of society can be reshaped in an enduring way, informed by different ideas about how power should be used for the common good, and serving the interests of a wider section of the population. The objective of a second Irish Republic is the lens through which this attempt to reshape power relations finds expression in contemporary Ireland. It has become clear to us in writing the book, and in particular in watching the dramatic political realignments of the 2011 general election, that much remains to be done to ensure that the reform of institutions now underway in Ireland will reshape power relations and move us beyond the weak liberal model that has plunged us into the current crisis. Civil society therefore faces determined struggles. Our hope is that this book may contribute to clarifying the options that are likely to inform these struggles over the foreseeable future. In introducing the option for an ecological socialist model, the book opens the debate to a wider horizon of options that is going to be forced upon us by the twin challenges of peak oil and the need radically to reduce greenhouse gas emissions. It is this that opens the prospect of a move beyond capitalism into a society in which prosperity and flourishing, rather than economic growth, define the agenda of politics. We have also, throughout the book, drawn attention to the deeply patriarchal nature of Irish capitalism and argued that whatever model emerges will have to be embedded in an ethic of care from which true gender equality can emerge. These challenges inevitably move us into a time when the dominant ideas that inform the structures of our societies, the ways in which people define their interests, and the institutions required to structure production and distribution will all need to be fundamentally reformulated. Nothing in this book would lead us to believe that Ireland has much to offer to this task. Instead, as so often in the past, we in Ireland appear to be arriving a little breathless and a little late at the scene of struggles for a more socially just form of capitalism and greater gender equality – struggles that have been fought and partly won elsewhere decades ago (even if these victories are progressively being overturned). But at least we are arriving, and it is better to do so late than to be seduced into inaction by the wiles of a financial and consumerist capitalism.

Finally, in the words of James Connolly, 'Ireland is nothing without her people'. We draw attention to the true potential of active citizenship and stress the role of the public sphere in expressing solidarity and interdependence (Gaynor 2009b; Cronin 2009). Sandel (2009) argues about the necessary social nature of public goods and spaces that enable human social relations to grow and develop and that foster a sense of care, love and solidarity or interdependence and so enable development of a 'politics of the common good' (Vail 2010: 326). O'Ferrall (2001: 136) draws on Arendt's argument that all individuals have the capacity 'not just to choose between prescribed alternatives but in cooperation and solidarity with others to call entirely new possibilities into existence', that citizens have 'the role of initiative rather than simply the role of choice'. The first Irish republic was built on the initiative of nineteenth-century civil activism; building the second republic requires an equivalent twenty-first century civic initiative.

References

Adams, D. (2010) 'Raise this question: Debate on republicanism still dominated by the split', *Irish Times*, 12 August, p.16.

Adshead, M. and Tonge, J. (2009) *Politics in Ireland: Convergence and Divergence in a Two-Polity Island* (Basingstoke: Palgrave Macmillan).

Adshead, M. and Robinson, N. (2009) 'Late development and State developmentalism – never the twain? Towards a political economy of "post-Celtic Tiger" Ireland', paper presented to the Political Studies Association annual conference, University of Manchester, 7–9 April.

Advocacy Initiative (2010) 'Overview of survey research', presented by Middlequarter & Montague Communications, Advocacy Initiative Conference, Ashling Hotel, Dublin, 10 June.

Allen, K. (2007) *The Corporate Takeover of Ireland* (Dublin: Irish Academic Press).

Allen, K. (2009) *Ireland's Economic Crash: A Radical Agenda for Change* (Dublin: Gill and MacMillan).

Allen, M. (2011) 'The political context', input to Claiming Our Future Planning Day, Tailors' Hall, Dublin, 23 March.

All-Party Oireachtas Committee on the Constitution (1997) *Second Progress Report: Seanad Eireann* (Dublin: Stationery Office).

Bacon, P. (2009) 'Over-capacity in the Irish hotel industry and required elements of a recovery programme', www.ihf.ie/documents/HotelStudyFinalReport101109.pdf.

Baker, J. (2003) *Poverty and Inequality: Applying an Equality Dimension to Poverty Proofing* (Dublin: Equality Authority).

Baker, J. and Sinnott, R. (2000) 'Simulating multi-option referendums in Ireland: Neutrality and abortion', *Irish Political Studies*, 15(1):105–25.

Baker, J., Lynch, K., Cantillon S. and Walsh, J. (2004) *Equality: From Theory to Action* (Basingstoke: Palgrave Macmillan).

Baker, M. and Tippin, D. (2004) 'More than just another obstacle: Health, domestic purposes beneficiaries and the transition to paid work', *Social Policy Journal of New Zealand*, 21:98–120.

Bacik, I. (2009) 'Women in politics', report of the Sub-Committee on Women's Participation in Politics of the Joint Committee on Justice, Equality, Defence and Women's Rights, October.

Bank of Ireland (2007) *Bank of Ireland Wealth Report* (Dublin: Bank of Ireland).

Bárcena, A. (2010a) 'Structural constraints on development in Latin America and the Caribbean: A post-crisis reflection', *CEPAL Review*, 100:7–27.

Bárcena, A. (2010b) 'The time for Latin America', www.eclac.cl/notes/65/Opinion.html, accessed 24 February 2011.

Barrington, K. (2011) 'Bowing to the bankers', *Sunday Business Post*, 13 February, p.15.

Barry, F. (2009) 'Public policymaking and the marketplace for ideas', paper presented to a conference on 'Transforming Public Services', Croke Park, Dublin, 15 September.

Barry, F., Bradley, J. and O'Malley, E. (1999) 'Indigenous and foreign industry: Characteristics and performance', in F. Barry (ed.) *Understanding Ireland's Economic Growth* (Basingstoke: Palgrave), pp.45–74.

Barry, U. (ed.) (2008) *Where Are We Now? Feminist Debate in Contemporary Ireland* (Dublin: TASC @ New Island).

Beesley, A. (2011) 'Angry Barroso points finger of blame at Irish institutions', *Irish Times*, 20 January, p.1.

Begg, D. (2005) 'New society requires new labour market standards', *Irish Times*, 17 December.

Bell, D. and Blanchflower, D. (2009) 'What should be done about rising unemployment in the UK?', www.bankofengland.co.uk/publications/ speeches/2009/speech379paper.pdf, accessed 30 April 2010.

Bertelsmann Foundation (2011) *Sustainable Governance Project* (Berlin: Bertelsmann Foundation).

Birrell, D. (2006) 'The review of public administration in NI: Some policy implications and comparisons', address to Irish Social Policy Association Conference, October.

Bissett, J. (2008) *Regeneration and Public Private Partnerships* (Dublin: TASC @ New Island).

Block, F. (2010) 'Keynes lost and found', *Dissent*, Spring: 110–13.

Boucher, G. and Boyle, N. (2007) 'The institutional capacity of the Irish state: Development planning, infrastructural planning and training policy 1987–2007', paper presented at the Political Studies Association Ireland Annual Conference, Dublin, 19 October.

Boyd-Barrett, R. (2010) 'Time for a new alliance', *Village Magazine*, June/July:13.

Boyle, N. (2005) *FÁS and active labour market policy 1985–2004*, Studies in Public Policy, 17 (Dublin: The Policy Institute, Trinity College).

Boyle, R. (2009) 'The changing face of the Irish public service', in M. Mulreany (ed.) *Serving the State: The Public Sector in Ireland* (Dublin: IPA), pp.11–28.

Bradley, J. (2002) 'The computer sector in Irish manufacturing: Past triumphs, present strains, future challenges', *Journal of the Statistical and Social Inquiry Society of Ireland*, 31:26–73.

Bradley, J. (2006) 'An island economy or island economies? Ireland after the Belfast agreement', Working Paper 22 (Dublin: Institute for British–Irish Studies/Belfast: Centre for International Borders Research).

Breathnach, C. (2005) 'Does the concept of social capital provide an empowering network for national social partnership?', paper presented to Policy Institute seminar, Trinity College Dublin, 25 May.

Bruton, J. (2011) 'A letter to President Barroso of the European Commission', downloaded from www.johnbruton.com, March.

Bua, A. (2009) 'Realising online democracy: A critical appraisal of online civic commons', Compass Think Piece No 49, www.compassonline.org.

Burawoy, M. (2003) 'For a sociological Marxism: The complementary convergence of Antonio Gramsci and Karl Polanyi', *Politics and Society* 31(2):193–261.

Byrne, E. (2009) 'Legal and moral corruption', http://elaine.ie/2009/07/31/defini-tions-and-types-of-corruption/, cited from Byrne, E. (2007) *The Moral and Legal Development of Corruption: Nineteenth and Twentieth Century Corruption in Ireland*, Ph.D. thesis, University of Limerick.

Byrne, E. (2011) *A Crooked Harp: Political Corruption in Ireland 1800–2010* (Manchester: Manchester University Press).

Byrne, E., Farrell, D., O'Malley, E., Suiter J. and Wall, M.(2010) 'Path to rebuilding Republic should start with citizens' assembly', *Irish Times*, 26 November, www.irishtimes.com/newspaper/opinion/2010/1126/1224284180307.html.

Canzani, A. (2010) 'Un país suavamente ondulado', *Nueva Sociedad*, 225:18–30.

Caramani, D. (2004) *The Nationalization of Politics: The Formation of National Electorates and Party Systems in Western Europe* (Cambridge: Cambridge University Press).

Carnegie Trust (2007) *Inquiry into the Future of Civil Society in the UK and Ireland* (London: Carnegie UK Trust).

Carney, G. and Harris, C. (2011) 'Deliberative democracy and political reform', 30 March, http://politicalreform.ie/2011/03/30/deliberative-democracy-and-political-reform/.

Carroll, S. and Wall, M. (2009) 'Unions not planning to oust government – Begg', *Irish Times*, 17 December, p.9.

Carswell, S. (2009) 'Reforms spell end of light-touch era', *Irish Times*, 19 June, 'Business this week' supplement, p.5.

Carswell, S. (2011) 'At long last, an endgame for our shattered banks', *Irish Times*, 1 April, p.20.

Casey, M. (2009) 'Boom growth came too easy – now we'll have to graft', *Irish Times*, 8 May, p.13.

Casey, M. (2010) *Ireland's Malaise: The Troubled Personality of the Irish Economy* (Dublin: Liffey Press).

Castañeda, J.G. (1994) *Utopia Unarmed: The Latin American Left after the Cold War* (New York: Vintage Books).

Castells, M. (2001) 'Information Technology and Global Capitalism', in W. Hutton and A. Giddens (eds) *On the Edge: Living with Global Capitalism* (London: Vintage), pp.52–74.

Cerny, P.G. (2000) 'Structuring the political arena: Public goods, states and governance in a globalizing world', in R. Palan (ed.) *Global Political Economy: Contemporary Theories* (London: Routledge), pp.21–35.

Chari, R. and McMahon, H. (2003) 'Reconsidering the patterns of organised interests in Irish policy making', *Irish Political Studies*, 18(1):27–50.

Chubb, B. (1982) *Government and Politics of Ireland*, 2nd edn (Harlow: Longman).

Claiming Our Future (2010) 'Results from first ever consensus deliberation', 30 October, http://www.claimingourfuture.ie/who-we-are/results-from-the-30th-oct/, accessed 3 April 2011.

Clancy, P. and Murphy, G. (2006) *Outsourcing Government: Public Bodies and Accountability* (Dublin: TASC @ New Island).

Clifford, M. (2011) 'Too close for comfort, but that's the way crony capitalism is done in Ireland', *Sunday Tribune*, 30 January, www.tribune.ie/article/2011/jan/16/too-close-for-comfort-but-thats-the-way-crony-capi/.

Coakley, J. (2004) 'Society and Political Culture', in J. Coakley and M. Gallagher (eds) *Politics in the Republic of Ireland*, 4th edn (London: Routledge), pp.36–71.

Coakley, J. and Gallagher, M. (eds) (2010) *Politics in the Republic of Ireland*, 5th edn (London: Routledge).

Coffey, T. (2011) 'A 10 point manifesto: Towards a second republic', a collection of discussion papers on options to transform governance and leadership in the Irish Republic for the better (Dublin: Dublin City Business Association).

Collins E (2009) 'International competitiveness and the new economy: The role of equality and diversity', TASC Think Piece No. 23 (Dublin : TASC).

Collins, M., Healy, S. and Reynolds, B. (2010) *An Agenda for a New Ireland: Policies to Ensure Economic Development, Social Equity and Sustainability* (Dublin: Social Justice Ireland).

Collins, N. and O'Shea, M. (2003) 'Clientelism: Facilitating rights and favours', in M. Adshead and M. Millar (eds) *Public Administration and Public Policy in Ireland: Theory and Methods* (London: Routledge), pp.88–107.

Combat Poverty Agency (2007) *Stories from 'Silent People and Other Stories'*(Dublin: CPA).

Comptroller and Auditor General (2009) 'Advertising and promotion in FÁS', Special Report 66 (Dublin: Stationery Office).

Comptroller and Auditor General (2010) 'Accounts of the Public Services 2009: Vote Management', report of the Comptroller and Auditor General, vol.2 (Dublin: Stationery Office).

Connaughton, B. (2010) 'Symptom or Remedy? Mediating Characteristics of the Irish Central Bureaucracy and their Influence on the Strategic Capacity of a "Small" State', *Halduskultuur–Administrative Culture*, 11(1):110–26.

Connolly, E. (2004) 'The government and the governmental system', in J. Coakley and M. Gallagher (eds) *Politics in the Republic of Ireland*, 4th edn (London: Routledge), pp.328–51.

Connolly, E. (2007) 'The institutionalisation of anti-poverty and social exclusion policy in Irish social partnership', Research Working Paper Series 07/01 (Dublin: Combat Poverty Agency).

Connolly, E. and O'Halpin, E. (1999) 'The government and the governmental system', in J. Coakley and M. Gallagher (eds) *Politics in the Republic of Ireland*, 3rd edn (London: Routledge), pp.249–70.

Connolly, L. and Hourigan, N. (eds) (2006) *Social Movements and Ireland* (Manchester: Manchester University Press).

Constitution Review Group (1996) 'Report of the Constitution Review Group' (Dublin: Stationery Office).

Cooper, M. (2009) *Who Really Runs Ireland? The Story of the Elite Who Led Ireland from Bust to Boom and Back Again* (Dublin: Penguin Ireland).

Cousins, M. (2005) *Explaining the Irish Welfare State* (Lewiston, N.Y.: Edwin Mellen Press).

Cousins, M. (2007) 'Political budget cycles and social security budget increases in the Republic of Ireland, 1923–2005', MPRA Paper No. 5359, June.

Cox, L. (2010) 'Another world is under construction: Social movement responses to inequality and crisis', paper presented to conference on 'Equality in a time of crisis', Egalitarian World Initiative/UCD School of Social Justice, University College Dublin, 7 May.

Cox, P. (2010) 'What can we learn from best practice elsewhere in the EU?', address given to Irish Parliamentary Society seminar 'The Dáil of Tomorrow', Dáil Eireann, 21 February.

Cronin, M. (2009) 'Active citizenship and its discontents', in D. O'Broin and P. Kirby (eds) *Dissent, Power and Democracy* (Dublin: A. & A. Farmer), pp.62–78.

Crowley, N. (2010) *Empty Promises: Bringing the Equality Authority to Heel* (Dublin: A. & A. Farmer).

Cruddas, J. and Rutherford, J. (2010) 'The common table', in R. Williams and L. Elliott (eds) *Crisis and Recovery: Ethics, Economics and Justice* (Basingstoke: Palgrave Macmillan), pp.54–76.

CSO (2000) *That was then, this is now: Change in Ireland, 1949–1999* (Dublin: Central Statistics Office).

CSO (2009) 'Measuring Ireland's progress' (Dublin: Central Statistics Office).

CSO (2010a) 'Survey on income and living conditions (SILC) 2009', April (Dublin: Central Statistics Office).

CSO (2010b) 'Quarterly household survey Q3 2010' (Dublin: Central Statistics Office).

CSO (2010c) 'Population and migration estimates', April (Dublin: Central Statistics Office).

CSO (2010d) 'Vital statistics', April (Dublin: Central Statistics Office).

CSO (2011) 'Live register', March (Dublin: Central Statistics Office).

Cullen, M. (2008) 'The potential of civic republicanism', *The Citizen*, 1:8–10.

Dahl, R. (2005) 'What political institutions does large-scale democracy require?', *Political Science Quarterly*, 120(2):187–97.

Dahl, R. (2007) *On Democracy* (New Haven, Conn. and London: Yale University Press).

Dahlgren, P. (2005) 'The Internet, public spheres, and political communication: Dispersion and deliberation', *Political Communication*, 22(2):147–62.

Dalton, G. (ed.) (1968) *Primitive, Archaic and Modern Economies: Essays of Karl Polanyi* (New York: Anchor Books).

Daly, S. (2007) 'Mapping civil society in the Republic of Ireland', *Community Development Journal*, 43(2):157–76.

Davies, H. (2010) *The Financial Crisis: Who Is to Blame?* (Cambridge: Polity Press).

De Buitlear, D., Ó Brolcháin, D. and Roden, J. (1998) 'Institutional reform', in S. Healy and B. Reynolds (eds) *Social Policy in Ireland: Principles, Practice and Problems* (Dublin: Oaktree Press), pp.371–85.

De Burca, D. (2010) 'Time for a new Party', *Village* Magazine, June/July:12.

Department of Justice (2010) 'Organised and White Collar Crime', white paper on crime, discussion document no.3, Department of Justice and Law Reform (Dublin: Stationery Office).

Department of the Environment, Heritage and Local Government (2008) *Housing needs Assessment*, (Dublin: Government of Ireland).

Department of the Taoiseach (2011) 'Programme for government', www.taoiseach. gov.ie/eng/Publications/Publications_2011/Programme_for_Government_2011. html, accessed May 2011.

Desmond, B. (2011) 'What recommendations for Dáil reform have yet to be implemented?', presentation to seminar 'The Dáil of Tomorrow', Irish Parliamentary Society, Dáil Eireann, 21 February.

Doherty, M. (2011) 'Crisis and response of social partnership in Ireland', paper presented to Session 1, 'Trade Unions, Industrial Relations and the Crisis', research symposium on 'Employment and the Crisis: Work Migration and Unemployment', Trinity College Dublin, 11 March.

Dorr, N. (2002) 'Ireland at the United Nations', in B. Tonra and E. Ward (eds) *Ireland in International Affairs: Interests, Institutions and Identities* (Dublin: Institute of Public Administration), pp.104–28.

Doyle, M. (2009) 'On slow road to recovery', *Irish Times*, 'Business This Week' supplement, 9 October, p.7.

Drucker, J. (2010) 'Google 2.4% rate shows how $60 billion lost to tax loopholes', www.bloomberg.com/news/2010-10-21/google-2-4-rate-shows-how-60-billion-u-s-revenue-lost-to-tax-loopholes.html.

Drudy, P.J. and Punch, M. (2005) *Out of Reach: Inequalities in the Irish Housing System* (Dublin: TASC @ New Island).

Duncan, G. and Chapman, J. (2010) 'New millennium, new public management and the New Zealand model', *Australian Journal of Public Administration*, 69(3):301–13.

Dunphy, R. (1995) *The Making of Fianna Fáil Power in Ireland, 1923–1948*(Oxford: Clarendon Press).

Duwurry, N. (2011) 'Gender employment and recession trends and impacts', paper presented to research symposium 'Employment in the Crisis: Work, Migration and Unemployment', Trinity College Dublin, 11 March.

EAPN (ed.) (2010) *Ireland and the European Social Inclusion Strategy: Lessons Learned and the Road Ahead* (Dublin: EAPN, Ireland).

Edwards, M. (2004) *Civil Society* (Cambridge: Polity Press).

EPA (Environmental Protection Agency) (2008) 'Ireland's Environment 2008' (Wexford: Environmental Protection Agency).

Erne, R. (2011) 'European Unions after the global crisis', in L. Burroni, M. Keune and G. Meardi (eds) *Economy and Society in Europe: A Relationship in Crisis* (Cheltenham: Edward Elgar), http://ucd-ie.academia.edu/RolandErne/ Papers/253800/European_Unions_after_the_Crisis, accessed 3 April, pp.1–24.

Esping-Anderson, G. (1990) *The Three Worlds of Welfare Capitalism* (Cambridge: Polity Press).

European Commission (2009) 'Statistical annex of the European economy'(Brussels: European Commission).

European Commission (2010) 'More women in senior positions: Key to economic stability and growth' (Brussels: European Commission).

Evans, M. and Coen, G. (2003) 'Elitism and agri-environmental policy', in M. Adshead and M. Millar (eds) *Public Administration and Public Policy in Ireland: Theory and Methods* (London: Routledge), pp.1–20.

Fahey, T. (2010) 'The welfare state: An overview', in B. Reynolds, S. Healy and M. Collins (eds) *The Future of the Welfare State* (Dublin: Social Justice Ireland), pp.1–20.

Farrell, D. (2008) 'Commentary', in C. McGrath and E. O'Malley (eds) *Irish Political Studies Reader: Key Contributions* (London: Routledge), pp.216–22.

Farrell D. (2010) 'Irish electoral reform: Three myths and a proposal', MacGill Summer School, 'Reforming the Republic', July, http://politicalreformireland. files.wordpress.com/2010/07/irish_electoral_reform-2.pdf, accessed 3 April 2011.

Feasta (2005) 'Growth: The Celtic cancer', *Feasta Review*, 2 (Dublin: Feasta).

Feeney, P. (2003) 'The media in Ireland: A distorted vehicle for political communication', in D. De Buitlear and F. Ruane (eds) *Governance and Policy in Ireland: Essays in Honour of Miriam Hederman O'Brien* (Dublin: IPA), pp.73–90.

Ferguson, N. (2008) *The Ascent of Money: A Financial History of the World* (London: Allen Lane).

Ferriter, D. (2004) *The Transformation of Ireland 1900–2000* (London: Profile Books).

Financial Times (2008) '"I made a mistake", admits Greenspan', *Financial Times*, 24 October, p.6.

Fine Gael (2011) 'New politics', www.finegael.org/upload/NewPolitics.pdf.

Fischer, C. (2011) 'Revisioning Ireland: Lessons from feminist care ethics', *Studies*, 100(397), pp.63–72.

FitzGerald, G. (2008) 'End of asset boom reveals foolishness of tax cuts', *Irish Times*, 11 October, p.14.

Flood, F. (2002) 'The second interim Report of the Tribunal of Inquiry into Certain Planning Matters and Payments: Final Report' (Dublin: Stationery Office).

Forfás (2010) 'Profile of employment and unemployment', February (Dublin: Forfás).

Foster, R.F. (1989) *The Oxford Illustrated History of Ireland* (Oxford: Oxford University Press).

Foster, R.F. (2008) *The Luck of the Irish: A Brief History of Ireland from 1970* (Oxford: Oxford University Press).

Gallagher, L.A., Doyle, E. and O'Leary, E. (2002) 'Creating the Celtic Tiger and Sustaining Economic Growth: A Business Perspective', in D. McCoy, D. Duffy, J. Hore and C. MacCoille (eds) *Quarterly Economic Commentary* (Dublin: Economic and Social Research Institute), Spring:63–81.

Gallagher, M. (1987) 'Does Ireland need a new electoral system', *Irish Political Studies*, 2:27–48.

Gallego, A. (2007) 'Inequality in political participation: Contemporary patterns in European Countries', Centre for the Study of Democracy, UCLA, 07/01.

Gamble, A. (2009) *The Spectre and the Feast* (Basingstoke: Palgrave Macmillan).

Gannon, B. and Nolan, B. (2004) *The Dynamics of Disability and Social Inclusion in Ireland* (Dublin: National Disability Authority).

Garvin, T. (1987) 'The politics of language and literature in pre-independent Ireland', *Irish Political Studies*, 2:49–63.

Garvin, T. (1991) 'Democracy in Ireland: Collective somnolence and public policy', *Administration*, 39:42–54.

Gaynor, N. (2009a) 'In-active citizenship and the depoliticization of community development in Ireland', *Community Development Journal*, 46(1):9–36.

Gaynor, N. (2009b) 'Deepening democracy within Ireland's social partnership', *Irish Political Studies*, 24(3):303–19.

Geoghegan, M. and Powell, F. (2009) 'Community development, the Irish state and the contested meaning of civil society', in D. Ó Broin and P. Kirby (eds) *Power, Dissent and Democracy: Civil Society and the State in Ireland* (Dublin: A. & A. Farmer), pp.95–110.

Gilmore, E. (2010) 'Building a republic that reflects the ideals and ambitions of its founders', speech to MacGill summer school, 23 July, www.labour.ie/press/listing/127991694920337939.html.

Goede, M. de (2004) 'Repoliticizing financial risk', *Economy and Society*, 33(2):197–217.

Gormley-Heenan, C. and Devine, P. (2010) 'The "us" in trust: Who trusts Northern Ireland's political institutions and actors?', *Government and Opposition*, 45:143–65.

Gottheil, F. (2003) 'Ireland: What's Celtic about the Celtic Tiger?', *Quarterly Review of Economics and Finance*, 43:720–37.

Grugel, J. and Riggirozzi, M.P. (2007) 'The return of the state in Argentina', *International Affairs*, 83(1):87–107.

Guiomard, G. (1995) *The Irish Disease and How to Cure It: Common-Sense Economics for a Competitive World* (Dublin: Oak Tree Press).

Habermas, J. (2006) 'The public sphere', in R.E. Goodin and P. Pettit (eds) *Contemporary Political Philosophy: An Anthology*, 2nd edn (Oxford: Blackwell Publishing), pp.103–6.

Hall, P.A. and Soskice, D. (2001) 'An Introduction to Varieties of Capitalism', in P.A. Hall and D. Soskice (eds) *Varieties of Capitalism: The Institutional Foundations of Comparative Advantage* (New York: Oxford University Press), pp.1–68.

Hardiman, N. (2006) 'Politics and social partnership: Flexible network governance', *Economic and Social Review*, 37(3):343–74.

Hardiman, N. (2009) 'The impact of the crisis on the Irish political system', paper presented to the Royal Irish Academy Committee for International Affairs conference, 'International Politics and the Global Economic Crisis', Dublin, 5 November.

Hardiman N. (ed.) (2011) *Irish Governance in Crisis* (Manchester: Manchester University Press).

Harvey, B. (2009) 'Ireland and civil society: Reaching the limits of dissent', in D. O'Broin and P. Kirby (eds) *Power, Dissent and Democracy: Civil Society and the Irish State* (Dublin: A. & A. Farmer), pp.25–34.

Harvey, B. (2010) 'Community development along the border: An instrument for the development of the cross-border region?' *Journal of Cross-Border Studies in Ireland*, 5:34–43.

Hay, C. (2004) 'Ideas, interests and institutions in the comparative economy of great transformations', *Review of International Political Economy*, 2(1):204–26.

Hay, C. (2009) 'The winter of discontent thirty years on', *Political Quarterly*, 80(4):545–52.

Hayes, B. and McAllister, I. (2008) 'Who voted for peace? Public support for the 1998 Belfast Agreement', in C. McGrath and E. O'Malley (2008) *Irish Political Studies Reader: Key Contributions* (London: Routledge), pp.310–34.

Hermann, C. (2007) 'Neoliberalism in the European Union', FORBA Discussion Paper 3/2007 (Vienna: Forschungs- und Beratungsstelle Arbeitswelt).

Higgins, M. (2007) *Causes for Concern: Irish Politics, Culture and Society* (Dublin: Liberties Press).

Honohan, I. (2001a) 'Friends, strangers or countrymen? The ties between citizens as colleagues', *Political Studies*, 49:51–69.

Honohan, I. (2001b) 'Freedom as citizenship: The republican tradition in political theory', *The Republic*, 2:7–25.

Honahan, P. (2010) 'The Irish banking crisis: Regulatory and financial stability policy 2003–2008', a report to the Minister for Finance by the governor of the Central Bank (Dublin: Department of Finance).

Hout, M. (2007) 'Maximally maintained inequality revisited: Irish educational mobility in comparative perspective', in P.M. NicGhiolla and E. Hilliard (eds) *Changing Ireland, 1989–2003* (Dublin: Liffey Press), pp.21–41.

Humphreys, R. (2009) *Countdown to Unity: Debating Irish Reunification* (Dublin: Irish Academic Press).

Hyman, R. (2011) 'The European context', paper presented to Session 1, 'Trade Unions, Industrial Relations and the Crisis', research symposium on 'Employment and the Crisis: Work Migration and Unemployment', Trinity College Dublin, 11 March

ICTU (2010) 'Embarrassment of riches', *Peoples Voice* (Dublin: ICTU), 27 November, p.22, www.ictu.ie/download/pdf/peoples_voice_201011.pdf.

IMF (2003) 'Vulnerability indicators: A factsheet', www.imf.org/external/np/facts/vul.html.

IMF (2009) 'Ireland: IMF country report', No. 09/195 (Washington DC: IMF).

IMF (2011) 'Country report: Iceland', No. 11/16 (Washington DC: IMF).

Ireland (1997) 'National anti-poverty strategy (NAPS)' (Dublin: Stationery Office).

Ireland (2007) 'National action plan for social inclusion 2007–2010' (Dublin: Office for Social Inclusion).

Ireland (2009) 'Report of the Commission on Taxation' (Dublin: Stationery Office).

Ireland First (2011) 'A blueprint for Ireland's recovery', March, www.irishtimes.com/focus/2011/blueprint/index.pdf.

Irish Times (2010) 'Renewing the Republic', final editorial, 3 April, p.15.

Irish Times (2011) 'Normal politics at last', editorial, 2 April, p.15.

Is Féidir Linn (2009) 'Manifesto: Shaping our future', http://www.isfeidirlinn.org/page/manifesto-1, accessed 3 April 2011.

Jackson, T. (2009a) *Prosperity without Growth: Economics for a Finite Planet* (London: Earthscan).

Jackson, T. (2009b) *Prosperity without Growth? The Transition to a Sustainable Economy* (London: Sustainable Development Commission).

Johnston, H. (2005) 'Poverty in Ireland: The issues', paper delivered to the Irish Association for Cultural, Economic and Social Relations, Mansion House, Dublin, 14 April.

Johnston, H. (2010) 'Instruments for implementation', in EAPN (ed.) *Ireland and the European Social Inclusion Strategy: Lessons Learned and the Road Ahead* (Dublin: EAPN), pp.130–45.

Katzenstein, P.J. (2003) 'Small States and Small States Revisited', *New Political Economy*, 8(1):9–30.

Katzenstein, P.J. (2006 [1985]) 'Small states in world markets: Industrial policy in Europe', in C. Ingebritsen, I. Neumann, S. Gstohl and J. Beyer (eds) *Small States in International Relations* (Seattle: University of Washington Press and Reykjavik: University of Iceland Press), pp.193–217; original (1985) *Small States in World Markets* (Ithaca, N.Y.: Cornell University Press).

Keane, F. (2011) 'History that wouldn't go away', *Irish Times*, 'Saturday Weekend Review', 5 February, p.3.

Kearney, A.T. (2001) 'Measuring globalization', *Foreign Policy*, January/February:56–65.

Kearney, A.T. (2002) 'Globalization's Last Hurrah?', *Foreign Policy*, January/February:38–51.

Kearney, A.T. (2003) 'Measuring Globalization: Who's Up, Who's Down?', *Foreign Policy*, January/February:60–72.

Kearney, A.T. (2004) 'Measuring Globalization: Economic Reversals, Forward Momentum', *Foreign Policy*, March/April:54–69.

Kearney, A.T. (2005) 'Measuring Globalization: The Global Top 20', *Foreign Policy*, May/June:52–60.

Kearney, A.T. (2006) 'The Globalization Index', *Foreign Policy*, November/December:74–81.

Kearney, A.T. (2007) 'The Globalization Index', *Foreign Policy*, November/December:68–76.

Kelleher, P., O'Connor, M. and Pillinger, J. (2009) 'Sex trafficking and prostitution: The experiences of migrant women in Ireland' (Dublin: Health Service Executive/Ruhama).

Kelly, A. and Teljeur, C. (2004) 'A new national deprivation index for health and health services', Small Area Health Research Unit, Department of Public Health and Primary Care (Dublin: TCD).

Kelly, M. (2011) 'Ireland's future depends on breaking free from bailout', *Irish Times*, 7 May, p.13.

Kelly, P. (2011) 'Commentary', NESC symposium 'Challenges for Ireland in the European Union', Royal College of Physicians, Dublin, 26 January.

Kennedy, K., Giblin, T. and McHugh, D. (1988) *The Economic Development of Ireland in the Twentieth Century* (London: Routledge).

Keynes, J.M. (2007 [1936]) *The General Theory of Employment, Interest and Money* (Basingstoke: Palgrave Macmillan).

Kiander, J. (2010) 'The Great Depression of Finland 1990–1993: Causes and consequences', paper presented to ESRI Policy Conference, 'The Labour Market in Recession', ESRI, Dublin, 28 April.

Kilmurray, A. (2010) 'Thoughts from the Border', paper presented to Rowntree Trust Seminar, Jurys Hotel, Dublin, 20 June.

Kingston, S. (ed.) (2010) *Aspirations for Ireland: New Ways Forward* (Dublin: Columba Press).

Kinsella, R. and Kinsella, M. (2011) 'Unemployment: Scarring a generation', *Studies*, 100(397):93–102.

Kirby, P. (2002) *The Celtic Tiger in Distress: Growth with Inequality in Ireland*, International Political Economy Series (Basingstoke: Palgrave).

Kirby, P. (2003) *Introduction to Latin America: Twenty-First Century Challenges* (London: Sage).

Kirby, P. (2006) *Vulnerability and Violence: The Impact of Globalisation* (London: Pluto Press).

Kirby, P. (2008) 'Explaining Ireland's development: Economic growth with weakening welfare', Social Policy and Development Paper No. 36 (Geneva: United Nations Research Institute for Social Development).

Kirby, P. (2009) 'The competition state: Lessons from Ireland', Limerick Papers in Politics and Public Administration, No. 1.

Kirby, P. (2010) *Celtic Tiger in Collapse: Explaining the Weaknesses of the Irish Model* (Basingstoke: Palgrave Macmillan).

Kirby, P. and Murphy, M.P. (2008a) 'Ireland as a "competition state"', in M. Adshead, P. Kirby and M. Millar (eds) *Contesting the State: Lessons from the Irish Case* (Manchester: Manchester University Press), pp.120–42.

Kirby, P. and Murphy, M.P. (2008b) *A Better Ireland Is Possible* (Galway: Community Platform).

Kirby P. and Murphy, M.P. (2011) 'Globalisation and models of state: Debates and evidence from Ireland', *New Political Economy*, 16(1):19–39.

Kitchin, R. (2010) 'Decentralisation: Halt, reverse, modify or proceed as planned?', http://irelandafternama.wordpress.com/category/uncategorized.

Kitchin, R. (2011) 'Roundtable plenary: Property and the crisis of planning and the market', 'Understanding the crisis – political economy and property' (Maynooth: NIRSA), 10 February.

Kitchin, R., Gleeson, J., Keaveney, K. and O'Callaghan, C. (2010) 'A haunted landscape: Housing and ghost estates in post-Celtic Tiger Ireland' (Maynooth: NIRSA).

Krugman, P. (2009) 'Erin Go Broke', *New York Times*, 20 April.

Krugman, P. (2010) 'Eating the Irish', *New York Times*, 25 November.

Laffan, B. and O'Donnell, R. (1998) 'Ireland and the growth of international governance', in W. Crotty and D. Schmitt (eds) *Ireland and the Politics of Change* (London: Longman), pp.156–77.

Laffan, B. and O'Mahony, J. (2008) *Ireland and the European Union* (Basingstoke: Palgrave Macmillan).

Laver, M. (1998) 'A new electoral system for Ireland', Studies in Public Policy No. 2 (Dublin: The Policy Institute).

Leahy, P. (2009) *Showtime: The Inside Story of Fianna Fáil in Power* (Dublin: Penguin Ireland).

Lee, J. (1989) *Politics and Society in Ireland 1912–1985*(Cambridge: Cambridge University Press).

Leonard, L. (2010) *The Environmental Movement in Ireland* (Dordrecht: Springer).

Lewis, M. (2011) 'When Irish eyes are crying', *Vanity Fair*, March.

Lijphart, A. (1991) 'Constitutional choices for new democracies', *Journal of Democracy*, 2(1):72–84.

Lijphart, A. (1999) *Patterns of Democracy: Government Forms and Performance in Thirty-Six Countries* (Yale: Yale University Press).

Loftus, C. (2010) 'How The Poor Were Made to Pay: An Analysis of the Impact of the December 2009 Budget' (Dublin: The Poor Can't Pay).

Lynch, K. (2006) 'Neo-liberalism and marketisation: The implication for higher education', *European Education Research Journal*, 5(1):1–17.

Lynch, K. (2007) 'How much inequality is there and who cares?', paper presented to 'Realising Equality and Inclusion: Building better policy and practice', Pobal Conference, Croke Park, Dublin, 22 November.

Lynch, K. and Lyons, M. (2008) 'The gendered order of caring', in U. Barry (ed.) *Where are We? New Feminist Perspectives on Women in Contemporary Ireland* (Dublin: TASC @ New Island), pp.163–83.

Lyons, B. (2009) 'The power of one', *Irish Times*, 22 June, p.11.

MABS (2010) 'MABS response to the Law Reform Commission's final report on debt management and debt enforcement' (Dublin: MABS), 15 December.

MacCarthaigh, M. (2005) *Accountability in Irish Parliamentary Politics* (Dublin, Institute of Public Administration).

MacCarthaigh, M. and Manning, M. (eds) (2010) *The Houses of the Oireachtas Parliament in Ireland* (Dublin: Institute of Public Administration).

MacSharry, R. and White, P. (2000) *The Making of the Celtic Tiger: The Inside Story of Ireland's Boom Economy* (Cork: Mercier Press).

Maguire, R. (2010) 'White collar crime: The business of crime', in J. Hogan, P.F. Donnelly and P.K. O'Rourke (eds) *Irish Business and Society: Governing, Participating and Transforming in the 21st Century* (Dublin: Gill & Macmillan), pp.172–93.

Mair, P. (1992) 'Explaining the absence of class politics in Ireland', in J.H. Goldthorpe and C.T. Whelan (eds) *The Development of Industrial Society in Ireland* (Oxford: Oxford University Press), pp.383–410.

Mair, P. (2010) 'The paradoxes of Irish politics', address given to the MacGill summer school, 'Reforming the Republic', July, http://politicalreformireland. files.wordpress.com/2010/07/paradoxes-and-problems-of-modern-irish-politics-glenties-2010.pdf, accessed 3 April 2011.

Martin, S. (2010) 'Monitoring Irish government', in E. O'Malley (ed.) *Governing Ireland* (Dublin: Institute of Public Administration).

Maxwell, N. and Dorrity, C. (2010) 'Access to third level education: Challenges for equality of opportunity in post-Celtic Tiger Ireland', *Irish Journal of Public Policy*, 2(1).

McCabe, C. (2009) 'Unemployment and class in Ireland: An analysis of the quarterly household survey, Q1 2009', http://dublinopinion.com/2009/08/02/unemployment-and-class-in-ireland-an-analysis-of-the-quarterly-household-survey-q1-2009/, accessed 3 April 2011.

McCall, M. (2009) 'Review symposium: Best of times? The social impact of the Celtic Tiger', *Economic and Social Review*, 39(2)157–69.

McCarthy, C. (2009) 'Report of the Special Group on Public Service Numbers and Expenditure Programmes' (Dublin: Stationery Office).

McCarthy, D. (1998) 'The genesis and evolution of the Irish state's commitment to partnership at local level', in P. Kirby and D. Jacobson (eds) *In the Shadow of the Celtic Tiger* (Dublin: Dublin City University Press), pp.39–49.

McCarthy, J. (2010) 'It is time Irish women let off a little bit of steam', *People's Voice* (Dublin: ICTU):8

McCashin, A. (2004) *Social Security in Ireland* (Dublin: Gill & Macmillan).

McCaughren, S. (2011) 'Business leaders working on a proposal for recovery', *Sunday Business Post*, 8 February, www.insideview.ie/irisheyes/2011/02/sunday-news-with-an-election-outside.html#tp.

McCoy, S., Byrne, D., O'Connell, P., Kelly, E. and Doherty, C. (2010) 'Hidden disadvantage? A study on the low participation in higher education by the lower non-manual group' (Dublin: HEA).

McDonald, F. and Sheridan, K. (2009) *The Builders* (London: Penguin).

McGauran, A.M. (2005) 'Plus ça change…? Gender mainstreaming of the Irish National Development Plan', *Studies in Public Policy No.15* (Dublin: Policy Institute, Trinity College).

McGinnity, F. and Russell, H. (2007) 'Work rich, time poor? Time-use of women and men in Ireland', *Economic and Social Review*, 38(3):323–54.

McGrath, C. and O'Malley, E. (2008) *Irish Political Studies Reader: Key Contributions* (London: Routledge).

McGraw, S. (2008) 'Managing change: Party competition in the new Ireland', *Irish Political Studies*, 23(4):627–48.

McGreevy, R. and Holland, K. (2011) 'Tenants' human rights breached by poor condition of flats complex', *Irish Times*, 'Health Supplement', 29 March, p.3.

McManus, J. (2009) 'Patrick Neary's departure a repudiation of our approach to regulation', *Irish Times*, 12 January, p.18.

McManus, J. (2011) 'What Moriarty tells us about doing business in Ireland', *Irish Times*, 28 March, p.17.

McMenamin, P. (2008) 'Taxpayer continues to subsidise fee-paying schools while cutting disadvantaged provision', www.tui.ie/Taxpayer_Continues_to_Subsidise_Fee_Paying_Schools_While_Cutting_Disadvantaged_Provision/Default.368.html.

McWilliams, D. (2010) *Follow the Money* (Dublin: Gill and Macmillan).

Meade, R. (2005) 'We hate it here, please let us stay! Irish social partnership and the community/voluntary sector's conflicted experiences of recognition', *Critical Social Policy*, 25(3):349–73.

Merrill Lynch and Capgemini (2010) 'World wealth report', Merrill Lynch and Capgemini/Bank of America Corporation, www.it.capgemini.com/m/it/doc/pubbl/wwr_2010.pdf.

Mitchell, G. (2011) *By Dáil Account: Auditing of Government, Past, Present and Future* (Dublin: IPA).

Mjøset, L. (1992) 'The Irish economy in a comparable institutional perspective' (Dublin: NESC).

Morris Tribunal (2008) 'Report of the Tribunal of Inquiry into complaints concerning some Gardai of the Donegal division' (Dublin: Stationery Office).

Mulholland, J. (ed.) (2010) 'The MacGill report: Reforming the Republic (Cloughjordan; Environmental Publications).

Müller, M. and Myllyntaus, T. (eds) (2007) *Pathbreakers: Small European Countries Responding to Globalisation and Deglobalisation* (Oxford: Peter Lang).

Murphy, A. (2010) 'ECB shift from lender of last resort casts doubt on independence', *Irish Times*, Business This Week supplement, 26 November 2010, p.3.

Murphy, G. (2006) 'Assessing the relationship between neoliberalism and political corruption: The Fianna Fáil–Progressive Democrat coalition, 1997–2006', *Irish Political Studies*, 21(3):297–317.

Murphy, M.C. (2010) 'Northern Ireland and the Republic of Ireland: A changed relationship', in J. Hogan, P.A. Donnelly and B.K. O'Rourke (eds.) *Irish Business and Society: Governing, Participating and Transforming in the 21st Century* (Dublin: Gill & McMillan), pp.398–416.

Murphy, M.P. (2006) *Domestic Constraints on Globalisation: A Case Study of Irish Social Security 1986–2006*, unpublished Ph.D. thesis, Dublin City University.

Murphy Report (2009) 'Report by Commission of Investigation into Catholic Archdiocese of Dublin' (Dublin: Government Publications).

Murray, P. (2008) 'Americanisation and Irish industrial development 1948–2008', NIRSA Working Paper No. 42.

Navarro, V. (2010) 'Existen alternativas a los recortes', *Público.es*, downloaded from www.vnavarro.org, accessed 4 March 2011.

Navarro, V. (2011) 'El dogma neoliberal domina la Unión Europea', *Sistema Digital*, downloaded from www.vnavarro.org, accessed 4 March 2011.

NESC (National Economic and Social Council) (2005) 'The developmental welfare state', report no.113 (Dublin: Stationery Office).

NESC (National Economic and Social Council) (2006) 'People, productivity, purpose', report no.114 (Dublin: Stationery Office).

NESDO (National Economic and Social Development Office) (2009) 'Ireland at another turning point: Reviving development, reforming institutions and liberating capabilities' (Dublin: NESDO).

Newenham, P. (2011) 'Inquest into hypothermia death told of heating complaints', *Irish Times*, 25 February, p.4.

Nyberg, Peter (2011) 'Misjudging risk: Causes of the systemic banking crisis in Ireland', report of the Commission of Investigation into the Banking Sector in Ireland (Dublin: Department of Finance).

Oakley, R. (2009) 'Second FAS boss in huge pension deal', *Sunday Times*, 18 October, www.timesonline.co.uk/tol/news/world/ireland/article6879640.ece, accessed 3 April 2011.

O'Brennan, J. (2010) 'Ireland and the European Union: Mapping domestic modes of adaptation and contestation', in J. Hogan, P.F. Donnelly and B.K. O'Rourke (eds) *Irish Business and Society: Governing, Participating and Transforming in the 21st Century* (Dublin: Gill & Macmillan), pp.379–87.

O'Brien, A. (2010) 'The Irish tourism industry', paper presented to 'Liberalism in Crisis: US, UK and Ireland', Department of Sociology, NUI Maynooth, 6 May.

O'Brien, A. (2011) *The Politics of Tourism Development: Booms and Busts in Ireland* (Basingstoke: Palgrave Macmillan).

O'Brien, D. (2009) *Ireland, Europe and the World* (Dublin: Gill and Macmillan).

O'Brien, D. (2011a) 'Economic crash hits Iceland more than Ireland – except on jobs', *Irish Times*, 'Business This Week' supplement, 18 February, p.4.

O'Brien, D. (2011b) 'Ministerial inertia at heart of economic catastrophe', *Irish Times*, 18 April, p.14.

O'Brien, J. (2009) 'After hubris always comes catastrophe', *Irish Times*, 9 February 2009, p.11.

O'Brien, M. (2001) *De Valera, Fianna Fáil and the Irish Press* (Dublin: Irish Academic Press).

O'Brien, M. (2004) 'Workfare: Not Fair for Kids', a review of compulsory work polices and their effects on children (Auckland: Child Poverty Action Group).

Ó Broin, D. and Waters, E. (2007) *Governing Below the Centre: Local Governance in Ireland* (Dublin: TASC @ New Island).

Ó Broin, D. (2009) 'Institutionalising social partnership in Ireland', in D. Ó'Broin and P. Kirby (eds) *Power, Dissent and Democracy: Civil society and the state in Ireland* (Dublin: A. &A. Farmer), pp.111–25.

Ó Broin, E. (2009) *Sinn Féin and the Politics of Left Republicanism* (London: Pluto Press).

Ó Broin, E. (2010) 'Sharing the burden', www.irishleftreview.org/2010/11/08/sharing-burden/.

Ó Broin, E. (2011) 'The future of the Irish Left: Policies, Political Strategies and future possibilities', presentation at 'Political change and people power: New political possibilities in Ireland for all left-wing parties in partnership with civil society', 5 February, Gresham Hotel, Dublin.

Ocampo, J.A. (2010) 'How Well has Latin America fared during the global financial crisis?', James A. Baker III Institute for Public Policy, Rice University, www.itf.org.ar/pdf/lecturas/lectura56.pdf.

O'Carroll, J.P. (2002) 'Culture lag and democratic deficit in Ireland: Or, Dat's outside de terms of d'agreement', *Community Development Journal*, 37(1):10–20.

Ó Cinnéide, S. (1972) 'The extent of poverty in Ireland', *Social Studies*, 1(4):381–400.

Ó Cinnéide, S. (2005) 'The EU and the Irish welfare state', Colmcille Winter School, Gartan, Co. Donegal, 26 February.

Ó Cinnéide, S. (2010) 'From poverty to social inclusion: The EU and Ireland', in EAPN (ed.) *Ireland and the European Social Inclusion Strategy: Lessons Learned and the Road Ahead* (Dublin: EAPN), pp.18–35.

O'Connell, P. and Rottman, D. (1992) 'The Irish welfare state in comparative perspective', in J. Goldthorpe and C.T. Whelan (eds) *The Development of Industrial Society in Ireland* (Oxford: The British Academy), pp.205–39.

O'Connor, M. (2009) 'Profit and loss: The politics of "health reform" in Ireland', *The Citizen*, 2:22–8.

O'Connor, P. (2008) 'The patriarchial state', in M. Adshead, P. Kirby and M. Millar (eds) *Contesting the Irish State* (Manchester: Manchester University Press), pp.143–65.

Ó Dochartaigh, N. (2008) 'Commentary', in C. McGrath and E. O'Malley (eds) *Irish Political Studies Reader: Key Contributions* (London: Routledge), pp.343–8.

O'Donnell, R. (1999) 'Reinventing Ireland: From sovereignty to partnership', Jean Monnet inaugural lecture, University College Dublin, 29 April.

O'Donnell, R. (2000) 'The new Ireland in the new Europe', in R. O'Donnell (ed.) *Europe: The Irish Experience* (Dublin: Institute for European Affairs), pp.161–214.

O'Donnell, R. and Thomas, D. (1998) 'Partnership and policymaking', in S. Healy and B. Reynolds (eds) *Social Policy in Ireland* (Dublin: Oak Tree Press), pp.117–46.

OECD (1999) 'Economic surveys: Ireland 1999'(Paris: OECD).

OECD (2008) 'Public management reviews – Ireland: Towards an integrated public service' (Paris: OECD).

OECD (2011) 'Doing better for families' (Paris: OECD).

O'Ferrall, F. (2001) 'Civic republican citizenship and voluntary action', *The Republic*, 2 ('The Common Good: Republicanism in Theory and Practice') (Dublin: The Ireland Institute), pp.126–37.

O'Ferrall, F. (2010) 'Visioning the new civic republic: Questions and implications for Ireland', Flourishing Society Series (Dublin: TASC).

Office for Social Inclusion (2009) 'National social inclusion strategy report on vulnerable communities' (Dublin: Government of Ireland).

Ó Gráda, C. (1994) *Ireland, a New Economic History 1780–1939* (Oxford: Clarendon Press).

Ó Gráda, C. (1997) *A Rocky Road: The Irish Economy since the 1920s* (Manchester: Manchester University Press).

O'Halloran, M. (2009) 'Problems found in more FAS courses', *Irish Times*, 16 October, p.8.

O'Halpin, E. (1998) 'A changing relationship? Parliaments and government in Ireland', in P. Norton (ed.) *Parliaments and Governments in Western Europe* (London: Frank Cass), pp.123–41.

O'Hanlon, G. (2010) 'A new economic paradigm', *Working Notes*, 64 (Dublin: Jesuit Centre for Faith and Justice), pp.3–9.

Oireachtas Committee on Constitutional Reform (2010) 'Report of the Oireachtas Committee on Constitutional Reform' (Dublin: Stationery Office).

Ólafsson, T.T. and Pétursson, T.G. (2010) 'Weathering the financial storm: The importance of fundamentals and flexibility', SEM Economics Working Paper 2010-17, School of Economics and Management, Aarhus University.

O'Mahony, P. (2008) 'The Public Reaction of Sympathy and Outrage at the Killing of Shane Geoghan', *Irish Left Review*, 21 November, www.irishleftreview.org/2008/11/21/public-reaction-sympathy-outrage-killing-shane-geoghan/.

O'Malley, E. (2006) 'Ministerial selection in Ireland: Limited choice in a political village', *Irish Political Studies*, 21:319–36.

O'Malley, E. (ed.) (2010) *Governing Ireland* (Dublin: Institute of Public Administration).

O'Neill, G. (2010) *2016: A New Proclamation for a New Generation* (Dublin: Mercier).

Ó Riain, S. (2000) 'The flexible developmental state: Globalization, information technology, and the Celtic Tiger', *Politics and Society*, 28(2):157–93.

Ó Riain, S. (2004) *The Politics of High-Tech Growth: Developmental Network States in the Global Economy* (Cambridge: Cambridge University Press).

Ó Riain, S. (2008) 'Competing state projects in the contemporary Irish political economy', in M. Adshead, P. Kirby and M. Millar (eds) *Contesting the State: Lessons from the Irish Case* (Manchester: Manchester University Press), pp.165–86.

Ó Riain, S. (2009) 'Class and unemployment decline', www.progressive-economy.ie/2009/06/class-and-employment-decline.html.

Ó Riain, S. and O'Connell, P.J. (2000) 'The role of the state in growth and welfare', in B. Nolan, P.J. O'Connell and C.T. Whelan (eds) *Bust to Boom? The Irish Experience of Growth and Inequality* (Dublin: Institute for Public Administration), pp.310–39.

O'Sullivan, M.J. (2006) *Ireland and the Global Question* (Cork: Cork University Press).

O'Toole, F. (2009) *Ship of fools: How stupidity and corruption sank the Celtic Tiger* (London: Faber and Faber).

O'Toole, F. (2010) *Enough is Enough: How to Build a New Republic* (London: Faber and Faber).

O'Toole, F. (2011) 'Everything and nothing has changed', *Irish Times*, 'Weekend Review', 12 March, p.1.

Pentony, S. (2010) 'The role of the economy in the flourishing society', Flourishing Society Series (Dublin: TASC).

Pettit, P. (2005) 'From republican theory to public policy', in M. Jones (ed.) *The Republic* (Dublin: Mercier/RTE), pp.130–47.

Pierson, C. (2004) *The Modern State*, 2nd edn (London: Routledge).

Pillinger, J. (2007) *The Feminisation of Migration: Experiences and Opportunities in Ireland* (Dublin: Immigrant Council of Ireland).

Piven, F.F. (2008) 'Can power from below change the world', *American Sociological Review*, 73(1):1–17.

Polanyi, K. (1977) *The Livelihood of Man* (New York: Academic Press).

Polanyi, K. (2001[1944]) *The Great Transformation* (Boston: Beacon Books).

Pollack, A. (ed.) (2010) *Journal of Cross Border Studies in Ireland No. 5* (Armagh: Centre for Cross Border Studies).

Pollack, A. (ed.) (2011) *Journal of Cross Border Studies in Ireland No. 6* (Armagh: Centre for Cross Border Studies).

Pollitt, C. (2005) 'International experience of public management reform', *Inside Government*, September, pp.4–6.

Pollitt, C. and Bouckaert, G. (2004) *Public Management Reform: A Comparative Analysis* (Oxford: Oxford University Press).

Powell, F. (2007) *The Politics of Civil Society* (Bristol: Policy Press).

Prasad, M. (2009) 'Three theories of the crisis', *Accounts*, 8(2):1–4.

Price Waterhouse Coopers (2010) 'Annual Review', *Irish Times*, 'Business Supplement', 31 December.

Programme for Government (2011) 'Government for National Recovery 2011–2016' (Dublin: Stationery Office).

Pye, R. (2011) 'Stop Brussels elite from ransacking our country', *Irish Times*, 6 May, p.16.

Rapley, J. (2004) *Globalization and Inequality: Neoliberalism's Downward Spiral* (Boulder, Colo.: Lynne Rienner).

Redmond, D., Crossan, V., Moore, N. and Williams, B. (2007) 'Dublin as an emergent global gateway: Pathways to creative and knowledge-based regions', paper presented to project 'Accommodating Creative Knowledge: Competitiveness of European Metropolitan Regions within the Enlarged Union', AMIDSt, University of Amsterdam.

Regling, K. and Watson, M. (2010) 'A preliminary report on the sources of Ireland's banking crisis' (Dublin: Government Publications).

Roden, J., De Buitleir, D. and Ó Brolcháin, D. (1986) 'A design for democracy', *Administration*, 34(2):148–63.

Rosales, J. (2010) 'Caracterización e impactos sectoriales y sociales de la crisis económica 2008–2009: Lecciones aprendidas y retos de política económica'(San José: Estado de la Nación).

Ross, S. (2008) 'FAS: The 20m-a-week quango', www.shane-ross.ie/archives/340/fas-the-e20m-a-week-quango/', accessed 3 April 2011.

Ross, S. (2009) *The Bankers* (Dublin: Penguin Ireland).

Roubini, N. (2009) 'Nouriel Roubini on Latin America's 2010 outlook', interview, Council of the Americas, http://www.as-coa.org/article.php?id=2090, accessed 21 February 2011.

Ruane, F. (2007) 'Foreword', in T. Fahey, H. Russell and C. Whelan (eds) *Best of Times? The Social Impact of the Celtic Tiger* (Dublin: IPA), pp.i–vii.

Ruggie, J. (2003) 'Taking embedded liberalism global: The corporate connection', in D. Held and M. Koenig-Archibugi (eds) *Taming Globalization: Frontiers of Governance* (Cambridge: Polity Press), pp.93–129.

Russell, H., Maître, B. and Donnelly, C. (2011) 'Financial exclusion and over-indebtedness in Irish households' (Dublin: ESRI).

Ryan, A.B. (2009) *Enough is Plenty: Public and Private Policies for the 21st Century* (Alresford, Hampshire: O-Books)

Ryan, A.B (2010) Enough: Foundation for a moral and ecological Economics *Working Notes* No 64 (Dublin: Jesuit Centre for Faith and Justice) pp.10–14.

Ryan, N. (2010) 'Why are all the best jobs in Irish radio and television still the preserve of men?', TASC Think Piece no.25 (Dublin TASC).

Ryan Report (2009) 'Commission to Inquire into Child Abuse' (Dublin: Government Publications).

Sabel, C. (1996) *Ireland: Local Partnerships and Social Innovation* (Paris: OECD).

Sandel, M. (2009) 'A new citizenship', BBC Reith Lectures 2009, www.bbc.co.uk/iplayer/episode/b00l0y01/The_Reith_Lectures_Michael_Sandel_A_New_Citizenship_2009_Morality_in_Politics/.

Scandrett, E. (2011) 'What can we learn from popular struggle?', presentation to workshop 'Beyond the crisis: Global justice, equality and social movements', Seomra Sproai, Dublin, 7 May.

Scharpf, F. (2000) 'Economic changes: Vulnerabilites and institutional capabilities', in F. Scharpf and V. Schmidt (eds) *Work and Welfare in the Open Economy, vol.1: From Vulnerability to Competitiveness* (Oxford: Oxford University Press), pp.21–124.

Schick, A. (1996) 'The Spirit of Reform: Managing the New Zealand State Sector in a Time of Change', report prepared for the State Services Commission, Wellington, New Zealand.

Schmidt, V. (2000) 'Values and discourse in the politics of adjustment', in F. Scharpf and V. Schmidt (eds) *Work and Welfare in the Open Economy, vol. 1: From Vulnerability to Competitiveness* (Oxford: Oxford University Press), pp.229–309.

Schwartz, H. and Seabrooke, L. (2008) 'Varieties of residential capitalism in the international political economy: Old welfare states and the new politics of housing', *Comparative European Politics*, 6:237–61.

Sen, A. (1999) *Development as Freedom* (Oxford: Oxford University Press).

Shaver, S. and Bradshaw, J. (1995) 'The recognition of wifely labour by welfare states', *Social Policy and Administration*, 29(1):10–25.

Silva, E. (2009) *Challenging Neoliberalism in Latin America* (Cambridge: Cambridge University Press).

Simon Community (2010) 'Experiencing increase in people needing help', press release, 7 September (Dublin: Simon Community).

Sinnott, R. (1999) 'The electoral system', in J. Coakley and M. Gallagher (eds) *Politics in the Republic of Ireland*, 3rd edn (London: Routledge), pp.99–126.

Skidelsky, R. (2009) *Keynes: The Return of the Master* (New York: Public Affairs).

Skidmore, P. (2009) 'Polls apart: Democracy in an age of inequality', www.compassonline.org.uk/publications/thinkpieces/item.asp?d=232.

Slattery, L. (2010a) 'Exchequer deficit deepens by €11.9bn', *Irish Times*, 6 January, p.16.

Slattery, L. (2010b) 'Winners and losers', *Irish Times*, 'Weekend Review', 31 December, www.irishtimes.com/newspaper/finance/2010/1231/1224286534463.html.

Slí Eile (2010) 'Changing the political, institutional and legal framework for a civic republic', Flourishing Society Series (Dublin: TASC).

Smeeding, T. and Nolan, B. (2004) 'Ireland's income distribution in comparative perspective', LIS Working Paper Series No. 395, December (Luxembourg: LIS).

Smith, G. (2010) 'Political Corruption in Ireland', in J. Hogan, P.F. Donnelly and P.K. O'Rourke (eds) *Irish Business and Society, Governing, Participating and Transforming in the 21st Century* (Dublin: Gill & Macmillan), pp.194–215.

Smith, M. (2009) 'Analysis Note: Gender Equality and the Recession', prepared for European Commission's Network of Experts on Employment and Gender Equality Issues (accessed through the European Commission's Directorate-General for Employment, Social Affairs and Equal Opportunities).

Smith, N. (2005) *Showcasing Globalisation? The Political Economy of the Irish Republic* (Manchester: Manchester University Press).

Smyth, J. (2006) 'Moving the immovable: The civil rights movement in Northern Ireland', in L. Connolly and N. Hourigan (eds) *Social Movements and Ireland* (Manchester: Manchester University Press), pp.106–23.

Social Justice Ireland (2009) *Beyond GDP: What is Progress and How Should It Be Measured?* (Dublin: Social Justice Ireland).

Social Justice Ireland (2011) 'Policy briefing, January 2011' (Dublin: Social Justice Ireland).

Solt, F. (2008) 'Economic inequality and democratic political engagement', *American Journal of Political Science*, 52(1):48–60.

Sørensen, G. (2010) 'Globalisation and development: Ireland and Denmark in comparative perspective', in M. Boss (ed.) *The Nation-State in Transformation: Economic Globalisation, Institutional Mediation and Political Values* (Aarhus: Aarhus University Press), pp.233–43.

Standards in Public Office Commission (2010) 'Annual Report 2009' (Dublin: SIPOC), www.sipo.gov.ie/en/Reports/AnnualReports/AnnualReport2009/std_eng/chapter3.html.

Stapleton, L., Lehane, M. and Toner, P. (eds.) (2000) 'Ireland's environment: A millennium report' (Wexford: Environmental Protection Agency).

Steck, G., Grimm, M., Heise, M., Holzhausen, A. and Sauter, N. (2010) 'Allianz global wealth report 2010' (Munich: Allianz).

Suttner, R. (2006) 'Party dominance "theory": Of what value?', *Politikon*, 33(3):277–97.

Sweeney, A. (2009) *Banana Republic: The Failure of the Irish State and How to Fix It* (Dublin: Gill & Macmillan).

Sweeney, P. (2003) 'Globalisation: Ireland in a global context', in M. Adshead and M. Millar (eds) *Public Administration and Public Policy in Ireland* (London: Routledge), pp.201–18.

Sweeney, P. (2009) 'What we need for recovery is a major Keynesian-style stimulus package', *Irish Times*, 31 January, p.15.

Taft, M. (2009) 'Money, money, everywhere but here', Progressive-Economy@TASC 2009 Review (Dublin: TASC), pp.28–31.

Taft, M. (2011) 'Flying with pigs', 'Notes on the Front' blog post, http:// notesonthefront.typepad.com/politicaleconomy/2011/02/when-i-re-tweeted-labour-councillor-cian-ocallaghans-news-statement-calling-on-labour-not-to-enter-coalition-with-fine.html, accessed 3 April 2011.

TASC (2009) 'Hierarchy of earnings, attributes and privilege analysis' (Dublin: TASC).

TASC (2010a) *Mapping the Golden Circle* (Dublin: TASC).

TASC (2010b) 'The solidarity factor: Public responses to economic inequality in Ireland' (Dublin: TASC).

Taskforce on Active Citizenship (2007) 'The concept of active citizenship' (Dublin: Taskforce on Active Citizenship).

Teague, P. and Donaghey, J. (2009) 'Social partnership and democratic legitimacy in Ireland', *New Political Economy*, 14(1):49–69.

Timonen, V. (2003) 'Irish social expenditure in a comparative international context' (Dublin: Combat Poverty Agency and Institute of Public Administration).

Tonge, J. (2005) *The New Northern Ireland Politics* (Basingstoke: Palgrave Macmillan).

Tonra, B. (2002) 'Irish foreign policy', in W. Crotty and D.E. Schmitt (eds) *Ireland on the World Stage* (Harlow: Longman), pp.24–45.

Transparency International (2010) 'National integrity systems country study for Ireland 2009', www.transparency.ie/resources/nis09.htm, accessed 3 April 2011.

UN (2003) 'Report on the world social situation: Social vulnerability, sources and challenges' (New York: United Nations Department of Economic and Social Affairs).

UNDP (2010) 'Human development report 2010: The real wealth of nations' (Basingstoke: Palgrave Macmillan).

Vail, J. (2010) 'Decommodification and egalitarian political economy', *Politics and Society*, 38:310–46.

Village (2010) 'Our latest problem: The quality of the Irish debate', *Village Magazine*, June/July, pp.80–5.

Walsh, A. (2011) 'Roundtable plenary: Property and the crisis of planning and the market', paper presented to 'Understanding the crisis – political economy and property', Maynooth, NIRSA, 10 February.

Walsh, J. (2009) 'Political protection for many state agencies unacceptable', *Irish Times*, 16 October, www.irishtimes.com/newspaper/ireland/2009/1016/1224256787616.html, accessed 3 April 2011.

Webb, N. (2011) '*Sunday Independent* Rich List' supplement, 12 March.

Whelan, C.T. and Maître, B. (2010) 'Protecting the vulnerable: Poverty and social exclusion in Ireland as the economic crisis emerged', Working Papers 2010:23, Geary Institute, University College Dublin.

Whelan, K. (2010) 'Policy lessons from Ireland's latest depression', *Economic and Social Review*, 41(2):225–54.

Wilkinson, R. and Pickett, K. (2009) *The Spirit Level: Why More Equal Societies Almost Always Do Better* (London: Allen Lane).

Williams, B. (2011) 'Roundtable plenary: Property and the crisis of planning and the market', paper presented to 'Understanding the crisis – political economy and property', Maynooth, NIRSA, 10 February.

World Bank (2000) 'World development report 2000–01: Attacking poverty' (New York: Oxford University Press).

Wright, Rob (2010) 'Strengthening the capacity of the Department of Finance', report of the Independent Review Panel (Dublin: Department of Finance).

Young I.M. (2006) 'Polity and group difference : A critique of the ideal of universal citizenship', in R.E. Goodin and P. Pettit (2006) *Contemporary Political Philosophy: An Anthology*, 2nd edn (Oxford: Blackwell Publishing), pp.248–63.

Zimmerman, J.F. (2008) 'Freedom of information in Ireland', *Administration*, 56(2):19–39.

Index

Compiled by Sue Carlton